Asian Economic and Financial Integration in Global Framework

Asian Economic and Financial Integration in Global Framework

Pradeep S. Chauhan

Fellow, South Asian Study Centre,
St. Antony's College,
University of Oxford, UK.

New Century Publications
New Delhi, India

NEW CENTURY PUBLICATIONS
4800/24, Bharat Ram Road,
Ansari Road, Daryaganj,
New Delhi – 110 002 (India)

Tel.: 011-2324 7798, 4358 7398, 6539 6605
Fax: 011-4101 7798
E-mail: indiatax@vsnl.com • info@newcenturypublications.com
www.newcenturypublications.com

Editorial office:
LG–7, Aakarshan Bhawan,
4754-57/23, Ansari Road, Daryaganj,
New Delhi – 110 002

Tel.: 011-4356 0919

First Published: **September 2009**

ISBN: **978-81-7708-224-1**

Published by New Century Publications and printed at Salasar Imaging Systems, New Delhi.

Designs: Patch Creative Unit, New Delhi.

PRINTED IN INDIA

Contents

About the Book

This book analyzes the nature of Asia's merging regionalism, providing a basis for understanding its dimensions and further discussion on ways to move forward. The dynamic and outward-looking style of Asian regionalism can have a significant impact in an increasingly globalized world. Regionalism can be a stabilizing factor when shocks arise, whether region-based or externally-imposed. Reflecting the diversity of economies and their histories, regional integration follows markedly different patterns across the world. Europe has a long history of regional integration, underpinned by a strong institutional framework. North America has chosen a free trade area arrangement that does not foresee the creation of supranational institutions. In Latin America, the initial objectives of a common market and coordinated economic policies of Mercado Commum de Sur (MERCOSUR) have suffered setbacks caused by financial turbulence in the region in the late 1990s. In Asia, trade integration has progressed at a rapid pace based on the exploitation of intra-regional comparative advantages.

The book examines all these global economic and monetary integration processes focusing on Asian monetary and financial integration. What is the status of integration in Asia in monetary, financial, trade and production networks? These aspects have been discussed and compared with successful European economic and monetary integration. To give a more extensive view to the readers, separate chapters have been included on North American Free Trade Agreement (NAFTA), MERCOSUR and African Economic and Monetary Integration. The work is useful for students, researchers, policy makers and all others who want to understand and assess the status, processes and challenges of economic and monetary integration.

Author's Profile

Dr. Pradeep S. Chauhan, a noted economist, is based at South Asian Study Centre, St. Antony's College, University of Oxford, UK as a Fellow. He is M.Phil. (Gold Medallist) and Doctorate in Economics. He has taught in many world-known universities and institutions in his 17 years of academic career. His scholarship ranges over the fields of international economics, economics of climate change and economic theory. His illustrious academic career includes a prestigious French Government Fellowship for which he pursued his research and teaching at Paris School of Economics, Paris. He was awarded Agatha Harrison Memorial Fellowship to pursue his research at the University of Oxford, UK.

Dr. Chauhan has published 3 books and completed many research projects. He is member of many national and international academic bodies including Kastler Foundation, France, International Forum of Young Scientists, Hungary and Indian Economic Association. He has presented papers at many national and international conferences and seminars.

Preface

It is widely recognized that the world economy has experienced an unprecedented intensification of economic and financial integration since the latter part of the 20th century. Developments such as trade and capital account liberalization, as well as technological innovation in transport and telecommunications, have increased the international exchange of factors of production and final products. What is less often recognized is that the process of globalisation has been accompanied by the strengthening of economic and financial linkages within geographic regions. Indeed the world economy is simultaneously becoming more regionalized and more globalized.

The trend towards regional integration has been supported in many areas by regional policy initiatives, particularly in the field of trade. The result is a proliferation of regional agreements that vary widely in breadth and depth.

Reflecting the diversity of economies and their histories, regional integration follows markedly different patterns across the world. Europe has a long history of regional integration, underpinned by a strong institutional framework. North America has chosen a free trade area arrangement that does not foresee the creation of supranational institutions. In Latin America, MERCOSUR's initial objectives of a common market and coordinated economic policies have suffered setbacks caused by financial turbulence in the region in the late 1990s, and the grouping is yet to recover momentum. In East Asia, trade integration has progressed at a rapid pace based on the exploitation of intra-regional comparative advantages. Only since the 1997-98 Asian Crisis has this market-led process been accompanied by closer inter-governmental coordination, which however, is embracing monetary and financial spheres as well as trade.

This book has examined all these global economic and monetary integration processes focusing on Asian Monetary and Financial Integration. What is the status of integration in Asia in monetary, financial, trade and production networks? These aspects have been discussed and compared with successful European economic and monetary integration. To give a more extensive view to the readers separate chapters have been included on NAFTA, MERCOSUR and African Economic and Monetary Integration.

The book is organized into 9 chapters.

Chapter 1 is devoted to the debate on regional economic integration with a discussion of it in Asian context.

Chapter 2 deals with the prospects and challenges of Asian economic integration vis-à-vis European integration. It discusses the political economy of European integration, its history and commitments to integration, pros and cons of trade creation and trade diversion and the role of institutions. Lessons for Asian economic integration have been drawn and discussed.

Chapter 3 assesses the progress towards Asian monetary and financial integration. It shows that financial integration in Asia is approaching through trade and production networks. Further, it examines the role of national authorities and multinational institutions for strengthening the financial markets and harmonizing regulations and mitigating the vulnerability that might arise from greater cross-boarder capital flows.

Chapter 4 explains and evaluates the nature and the driving forces of economic integration in Asia. In Europe, the process was driven by governments and their policies, including the early creation of regional institutions, which strengthened over time to become a driving force for integration in their own right. In Asia, where regional institutions are not well-developed, integration has progressed to a fairly high level through markets, multinational corporations and their production networks.

Chapter 5 is devoted to comparative analysis of Asian and European economic integration in terms of institution building.

European economic and monetary integration was led by strong institutions and government policies, which is clearly not the similar process in the Asian case.

Chapter 6 is focused on the role of China and India in the integration process. Given the size of their populations and strategic positions in international and regional relations, the two countries play fundamentally important, if not entirely dominating, roles. China and India must take the lead in promoting Asian economic integration.

Chapters 7, 8 and 9 review the functioning and performance of NAFTA, African Economic and Monetary Integration and MERCOSUR respectively.

This work would not have been possible without the valuable support and assistance received from various quarters and various persons. It gives me immense pleasure to place on record my deep and sincere thanks to all those individuals and institutions that helped me at various stages of the completion of this book.

I have great pleasure in acknowledging my gratitude to the Governing Body of St. Antony's College - to Professor Margaret Macmillan, the Warden and Mr. Alan Taylor, the Bursar who have always been very supportive and encouraging.

Thanks are also due to Dr. David Washbrook, Convener, South Asian Studies Seminars, University of Oxford for his valuable help and guidance at the beginning of my tenure at Oxford. I am also thankful to Dr. Nandini Gooptu, Fellow, St. Antony's College, University of Oxford and Professor Roger Guesnerie, Director, College de France.

I am indeed grateful and indebted to Professor M.M. Goel, Chairman, Department of Economics, Kurukshetra University for his constant and valuable support in my academic pursuits. It is my pleasure to thank Faculty of Economics, Kurukshetra University, especially Professor V.N. Attri, Dr. Neera Verma, Dr. Kuldeep Singh, Dr. R.K. Sudan, Dr. Ashok Chauhan, Dr. Sanjeev Bansal and Mr. Dara Singh.

I wish to express my deep sense of love, affection and indebtedness to my ever-charming and beloved wife Dr. Shivalli Chauhan, who has always inspired me and constantly provided me a hand of support and love. I express my hearty gratitude to my parents for the care and affection.

Finally, I am thankful to Mr. Sandeep Sury, Chief Executive, New Century Publications, New Delhi and his anonymous team of editors for standardizing and improving the format and presentation of the material contained in this book.

The necessary caveat stands: I, alone, am to blame for the flaws and deficiencies in this work.

August 2009
Oxford, UK.

Pradeep S. Chauhan

Abbreviations and Acronyms

ABF	Asian Bond Fund
ABMI	Asian Bond Markets Initiative
ADB	Asian Development Bank
AFTA	ASEAN Free Trade Area
AMC	Asset Management Company
AIA	ASEAN Investment Area
AEF	African Equatorial Francaise
AOF	African Occidental Francaise
APEC	Asia-Pacific Economic Cooperation
ASA	ASEAN Swap Arrangement
ASEAN	Association of Southeast Asian Nations
ASEAN+3	ASEAN plus People's Republic of China, Japan, and Republic of Korea
ASEM	Asia-Europe Meeting
BCP	Basel II Core Principles
BEAC	Bank of Central African States
BIMP-EAGA	Brunei Darussalam-Indonesia-Malaysia-Philippines–East Asia Growth Area
BIMSTEC	Bay of Bengal Institute for Multilateral-Sectoral Technical and Economic Cooperation
BSA	Bilateral Swap Arrangement
CEMAC	Economic and Monetary Union of Central Africa
CMI	Chiang Mai Initiative
COMESA	Common Market for Eastern and Southern Africa
EAC	East African Community
EAS	East Asian Summit
EASG	East Asian Study Group
EC	European Commission
ECSC	European Coal and Steel Community
ECOWAS	Community of West African States
EDC	European Defence Community

EEC	European Economic Community
EHP	Early Harvesting Programme
EFTA	European Free Trade Area
EMEAP	Executives' Meeting of East Asia and Pacific Central Banks
ESCAP	Economic and Social Commission for Asia and the Pacific
EPC	European Political Community
EU	European Union
FDI	Foreign Direct Investment
ETLS	ECOWAS Trade Liberalisation Scheme
FTA	Free Trade Agreement
GATT	General Agreement on Tariffs and Trade
GDP	Gross Domestic Product
GMS	Greater Mekong Subregion
HIPC	Highly Indebted Poor Community
IA	Integrating Asia
IAIS	International Association of Insurance Supervisors
IMF	International Monetary Fund
JKCIK	Japan, ASEAN, China, India, Korea
IOSCO	International Organization for Securities Commission
MERCOSUR	Mercado Commum de Sur (The Southern Cone Common Market)
MCP	Monetary Cooperation Programme
MDG	Millennium Development Goal
MNC	Multinational Corporation
NAFTA	North American Free Trade Agreement
NIE	Newly Industrializing Economy
NTB	Non-tariff Barriers
OECD	Organisation for Economic Co-operation and Development
PCT	Parts and Components Trade
PTA	Preferential Treaty Agreement

PPP	Purchasing Power Parity
PRC	People's Republic of China
RI	Regional Integration
RIAs	Regional Integration Agreements
RISDP	Regional Indicative Strategy Development Plan
RMA	Rand Monetary Agreements
ROORs	Rules-of-origin Requirements
SAARC	South Asian Association of Regional Countries
SADA	Southern African Development Community
SARS	Severe Acute Respiratory Syndrome
SAFTA	South Asian Free Trade Area
SAPTA	South Asian Preferential Trade Agreement
SRCB	Southern Rhodesia Currency Bond
SWF	Sovereign Wealth Fund
UEBOA	Monetary Agreement of West African Economic and Monetary Union
US	United States
UNCTAD	United Nation Conference on Trade and Development
VAR	Vector Auto Regression
WACH	West African Clearing House
WAMA	West African Meeting Agency
WAMI	West African Monetary Institute
WAMZ	West African Monetary Zone
WAUA	West African Unit of Account
WHO	World Health Organization
WTO	World Trade Organization

List of Tables in the Text

1

Regional Economic Integration and Asia

1.1 Introduction

Regional integration (RI) is a worldwide phenomenon of territorial systems that increase the interactions between their components and create new forms of organisation, co-existing with traditional forms of state-led organization at the national level. The processes of regional integration that emerged after WW II, were originally mostly about trade and economics, but it has become clear that, especially since the 1980s, with the so-called 'new regionalism' wave, regional integration can be seen as a multidimensional process that implies, next to economic cooperation, also dimensions of politics, diplomacy, security, culture, etc. Regional integration agreements (RIAs) are groupings of countries formed with the objective of reducing barriers to trade between members. They have long historical antecedents, sometimes being a stage to nation building (most famously in the Zollverein of nineteenth century Germany), and sometimes as part of colonial trading arrangements.

In the post-war period, developments were led by the European Union (EU, originally the European Economic Communities, founded in 1958), and in the 1960s and 1970s there was a number of rather inward looking (and largely unsuccessful) RIAs between developing countries. Since the mid-1980s there has been a dramatic increase in regional integration activity. Of the 194 RIAs notified to the General Agreement on Trade and Tariffs/World Trade Organization (GATT/WTO) at the beginning of 1999, 87 were notifications since 1990. Now almost all countries are members of at least one RIA, and more than one third of world trade takes place within such agreements. The new developments include the expansion and deepening of the EU; the construction of new and more open RIAs between developing countries; and the advent of RIAs in which both high income and developing countries are equal partners, lead by the North American Free Trade Area (NAFTA) which, in 1994, extended the Canadian-USA free trade agreement to Mexico. RIAs come in many shapes and sizes. They vary in income levels, in openness to trade, and in the share of trade that takes place within the RIA, (60 percent for the fifteen members of the EU, but just 10 percent for the eight members of the West African Economic and Monetary Union).

Structures vary, from the loose agreements to facilitate trade of the African Cross-Border Initiative and Asia Pacific Economic Cooperation (APEC forum, through to the deep integration of the EU, involving the construction of shared executive, judicial and legislative institutions. The focus of this article, in common with most of the economics literature, is on RIAs as mechanisms fcr trade liberalization, not addressing the integration of factor markets, monetary systems, or political institutions. Even with this focus, RIAs differ widely in structure. 'Free trade areas' remove internal tariff and non-tariff barriers, but permit members to retain independent external tariff policies. 'Customs unions' go further, in fully harmonizing external trade policy. And it is increasingly recognized that effective integration of markets requires more than reducing tariffs and quotas. Many other barriers such as differing national product standards and a host of minor border frictions-impede trade and support market segmentation, and some RIAs are now pursuing 'deep integration' policies to eliminate these barriers.

1.1.1 Trade Creation and Diversion of Economic Integration: The modern analysis of RIAs dates from Viner, who drew the distinction between the trade creating and trade diverting effects of RIA formation. The classical source of gains from trade is that global free trade allows consumers and firms to purchase from the cheapest source of supply, hence ensuring that production is located according to comparative advantage. In contrast, trade barriers discriminate against foreign supply, inducing domestic import competing producers to expand even though they have higher costs than do imports. This in turn starves domestic export sectors of resources and causes them to be smaller than they otherwise would be. Since a RIA liberalizes trade, reducing at least some of the barriers, doesn't it follow that it too will generate gains from trade? Viner's contribution was to show that the answer is; not necessarily. The gains from trade argument applies if all trade barriers are reduced, but need not apply to a partial—and discriminatory—reduction in barriers, as in a RIA. This is because discrimination between sources of supply is not eliminated, it is just shifted. If partner country production displaces higher cost domestic production then there will be gains—trade creation. But it is possible that partner country production may displace lower cost imports from the rest of the world, and this is welfare reducing trade diversion.

The analysis of trade creation and trade diversion constitutes one of the first formal analyses of the more general problem of 'second-best welfare economics'. Given that distortions remain in place in some activities in the economy, it is not necessarily the case that removing just some of the distortions (e.g. eliminating trade barriers on partner countries and leaving them in place on external countries) is welfare improving. In the literature on regional integration the response to the fundamental ambiguity created by the second-best took three main forms.

1.2 Regional Economic Integration and Regionalism

Integration is a gradual, virtually open-ended process of eliminating discriminatory policies and other obstacles to trade among partners, which is facilitated by clearly defined objectives. There are five main considerations to ensure the success of a process of integration: (i) put in place clear and shared objectives; (ii) proceed step by step, with the right initial step; (iii) define clear and feasible deliverables; (iv) be mindful of derogations granted to members as they are not free from costs; and (v) have a framework that allows parties to cope with shocks. An orderly integration process requires the implementation of a set of sequential steps. The first step is to choose the level of integration to be pursued, with clear ultimate objectives and a well-defined starting point. This step implies choosing from among the five different degrees of integration (see Balassa) ranging from a free trade area—the least ambitious objective—to full integration, the arrangement that imposes the most stringent requirements on members. The second step of integration requires the selection of the partners to be part of the arrangements, based, among other criteria, on their size and degree of heterogeneity.

The third step consists of selecting the degree of convergence of the process. In the European Community (EC) experience, trade integration moved along with social cohesion (i.e. EU Structural and Cohesion Funds), whereas monetary integration moved alongside nominal economic convergence. More generally, though, it is not clear whether convergence is a precondition for integration or rather, at least partly, a consequence of the process of integration itself. Ultimately, parties need to define the degree of flexibility characterising the process. The options available include integration "à la carte", multi-speed models, core/periphery models and full flexibility. The EC experience draws on the multi-speed framework, under which successive enlargements have been accommodated, and on the flexible setup, as reflected in open partnerships. In relation to the first step (i.e. the definition of the objectives to be pursued), so that the choice between a free trade area arrangement and a customs union arrangement represents the key decision parties need to make. This is because this fundamental choice works as a de facto test of political will, on account of the loss of sovereignty implied and the implementation difficulties.

In practice, free trade areas prevail in the world economy,

while there are very few partial customs unions–not to mention fully-fledged ones. Moreover, it has also been found that there is an argument in favour of the sound implementation of an FTA and of then moving towards an FTA+ (one which eliminates barriers but does not consider the creation of common policies and common institutions), rather than being more ambitious and proceeding with a poorly implemented customs union arrangement.

The conditions necessary for the outcome of integration should be resource-efficient. They relate to the type of products and degree of liberalisation covered under the integration process: (i) a broad product coverage; (ii) a high degree of internal liberalisation; and (iii) a low degree of external protection.

These provisions are enshrined in Article XXIV of the GATT regarding regional trade arrangements.

To illustrate this assessment, the European integration model can be used , first defined in terms of a successful customs union that deepened, enlarged and diversified over time, until it converged first towards a common single market and then towards today's Economic and Monetary Union. The pillars of the European customs union were (i) the elimination of barriers to trade; (ii) the creation of common policies, differentiating between allocative policies (such as single market, competition and industrial policies), redistributive policies (related to the agricultural and regional chapters) and macroeconomic stabilisation policies (monetary and fiscal policies); and (iii) the creation of common institutions (namely the Council as a legislative body, the Commission as an executive body, the Parliament as a co-legislative body and the Court of Justice as the judicial body).

These three pillars were implemented progressively in line with achieving incremental stages of integration. For instance, under the customs union phase, the removal of barriers covered the elimination of tariffs and quotas on goods.

1.3 Conceptual Definitions

Regionalism, regionalisation, regional economic integration, regional economic cooperation, regional trade agreements, free trade agreements, these and other similar terms appear frequently on newspapers, academic articles, and official documents when international trade, investment, or finance is concerned. In essence, they all refer to one phenomenon: the cross-border preferential economic initiatives undertaken by national governments or private sectors at regional or bilateral level, as opposed to multilateral initiatives which are conducted on the basis of non-discrimination under the auspice of the World Trade Organisation (WTO). [1]

Although these terms can be understood loosely and used interchangeably, it is important and useful to distinguish one term from another conceptually. Winters, when discussing the regionalism versus multilateralism debate, defines regionalism "loosely as any policy designed to reduce trade barriers between a subset of countries regardless of whether those countries are actually contiguous or even close to each other". [2] According to Lamberte, regionalism refers to "formal economic cooperation and economic arrangements of a group of countries aimed at facilitating or enhancing regional integration." [3] Regionalism is to be distinguished from regionalisation, which is "market-driven integration, spurred by unilateral reforms in individual economies within a particular region". [4] Literally, regionalisation also refers to the actions of building regionalism through public and/or official efforts. According to the Dictionary of Trade Policy terms developed by the WTO, regionalism is described as "actions by governments to liberalise or facilitate trade on regional basis, sometimes through free-trade areas or customs unions." [5]

Following these inspirations, economic regionalism can be roughly understood as (a) formal economic cooperative measures (b) undertaken by governments (c) to facilitate regional economic integration (d) which however is not necessarily confined to a geographical region. Put differently, regionalism can now be broadly characterised as the tendency towards the creation of preferential trade arrangements between a number of countries located in the same or even different regions, which discriminate against third countries.

1.3.1 Economic Integration and Balassa's Stages Approach: This naturally leads to the definition of economic integration. Bela Balassa, in his seminal work The Theory of Economic Integration, defines economic integration as a process and a state of affairs: "Regarded as a process, it encompasses measures designed to abolish discrimination between economic units belonging to different national states; viewed as a state of affairs, it can be represented by the absence of various forms of discrimination between national economies".

Balassa further explains the different forms of integration Economic integration … can take several forms that represent varying degrees of integration. There are free-trade area, a customs union, a common market, an economic union, and complete economic integration. In a free-trade area, tariffs (and quantitative restrictions) between the participating countries are abolished, but each country retains its own tariff against non-members. Establishing a custom union involves, besides the suppression of discrimination in the field of commodity movements within the union, the equalization of tariffs in trade with non-member countries. A higher form of economic integration is attained in a common market, where not only trade restrictions but also restrictions on factor movements are abolished. An economic union, as distinct from a common market, combines the suppression of restrictions on commodity and factor movements with some degree of harmonization of national economic policies, in order to remove discrimination that was due to disparities in these policies. Finally, total economic integration presupposes the unification of monetary, fiscal, social, and countercyclical policies and requires the setting-up of a supra-national authority whose decisions are binding for the member states.

Since its introduction, the Balassa-stages approach has been indispensable for an understanding of both the literature and practice of economic integration. The usage of this approach is widespread and the terms contained therein for describing the different degrees of integration, especially the free-trade area and customs union, have hence come into fairly standard usage. It is nonetheless important to note that, in light of the later theoretical and practical development of regionalism, the Balassa-stages approach should be amended and clarified in order to provide a more precise analytical framework for economic integration. For example, it should be understood that the Balassa-stages are presented sequentially for the purpose of analysis, and hence the sequence is not to be followed rigidly. Economic integration in Europe, for instance, started directly with a customs union instead of a free-trade area. Balassa's distinction between a common market and an economic union also presents a conceptual problem.

The European Union's experience shows that integration beyond custom union is difficult to define and conceptualise, and in this sense Balassa's third and fourth stages (common market and economic union) should be taken together. Furthermore, it is probably not necessary or useful to define the final stage as "total economic integration" with a supranational authority. It is more realistic to "envisage several partial 'unions' beyond the economic union, such as a tax union, a social union, a monetary union and a political union". Whether these sub-unions will work together toward the formation of a unitary state, as Balassa's final stage implies, is currently beyond the theoretical studies as well as the practice of economic integration.

In both the literature and legal instruments of economic integration, the term "single market" is becoming increasingly popular. The Single European Act of 1987 formally created a

Single Market in Europe that came into operation on 1 July 1987. [6] In the 2003 Declaration of Association of South East Asian Nations (ASEAN) Concord II (Bali Concord II), the heads of ASEAN countries adopted the goal that the "ASEAN Economic Community shall establish ASEAN as a single market and production base." [7]

Apparently, a single market is more than a common market, but how much more is an interesting question. The Single European Act describes it as "an area without internal frontiers in which the free movement of goods, persons, services and capital is ensured". Criticising the imprecision of this definition, Lloyd defines a single market "as one in which the Law of One Price must hold in all goods, services and factor markets", which means that "there should be a single price in the region wide market for every tradable commodity and factor, expressing all prices in a common currency and adjusting for the real costs of moving goods or factors between locations". [8] In essence, a single market requires not only the elimination of border measures and full national treatment of beyond-the-border measures applying to imports, but also harmonisation of rules and procedures across participating states. "Hence, a single market is synonymous with complete economic integration of the area". [9]

However, without becoming a unitary state, how complete the market can be remains a question beyond the reach of this chapter. Regionalism, as noted above, can be a cross-region phenomenon. For analytical purposes, it is useful to define regional economic integration as a dynamic process encompassing the integration of economies within a geographic region. Hence in this paper, "regional economic integration in Asia", "Asian regionalism" or "East Asian regionalism", or other similar terms, are all used to refer to the integration activities in the particular Asian region concerned.

1.4 Meaning of RTA sans FTAs

Economic integration is conducted through trade

agreements. It is important to define the concepts of "regional trade agreements" ("RTAs") and "free trade agreements" ("FTAs") which are to be used frequently in this paper. Following the usage of the WTO, this paper does not distinguish between regional trade agreements or free trade agreements, as, "in the WTO context... RTAs may be agreements concluded between countries not necessarily belonging to the same geographical region." [10] There is also no distinction made between bilateral trade agreements concluded between two parties and those agreements between more than two parties. They are instead all referred to as regional trade agreements or free trade agreements, with the two terms used interchangeably in this paper. [11] However, to the extent that RTAs also cover agreements between countries in different regions, Asian RTAs are used to mean those arrangements between countries in Asia.

Economic integration may be conducted through different approaches, each of which however also represents a different degree of integration. Three approaches may be distinguished in this regard. [12] First, there is sectoral integration, which is used to mean integration which is "(i) limited to particular industries or sectors of the economy or economies concerned; (ii) gradual, proceeding successively from sector to sector." Second, functional integration refers to integration which is "(i) gradual, proceeding successively from sector to sector; (ii) by means of price incentives operating in a free market." In its first aspect, functional integration is identical to the second sense of sectoral integration. However, the latter is more inclined to be used as distinct from general across-the-board integration. The last one is institutional integration, used to mean integration which is "by means of adaptations of national or international institutions (in the widest sense of the word, for example, monetary practices and arrangements)."

In the regionalism literature, the second sense of institutional has been more customary. Sectoral and/or functional integration is often characterised as "market-driven" integration whilst institutional integration is known as "policy-driven." It has been observed that regional economic integration in Europe under the auspice of the European Union (EU) corresponds more to the policy-driven model of institutional integration as, in Europe, "the origins of integration have been institutional in nature, and the development of institutions has been prominent throughout the process." [13] In contrast, integration in East Asia has been market- driven. Although the existing institutions in this region are fairly weak and ineffective, "Intra-industry trade in parts and components and foreign direct investment—conducted by corporations and encouraged by significant liberalisation—have been and continue to be the key driving forces of the established production-sharing system, of the evolution of these cross- border networks and of the fostering of regional cooperation and integration." [14] As will be discussed below, China is a major player in this production-sharing regime and plays a key role in shaping the market-driven integration in Asia.

It is, however, over-simplistic to characterise any of the two integration model as entirely market-driven or policy-driven. The role of market forces in European integration should never be underestimated. For instance, in the sense that the extent of regionalisation is commonly measured by the share of intra-regional trade in total trade, intra-regional trade in Western Europe (EU-15) had amounted to over 50 percent long of total volume of trade before the Single Market was formed in 1992. On the other hand, national governments in Asia, through inter-governmental cooperation, have been playing a significant role in the integration process, albeit Asian supranational institutions have not yet developed.

Lastly, it is fundamentally important to stress that, although regional integration requires the existence of substantial political will to cooperate, it does not necessarily include the political commitment to political integration or political union. In other words, "aspirations for political union are not a necessary precondition for building regional institutions that foster economic integration." [15] This is of course the experience of Europe, but it would be highly relevant in the Asian context as political integration in Asia is almost unattainable in the foreseeable future.

1.5 Do Regional Trade Arrangements Help or Hinder Multilateral Liberalisation?

The debate surrounding this question can be colourfully illustrated by recounting the famous exchange between two eminent economists, Larry Summers and Jadish Bhagwati, at a World Bank conference in 1992. Summers, the head of the Bank's research department at the time, was supposed to welcome Bhagwati as the keynote speaker with the customary 'few kind words'. Instead, Summers launched into a half hour discourse on what a good thing regional integration was. His most famous line was "I like all the 'isms', unilateralism, regionalism and multilateralism." Feeling quite upstaged, Bhagwati quietly fumed until it was his turn. Taking the floor, Bhagwati launched into an energetic attack on the Panglossian embrace of regionalism. Among his many dire predictions, he argued that regionalism would undermine the GATT-based world trading system, place small nations under the thrall of hegemonic powers, and even foster wars among trade blocs.

This debate—which has raged for more than a decade—brings to mind the Buddhist parable, 'The Blind men and the Elephant'. Once upon a time a wise Raja summoned all the men in his realm who were born blind and proceeded to present an elephant to them. To one he showed its ears, to another its tusk, to another its trunk, and so on. He then said, "Tell me blind men, what sort of thing is an elephant?" Each gave his view, and since each had felt the elephant with his own hands, each was stubbornly sure that he knew the true nature of an elephant. They began to quarrel and eventually came to blows over the matter.

The morale of this story applies directly to the regionalism debate. Liberalising on a regional basis means liberalising on a discriminatory basis. Therein lays the two-sided nature of regionalism. The "liberalisation" part in "discriminatory liberalisation" is generally good since it removes artificial barriers between domestic and some foreign producers. The "discrimination" part, by contrast, is generally bad since it creates new barriers between various foreign producers. Plainly then, one cannot know whether regionalism helps or hinders multilateralism based on pure logic. This brings us to the state of the debate.

1.5.1 Bhagwati School and Regionalism: The Larry-Summers school-of-thought looks at discriminatory liberalisation and sees liberalisation. An outcome it welcomes since it views regionalism as having a largely benign effect on the multilateral system. The Jagdish Bhagwati school looks at discriminatory liberalisation and sees discrimination. An outcome it views as a serious threat to the WTO-centred world trading system. It is better to first consider the logic behind the Bhagwati school's thinking.

The Bhagwati-school posits two key risks of regionalism (see for example his tract entitled "The dangerous drift to preferential trade agreements"):

- Regional liberalisation is a substitute for multilateral liberalisation, and this for two reasons: it dampens nations' enthusiasm for further multilateral liberalisation, and it diverts policy makers' attention from WTO rounds.
- Regionalism shifts power in worrying directions, specifically it fosters greater dominance of small nations by hegemonic powers, and it increases the chances of inter-bloc trade war.

1.5.2 Regionalism's Dark History: Regionalism and Fascism in Europe and Asia: The Bhagwati fears are based first and foremost on historical analysis. As Doug Irwin wrote "In the interwar period discriminatory trade blocs and protectionist bilateral arrangements contributed to the severe contraction of world trade that accompanied the Great

Depression". The latter wave of regionalism is often associated with the pursuit of beggar-thy-neighbour policies and substantial trade diversion. Worse yet, regionalism was associated with some of the most horrific episodes that humankind has ever witnessed—the WWII fascist regimes.

This may seem like an unnecessary diversion in a paper on regionalism and multilateralism in the 21st century, but it is not. When Jagdish Bhagwati and Anne Kruger write about the "dangerous drift" of regionalism, they have the interwar period in mind.

1.5.3 Fascism, Autarky and Regionalism: Fascism is organised around the primacy of the nation and when it comes to economic policy this means promoting national industry by, among other things, avoiding 'destructive competition.' High tariff barriers were an important part of this in the 1920s and 1930s. Of course, protectionism was embraced by all major states in those times, but with an important difference. Most nations viewed protection as a stop-gap measure to address the crisis of unemployment and/or as a reaction to foreign protectionism. In Fascist Italy, Germany and Japan, by contrast, international trade per se was viewed with suspicion. Indeed, national self-reliance, i.e. autarky, was an explicit goal of policy. The connections can be made most clearly by tracing out the logic linking fascism, autarky and regionalism in its most destructive expression—Hitler's territorial ambitions known as Lebensraumpolitik in German. Hitler, whose formative years were deeply marked by the economic disruptions in the 1920s and 1930s, was thoroughly suspicious of trade. He believed that the Great Depression was caused by an over production of manufactured goods and explicitly rejected the notion that a nation could prosper as an exporter of manufactured goods and an importer of food.

Moreover, while the Atlantic Europeans had prospered and industrialised with the help of captured overseas markets (colonialism), Germany's colonial ventures were economic disasters. The development of Germany's industry relied much more on the formation of a regional trade bloc among the hundreds of small states of the German Confederation–Bismarck's famous customs union (Zollverein). Hitler's suspicions of relying on foreigners via trade were confirmed when the League of Nations placed trade sanctions on the Italian fascist state in reaction to Italy's invasion of Northeast Africa.

Hitler's mistrust of trade interacted with his dual doctrines of 'race' and 'space' to produce a radical and particularly destructive trade policy. There was nothing new about his belief that his race was superior; many people believe this of their own race even today. The dangerous innovation was his view of history as a struggle among races, with a winner-take-all outcome being inevitable. Each race, he thought, had to balance its population and its living space. If a people choose to adjust its population to its living space, Hitler thought, decline and eventual enslavement by another race was inevitable.

"Hitler had no confidence in the possibility of increasing food production from available land. The struggle for existence in which the races of the world engaged, the basic element of life on earth, was fundamentally a struggle for space. In this struggle the stronger won, took the space, proliferated on that space, and then fought for additional space. Racial vitality and spatial expansion were directly related" (Weinberg 1996 p. 34).

In short, Hitler, viewed trade with suspicion and autarky as a merit, but he realised that Germany could not prosper in isolation. The solution, he decided, was to rearrange international boundaries so that international trade became domestic trade. Signing bilateral trade agreements with fellow fascists and future victim nations were stepping stones to military invasion.

Italian fascism pursued a similar logic towards a similar goal, but in Mussolini's case the end point was a new Roman Empire. Fortunately, Italian fascists failed to implement the territorial expansion phase as effectively as the Nazis. Japanese fascism followed a similar logic taking steps towards what eventually became the "Greater East Asia Co- Prosperity Sphere". In the Japanese case, apologists for imperialism sought to justify the regional trade bloc in terms of anti-Western imperialism. In all cases, fascism aimed to set up more or less autarky trade blocs designed primarily to further the economic and political power of the hegemonic power.

1.5.4 Non-fascist Trade Blocs: The regional arrangements formed between World Wars I and II by non-fascist nations were highly discriminatory, relying on high external tariffs to provide preferential market access. For example, France and Great Britain sought to consolidate their empires. France formed a customs union with members of its empire in 1928 and the Commonwealth system of preferences established by Great Britain in 1932. Smaller European nations reacted defensively. Hungary, Romania, Yugoslavia, and Bulgaria each negotiated preferential access for their agricultural goods with various European countries. Belgium, Denmark, Finland, Luxembourg, the Netherlands, Norway, and Sweden signed economic agreements throughout the 1930s. Outside of Europe, the United States forged almost two dozen bilateral commercial agreements during the mid-1930s, many of which involved Latin American countries.

1.5.5 Building Blocs: Logic and Hopes: Summers' argument is basically a reaction to Bhagwati's fears. Bhagwati recalls that regionalism lead to terrible outcomes in the past and makes the general point that regionalism might be a substitute for multilateralism. Summer's argument is to implicitly reject this historical analysis, adopting a what-me-worry attitude, instead. According to Summers' worldview, post-WWII regionalism has resulted in a great deal of tariff removal and there is no clear evidence that regionalism has sidetracked multilateralism in the capitals that matter.

1.5.6 Prima Facie Rejection of Fears: The Summers point of view has been strengthened by the world's experience over the past 15 years. There are three salient points in the prima facie argument that "all the 'isms' are good".

1980s and 1990s regionalism did not thwart the Uruguay round Bhagwati's warnings fell on attentive ears in the early 1990s. The Uruguay Round, which was scheduled to finish in 1991, dragged on and on. In contrast, preferential trade arrangements in European and the Western Hemisphere spread like wildfire. By the mid- 1990s, however, this journalistic reading of history seemed passé. The Round finished, the WTO was set up and the nations that were responsible for the final push for the WTO were exactly the ones who lead the wave of regionalism that Bhagwati asserted would undermine the Round. This leads to the second point.

Key multilateralist nations are also regionalists, and have been since World War II. Multilateral liberalisation since WWII has been wildly successful at cutting developed nations' industrial tariffs. Yet the nations that steered this multilateral liberalisation—the US, the UK, the EEC6, the Nordics and Canada—are the same ones that drove regional liberalisation since the 1958 Treaty of Rome, the 1960 Stockholm Convention, and the 1965 Canada-US Auto Pact. Japan is the exception that confirms the rule. Although Japan has always been a good citizen when it comes to the multilateral trade system, it was never a leader in the GATT Rounds and it was also never involved in regional trade arrangements until recently.

Moreover where GATT Rounds failed, the regional route also failed. Historically, developed nations resisted agricultural trade liberalisation both multilaterally and regionally, and developing nations resisted tariff-cuts on manufactures both multilaterally and regionally.

1.5.7 Multilateralism as a Response to Regionalism: Finally, a number of observers believe that regional integration efforts promoted multilateral liberalisation via 'competitive liberalisation' (to use Fred Bergsten's term). For example, most scholars believe that formation of the EEC induced the

US to push for multilateral tariff-cutting via the Kennedy Round. Kenen (1989) provides the textbook treatment, which entails two steps. First, the phase-in of EEC preferences harmed US exporters. Second, redressing the discrimination required multilateral liberalisation (the direct way to offset it, joining the EEC, was unthinkable). In this roundabout way, European regionalism created a burst of free-trade multilateralism among US exporters, and the US government followed suite. Similar arguments have been made that the EU's Single Market Programme (announced in 1985 and ratified in 1986) fostered the launch of the Uruguay. See Schiff and Winters (2003) for more examples.

A dynamic view of regionalism and multilateralism: For ten years, I've been pushing a more focused rejection of the Bhagwati fears. Building political economy models of trade liberalisation known as 'the domino theory of regionalism', and the 'Juggernaut theory of reciprocal liberalisation'.

Dominos and Juggernauts: To think about regionalism's role as a stumbling or building bloc, it is useful to answer two questions independently and then to hook them up in the next section. The questions are: "Why are countries eager to open markets regionally?" and; "Why has GATT/WTO multilateral talks been so successful at liberalising the industrial tariffs of industrialised nations?" We take these questions in turn.

Why does regionalism spread in waves? One oft-heard explanation for why regionalism is so popular rests on two assertions.

- Regional integration has prospered as an alternative to multilateralism since multilateral trade negotiations have become too cumbersome to deal with today's complex trade issues. (This argument, first introduced when the Uruguay Round proved difficult to conclude, as re-emerged as the Doha Round is proving difficult to conclude.)
- Regionalism is fostered by the United States' conversion from devoted multilateralist avid regionalist.

Both of these assertions are just plain wrong, as have argued by (Baldwin 1997). In Baldwin (1993, 1995), he proposed a very different answer–the domino theory of regionalism.

1.5.8 Domino Theory of Regionalism: This theory is simple. It starts with an idiosyncratic shock, such as deeper integration of an existing regional bloc or formation of a new FTA for political reasons. This triggers membership requests from countries that were previously happy to be non-members. Why? The stance of a country's government concerning membership in a regional bloc is the result of a political equilibrium that balances anti-membership and pro-membership forces. Among the pro-integration forces are firms that export to the regional bloc. Since closer integration within a bloc is detrimental to the profits of non-member firms (trade diversion), closer integration will stimulate the exporters to engage in greater pro integration political activity. If the government was previously close to indifferent (politically) to membership, the extra activity may tilt the balance and cause the country to join the bloc. If the bloc enlarges, the cost to the non-members increases since they now face a cost disadvantage in an even greater number of markets. This second round effect will bring forth more pro-integration political activity in non-members and thus may lead to further enlargement of the bloc. The new political equilibrium will involve an enlarged regional trading bloc. Meanwhile it would appear that regionalism was spreading like wildfire.

If the trade bloc is open to expansion, virtually all nations who depend heavily on the bloc will end up signing preferential trade agreements (this is what has happened in Europe and most of the Mediterranean Basin). If the bloc's natural enlargement 'burnpath' is barred, the new political economy flames may find vent in preferential arrangements among excluded nations (this is what happened when Mercosol was formed). Notice that such regionalism could occur despite any progress being made in ongoing multilateral talks, unless these also promised to fully offset the discrimination.

The basic idea is not new. With hindsight, one can discern a version of it in Jacob Viner's account of how dozens of German principalities and city-states were cajoled and coerced into joining Prussia's Zollverein between 1819 and 1867 (Viner 1950 Chapter V.3). But the notion is probably much older. Bismarck himself probably understood the political-economy dynamics of trade diversion. Be that as it may, it is important to minutely examine the internal logic of even the oldest ideas and this requires maths. Baldwin (1993), which deals with EU enlargement, was the first formal framework to explore the dynamic political-economy implications of trade diversion. Several subsequent studies—most notably Yi (1996), Ethier (1996) and Siedmann and Winter (1997)—have elaborated the basic framework.

A domino effect has occurred repeatedly in Europe (e.g. in 1961, 1973, 1986, and 1994), and in the Western Hemisphere with NAFTA, the Enterprise for the Americas Initiative, Mercosol, and it is just starting in East Asia. (See Baldwin and Wyplosz 2003) The arrangement of preferential trade arrangements in the world is not completely random. In the Western Hemisphere and Europe, the system resembles an old fashioned wagon wheel, where the hub is a large economy (the US, the EU, Brazil-Argentina, etc.) and the spokes are the FTAs linking smaller, nearby nations to the hub.

The world is full of hub and spoke trade arrangements. What are the political economy forces that so systematically yield hub-and-spoke bilateralism?

1.5.9 Mercantilist View of Trade Negotiations: From a political perspective, exports are good and imports are bad. While this idea is economic nonsense from the medium- or long-run perspective, the important fact is that this mistaken reasoning points governments in the right direction. It leads them to conduct trade negotiations based on an exchange of market access. Specifically, since exports are good and imports bad, if country A wants better access to country's B's markets, then country A is expected to 'pay' for this market access by opening its own market to B's exports.

1.5.10 Law of the Jungle, MFN Rules and FTAs: Usually, the market opening that result from this mistaken reasoning is good for all nations involved. A drawback of this mechanism, however, is that may create a sort of law of the jungle. That is, with market access as the currency of exchange, big countries are rich and small countries are poor. The rules of the GATT correct this imbalance with the principle of Most Favoured Nations (MFN) treatment. However, when it comes to negotiating regional trade arrangements, MFN does not apply, so the law of the jungle may prevail. Nations with big markets are strong and those with small markets are weak.

1.5.11 Political Economy of Hub and Spoke Bilateralism: The political economy forces created by this law of the jungle foster hub-and-spoke bilateralism. Take a country like the Czech Republic in the mid-1990s, before it joined the EU. On the pro-liberalization side, Czech exporters have a large interest in the EU market, but only a minor interest in the market of, say, Estonia. On the anti-liberalization side, Czech import-competing industries dislike imports whether they come for the EU, Estonia or elsewhere. Now consider the line-up of political forces inside the Czech Republic. Czech exporters are willing to fight quite hard for market opening with the big EU market. They are willing to fight much less hard for market opening with Estonia. In other words, there are strong political forces backing market opening with the "hub" but very little support for market opening with other "spokes".

Since Czech protectionists simply want to reduce import competition from any source, the protectionists are likely to win when it comes to blocking spoke-spoke liberalization, though they lose when it comes to hub-spoke liberalization. An interesting add-on effect may occur if foreign investment from the hub is important in the spoke economies. To attract foreign investors, the spoke governments may promise protection from imports. Moreover, given a credible trade agreement with the hub, it is much easier for the spoke government to promise long-term protection against import from other spoke economies. If this sort of pandering-for-investment protectionism becomes quite common, the spoke economies may end up 'Balkanized'. That is, foreign multinationals may be enticed into locating inefficiently small production facilities in each spoke economy. Having done this, the multinationals may become a new anti-liberalization force. Companies from the hub that have invested in inefficiently small facilities in several spoke economies may resist efforts to liberalize spoke-spoke trade. This may make the hub governments more reluctant to take any initiative in redressing hub-and-spoke bilateralism.

Why FTAs between developing nations usually fail? If some idiosyncratic event stirs a great wave of enthusiasm for brotherhood among the spoke economies, politicians in these countries may sign agreements promising to open spoke-spoke trade. Yet once the headlines fade and the enthusiasm wanes, the drab politics of protectionism usually reasserts itself. Promises are broken, or never fulfilled and the expected liberalization never appears. Moreover, since protectionist forces reappear in both spoke economies, the broken promises are generally accepted without protest. Note how different the situation is for spoke-hub trade arrangements. Exporters in both the hub and the spoke (but especially those in the spoke economies) care a good deal about access to each other's market. Accordingly, exporters would raise their voices if promises were not kept. That is to say, the same sort of backsliding that is common in spoke-spoke agreements will not be tolerated in hub-spoke trade deals.

1.5.12 Domino Effect Applied to Hub and Spoke Bilateralism: The domino theory asserts that the signing of one preferential trade arrangement triggers a chain reaction in that it tends to induce other such arrangements, with the force of this effect feeding on itself. The theory was originally conceived to account for NAFTA and the create pro-EU-enlargement pressures that emerged in the 1990s. But the theory can be extended to the specific case of hub-and-spoke bilateralism. The above political economy reasoning suggests that exports to the hub are the key to the domino effect in this case, even though the full problem is radically more complex. To illustrate the basic logic as simply as possible, we make the extreme assumption that exports to the hub are the only thing that matter. To be concrete, suppose we have three nation that are potentially spoke, spokes 1, 2 and 3, and one potential hub. For simplicity's sake, assume that all of the spokes are symmetric to each other. Presuming the hub initially imposes an MFN tariff of T on all three of its partners, the signing of the first hub-to-spoke FTA raise the price facing exporters based in the spoke nation that negotiated the FTA. However, the extra competition in the hub market means implies a price and sales drop for exporters in the excluded spokes.

When the second hub-spoke FTA is signed, three things happen to spoke exports. The second FTA signer sees its exports rise as the price it faces rises. The first FTA signer sees an erosion of its preference, so its export volume and price fall in the hub market. The remaining spoke sees its exports fall as the price it faces for exports to the hub also falls. When the third and final hub-spoke FTA is signed, two things happen. The first and second FTA signer see their exports fall as the price they face falls to the free trade price. The third FTA signer sees its export volume to the hub expand significantly, as all the discrimination is removed, and the price it earns on exports to the hub rises.

To summarise, when we focus only on spoke exports, we can say that the gain is greatest for the first signer, next biggest for the second signer and smallest for the last. This ordering has important implications. Let us suppose that for some reason or the other, the hub cannot, or at least might be able, to simultaneously negotiate all three FTAs simultaneously. To keep things simple, let us make the artificial but useful assumption that the hub can do one FTA per year. It is obvious from the discussion above that any spoke that believes it will eventually sign an FTA with the hub would like to be the first one to do so. Or, to put it more colloquially, there will be scramble for the head of the queue, once the spokes knows that the hub is open to FTAs. Moreover, the same scramble would occur even if the hub can negotiate many FTAs at once but there is a possibility that some of these might be put off, or that at some point the hub would stop signing FTAs. This is what happened when the US and Mexico announced their FTA in 1990. Within months, Chile, Brazil, Argentina, Uruguay and Paraguay all formally or informally approached the US with requests for FTAs. The Bush administration, fearing five separate battles with protectionists in Congress, discouraged these efforts and offered the Enterprise for the Americas Initiative (EAI) instead; this was launched in June 1990.

According to CEA (1991 p. 255), the EAI created a process leading to free trade agreements, the first step of which required nations to sign so-called Framework Agreements. These committed countries to reducing their investment restrictions, inter alia, in exchange for promises of closer US ties in the future. Although the Framework Agreements might be viewed as unilateral 'concessions' by mercantilists, 26 Latin American countries signed them in 1991.

The model discussed above leaves out two very important elements. First, it ignores the impact of FTAs on the spoke's economies. A full analysis would account for the political economy forces opposing an FTA with the hub. While these are surely important to the whole picture, post-war history shows that very few spoke economies can resist the appeal of an FTA with the hub, once the hub starts signing such agreements. The second aspect has greater relevance to recent regionalism, namely, the attitude of the hub to further FTAs. In Europe, where the EU is clearly the hub, this is not an issue since the EU has committed itself to what might be called open

FTA-ism. The EU will sign an FTA with almost any nation that is democratic and is willing to accept the EU's insistence that agricultural trade be excluded. In the Americas, where the US is the dominant hub, things are quite different. The US has been extremely reluctant to accede to the many FTA offers it has received. Plainly, it would be nice to have a convincing analysis of why the EU and US approaches are so different, but I suspect that the real answer is non-economic.

1.5.13 Explaining the GATT/WTO's Success: The standard account of multilateral liberalisation starts from the Prisoner's dilemma created by so-called optimal tariffs. That is, nations, just like firms, can use their market power to force down the price of the goods they buy. According to the textbook presentation, all nations can improve their terms of trade by imposing a tariff (although the potential improvement is very small for very small nations). Terms-of-trade changes, however, are worse than a zero-sum game. If all nations strive of better terms of trade, the 'size of the pie' shrinks and all may end up worse off. Or, to put it differently, every nation may gain by removing its tariff in concert with other nations.

This standard account is a nice story, but it fails to explain most of the big facts of multilateralism. Stylising the facts for rhetoric's sake, only rich nations liberalised and then only industrial goods. Moreover, the process took 40 years. The Juggernaut theory proposes a very different approach. The theory was first posited informally by Baldwin (1994) and Baldwin and Baldwin (1996) and formalised by Baldwin and Robert-Nicoud (2004).

1.5.14 Juggernaut Theory of Multilateral Liberalization: The Juggernaut theory asserts that liberalisation begets liberalisation, so once the liberalisation ball starts rolling, it is difficult or impossible to stop. [16] Here is the logic. Wind back the clock to 1947 when the GATT became active. At that moment, tariffs started at levels that were politically optimal. That is, tariff levels—like prices in a competitive market—balance the supply and demand for protection in the political market. The main demanders of import protection are import-competing firms and workers they employed. The government was the supplier of protection, but was reluctant to raise tariffs to autarkic levels since this would harm the general economic health of the nation.

How to get the Juggernaut rolling? Starting from this situation, announcement of multilateral tariff-cutting talks based on the principle of reciprocity alters the array of political forces inside each and every nation participating in the talks on the basis of reciprocity. And reciprocity is the key. Reciprocity turns each nation's exporters from bystanders in the tariff debate to fervent opponents of protection within their own nation. Why? The principle of reciprocity means exporters win the prize of better access to foreign markets only if home tariffs are lowered. Thus lobbying against domestic tariffs becomes a way of lowering foreign tariffs. Since this rearrangement of political forces goes on inside every nation involved in the talks, a new political equilibrium emerges. Tariffs are cut because now the supply of protection shifts in (exporters increase the marginal political cost to their government of maintaining any given level of tariffs), but the demand for protection is unchanged. Note that tariffs do not go to zero, but they are cut in all participating nations and these tariff cuts are phased in over a 5 to 10 year period.

The phase in of tariff cuts at home and abroad alters the economic landscape and this generates a sort of political economy momentum.

1.5.15 Economic Source of Political Economy Momentum: In all participating nations, export sectors expand output and employment as foreign tariffs come down, and import-competing sectors reduce production and employment as home tariffs are lowered. In economic terms, the long-run supply responses in the export and import-competing sector are greater than the short-run responses. Why does this matter? Although many factors affect a sector's political influence in tariff-setting, size always matters. That is, other things equal, a sector with lots of workers, lots of capital and lots of profit will have more influence. Since the export sectors in all nations have expanded while all of the import-competing sectors have shrunk the next GATT/WTO Round leads to a different outcome. A few years down the road, when another multilateral Round is launched, reciprocity again re-aligns the tariff-setting balance by turning exporters into anti-protectionists. But this time, the pro-tariff camp is systematically weaker in every nation and the pro liberalisation camp is systematically stronger in every nation. The result is that all participating governments find it politically optimal to cut tariffs, but again not to zero.

As these fresh tariff cuts are phased in the cycle is repeated. This process means that any sector in any nation that is included in the reciprocal trade talks will eventually get liberalised.

1.5.16 Exceptions that Prove the Rule: Oversimplifying to make a point, tariffs in the world can be summarised in three points: they are zero on industrial goods imported into rich nations, they are high on food imported into rich nations and they are high on industrial goods imported into poor nations. How does the Juggernaut theory account for these 'facts'?

Until the 1990s, GATT Rounds focused on manufactured goods, so it is no surprise that food was not liberalised. More specifically, the import competitors in the EU, US and Japan were so strong that they managed to take food tariffs off the bargaining table, so no one inside the EU, US and Japan gained from lobbying against food tariffs. In this way, food tariffs were shielded from the relentless crushing force of the Juggernaut effect.

Developing nations have participated in GATT/WTO Rounds, but not on the basis of reciprocity. Until the 1970s, the GATT was a rich-man's club. Most poor nations were colonies or newly independent states, few of which wanted to join. When the merit of membership did become to be appreciated by some developing nations in the 1970s, the GATT adopted its "Enabling Clause" which should have been called the 'disabling clause' since it disables most of the GATT's discipline for poor nations. The Enabling Clause meant that developing nations did not have to make tariff concessions in order to gain better market access. Or, more to the point, GATT Rounds did not turn developing country exporters from bystanders to free traders. Under these rules, the multilateral talks had no impact on the array of pro-trade and anti-trade political forces within developing nations. Little wonder, then, that they decided to stay with the initial level of their tariffs, which were after all politically optimal to begin with.

1.5.17 Multilateralism and Regionalism as Complements: Does recent regionalism threaten the future of the world trading system? The best guess is that because trade is already quite free in the major trading nations, few regional liberalisations are capable of creating important anti-liberalisation forces. For this reason, most regional deals will weaken the key opponents of free trade (import competitors) while simultaneously strengthening its key proponents (exporters). Regional integration will, therefore, foster multilateral liberalisation and vice versa, just as it has done for the past 40 years.

If this is right, regional deals are not building blocks or stumbling blocks. Regionalism is half of the trade liberalisation 'wheel' that has been rolling towards global free trade since 1958. The discussion, hereto, has been relatively abstract. Which turns now to the most important "news item" when it comes to regionalism: East Asian regionalism.

1.5.18 Likely Evolution of East Asian Regionalism: At the end of 2004, the first hints of the 'wildfire regionalism' can clearly be seen in East Asia. No one, however, is in charge. There is no overarching plan for managing it. Judging from the history of unplanned regionalism in other areas of the world, the most likely outcome will be hub-and-spoke regionalism for a very simple reason. Bilateral trade flows in Asia form a hub-and-spoke pattern. As argued above, the mercantilist forces that drive nations' trade policies tend to free up major trade routes, leaving minor trade routes un-liberalised. Because bilateral trade flows in Asia form a hub-and-spoke pattern, the future pattern of FTAs is likely to follow the same pattern. But who will be the hub in East Asia? The results of the calculations in Baldwin (2003) suggest that both Japan and China will naturally emerge as hubs.

1.5.19 East Asian Bicycle: Two Hubs, Many Spokes: Tying the Baldwin (2003) hub-ness findings to political economy reasoning, it seems likely that the pattern of FTAs that will be signed in the next ten years will have two hubs, Japan and China—something like a bicycle. Of course, our numerical results are not essential to this prediction; it would also be suggested by a careful examination of the regional trade patter. The merit of the rough quantification of "bilateral attractiveness" is that it provides some discipline on what is usually an unruly analysis. One just cannot think of, say, Singapore or Vietnam, as a hubs even if they signed an FTA with every East Asian nation.

A schematic drawing of this prediction for East Asian FTAs. While it does not show all the FTAs (e.g. Singapore has signed many bilateral FTAs), it stylised the implications of rampant bilateralism. Since ASEAN is not an effective free trade area, it is shown as a dashed and irregular shaped line.

Hub status is all about market access. For most industries, domestic market access is quite important, so it is worth noting the so-called 'border effect' (McCallum 1995). As it turns out, domestic firms have much, much better access to the domestic market than foreign firms do, even when those foreign firms have duty free access. Consequently, the market access provided to a firm in Korea may be much less than one in Japan or China, even if there are Korean FTAs with both China and Japan, but no Japan-China FTA.

Another problem arises when considering the 'law of the jungle' bilateral FTAs between big and small nations naturally tend to reflect the concerns of the big nation much more than those of small nations—after all, market access is the currency in an FTA negotiation, so negotiators from big-market nations can 'buy' more than those from small-market nations. Given this hard fact of bilateralism, a spoke's FTA with China and its separate FTA with Japan is likely to impose conditions that diminish the attractiveness of the spoke market.

While there many, many other possibilities, it seems to me that the two-hub scenario is the most likely for East Asia–unless something is done to prevent it. (See Baldwin 2002, 2003 for a discussion of various solutions.)

Because regional trade liberalisation is both discrimination (i.e. not MFN) and liberalisation, its implications are profoundly ambiguous. The regionalism-is-a-stumbling-bloc school focuses on the discrimination. The regionalism-is-a-building bloc school focuses on the liberalisation. Baldwin has argued that for the most part, reciprocal liberalisation of most kinds tends to strengthen pro-trade political economy forces while at the same time weakening the anti-trade political economy forces, and this within each of the participating nations. He observed that North-North regionalism is not a threat to the multilateral system since it has been accompanied by multilateral liberalisation for so long. North-South regionalism is also not a problem since the Southern partner ends up facing something close to world prices via the previous MFN liberalisation of the Northern partner. South-South regionalism, however, poses the possible that it will create new, politically power interest groups that will oppose multilateral liberalisation. In his view, the only South-South regional trade agreements that have the potential of becoming real stumbling blocs are to be found in the southern cone of South America and in East Asia. The dangers of this would be mitigated if these developing nations fully participated in the exchange of market access taking place in the Doha Round.

1.6 Regionalism versus Multilateralism: Debate in the Asian Context

1.6.1 Economic Impact of RTAs: Trade Creating or Trade Diverting: Regionalism, practiced mainly through RTAs/FTAs at this stage, is questioned by conventional economic theory for its benefits to both the contracting parties and the third countries outside the agreements. Using the words of Jacob Viner in his pioneering analysis of the economics of customs unions, the question is about the economic costs and/or benefits of a RTA "(a) for each of the [RTA participating] countries taken separately; (b) for the two combined; (c) for the outside world; and (d) for the world as a whole." [17]

The analytical framework of the economics of RTAs is still based on the key concepts of trade creation and trade diversion introduced by Viner. Trade creation takes place when, as a result of the removal of tariffs on intra-area trade, domestic production of a product is displaced by imports from another member of the RTA whose comparative advantage enables it to produce the goods at a lower cost. The preferential tariff rate established by a RTA. might also cause trade diversion, defined as a shift of production away from a lower-cost producer outside the RTA. to a higher-cost source of supply within it. [18]

Both the economic literature and empirical studies of the impact of RTAs lead to notoriously ambiguous results. With regard to the trade stimulating effects of RTAs on the participating members, the findings generally suggest that RTAs have a positive welfare consequence on the members. [19] This is because regional cooperation in the RTAs "offers one route to overcome the disadvantages of smallness, by pooling resources or combining markets". [20]

RTAs can first of all foster competition in an enlarged market, and as such they can increase efficiency of domestic firms which have to face greater competition brought about by the entry of foreign competitors in previously trade-protected sectors. There are also market-size effects associated with RTAs, in the sense that the combined size of the consumer base and the suppliers can offer significant scale effects. Further, RTA membership can make the participating countries more attractive to FDI as foreign investors will be induced to invest in the integrated market. [21]

Trade-diversion of RTAs is an issue that economists and policy-makers have long studied and debated. In this regard, Viner's seminal contribution was in showing that the formation of a RTA is not necessarily welfare-improving. As Bhagwati puts it, this serves to "destroy the common fallacy that a preferential move toward (total) free trade was necessarily welfare improving and thus to demonstrate that all preferential paths to (total) free trade were not monotonic in welfare". [22] However, the voluminous literature generated thereafter does not offer conclusive evidence as to whether, in any particular RTA or all the RTAs overall, trade creation will exceed trade diversion or vice versa. [23] For instance, regarding the enlargement of the European Union (to include Greece, Portugal, and Spain), the study of Bayoumi and Eichengreen finds no evidence of trade diversion, while another study by Wei and Frankel discovers "massive trade diversion". Not surprisingly, former U.S. Treasury Secretary Lawrence Summers, who is also a distinguished economist, offered the opinion that "trade diverting regional arrangements may be desirable despite their trade diverting effects", and concluded that he found "it surprising that this issue is taken so seriously—in most other situations, economists laugh off second best considerations and focus on direct impacts" [24]

A very recent staff study of the International Monetary Fund (IMF), using a widely adopted gravity model, suggests that Asian RTAs have not led to trade diversion as the rapid trade growth among members for RTAs was not associated with any decrease in trade with non-members. Further, compared to RTAs in other regions of the world, the study suggests that "the members of RTAs in Asia-especially

ASEAN-showed a higher degree of openness with non-members than other RTA countries outside the region do". [25] According to the IMF study, the fact that RTAs in Asia have been more trade-creating than other RTAs to date can be explained by another fact, which is that "regional trade integration in Asia followed a long period of unilateral liberalization during the 1980s and 1990s". This is in line with the economic theory that, to avoid the asymmetric distribution of the gains and losses of integration between regional members, the best solution is to lower the external trade barriers. [26]

1.6.2 WTO Constraints on RTAs: A RTA must comply with WTO rules if any of its contracting parties is a WTO Member. However, any RTA, because it incurs preferential treatments only amongst its members inter se, is, by definition, a violation of the principle of non-discrimination of the WTO, embodied in the most-favoured nation clause in WTO Agreements such as the General Agreement on Tariffs and Trade (GATT) and the General Agreement on Trade in Services (GATS). The draftsmen of the GATT and the WTO Agreements were well aware of this and therefore created several safe harbours to accommodate RTAs. Under the current WTO regime, RTAs are subject to three sets of rules. The first is Article XXIV of GATT 1947 which, as clarified in the Understanding on the Interpretation of Article XXIV of the GATT 1994, provides for the formation and operation of customs unions and FTAs on trade in goods. The so-called "Enabling Clause", formally called the Decision on Differential and More Favourable Treatment, Reciprocity and Fuller Participation of Developing Countries passed by the GATT Council in 1979, permits preferential trade arrangements in trade in goods between developing country Members. Finally, Article V of GATS, entitled "Economic Integration", governs the formation of RTAs in the area of trade in services. [27]

Are the above rules effective in terms of judging the

WTO-consistency of any RTA? It is noted that "RTAs are generally WTO-consistent", albeit "this is because the requirements of Article XXIV and the Enabling Clause and GATS are very weak and have never been enforced".37 This statement reveals the poverty of the WTO rules in containing regionalism, despite the WTO's view that it is an adversary of the multilateral trading system. Regarding whether RTAs can comply with WTO Rules, one commentator observes. Theoretically, the answer is yes. After all, if a country is a Member of the WTO, the obligation to comply with the rules of the multilateral trading system is mandatory.

However, a more useful answer is probably "no", because of the reasons implied in the above analysis. To summarise, firstly, the WTO rules on the introduction of RTAs are troublesomely ambiguous and cannot be followed in an operational way. It is the inadequacy of the WTO rules that is principally to blame, as opposed to Members' non-compliance (if any). Secondly, the nature of the WTO as a consensus-based institution prevents it from strengthening the enforcement of the existing rules. Roughly starting with the examination of the EEC which was given up in early GATT days due to a clash of political interests, and was never picked up again.

Although the reason behind the failure of enforcement is the divergent interpretations of WTO rules by Members, the real implication seems to be that almost no R.T.A. can ever be declared unlawful under the current WTO regime and that the process of CRTA examination can, in practice, be ignored. Experience shows that, to comply literally with GATT/WTO rules governing RTAs, Members involved in RTAs need only to notify the agreements to the WTO in a timely fashion either before or after their taking effect. Until the WTO substantially revises its rules governing regional economic integration, there is no imminent need for RTA members to worry about compliance with the substantive WTO requirements. In this sense, since China has already notified the WTO of its RTAs, it can be assumed that those RTAs are to be deemed compatible by the WTO unless the WTO can render adverse reports and recommendations.

1.6.3 The Systemic Problems: The explosive proliferation of RTAs is constructing an extremely network of different trading rules. The existence of several hundreds regional agreements has meant overlapping members for many countries, some of which are parties to dozens of agreements. However, the fear of Asian RTAs being detrimental to the interests of trading nations has caused the ADB, an enthusiastic promoter of Asian regionalism, to point out that the proliferation of a large number of bilateral FTAs can lead to the "Asian noodle bowl effect" highlighted by [ADB] President Kuroda following Professor Bhagwati's initial observation. There can be harmful effects caused by multiple rules of origin arising from overlapping agreements among members of different FTAs. Complex rules increase administrative and business costs, particularly for small and medium enterprises which have limited capacity to deal with them. Furthermore, if they have large transactions costs, such rules can deter foreign investment and trade.

The complex rules and procedures for trade related policies in RTAs have also caused grave concerns in the private sector. In a trade conference of the United Nations Economic and Social Commission for Asia and the Pacific (ESCAP), a Hong Kong businessman pointed out the troublesome consequences for the global production system created by RTAs.

It is however politically unrealistic to expect the trading nations to call a stop to the proliferation of RTAs, especially in light of the domino effect of regionalism, whereby countries participate in bilateral or regional trade arrangements to avoid marginalisation as more and more countries become members of in many situations more than one RTAs. [28] Further, the formation of rules of origin and other rules or procedures in a R.T.A. is influenced by many factors, including, significantly, the interest of domestic producers who expect exclusive protection from those rules that may help to prevent competition from foreign exporters. It is important to bear in mind that, for many domestic interests, the philosophy of trade is not yet "the freer, the better." In the global context, the burgeoning number of RTAs has contributed to the trend of adding greatly to the complexity of international trade and to the costs of trade. Realistically, it is impossible to avert the problems entirely, as, by definition, RTAs have different rules and systems. A more practical solution might lie in synthesising RTAs with the multilateral, namely the WTO, system, including the harmonisation of rules and convergence of procedures and standards. The general idea is that, under the guidance of the principles of the WTO, Asian RTAs should adopt common rules and procedures to the maximum extent, and conduct most- favoured-nation (MFN) based liberalisation whenever possible.

1.6.4 Making Regionalism Complementary to Multilateralism: There is little doubt that multilateral liberalisation is still the best approach to international trade and development. Without challenging this, regionalists argue that regionalism is the second-best approach for liberalisation, especially given the frustration caused by the slow and halting pace of multilateral trade negotiations conducted under the auspices of the WTO.

The fact that WTO constraints on RTAs are ineffective does not entail that RTAs should be WTO-inconsistent. On the contrary, efforts should be made to ensure that RTAs are "building blocks" rather than "stumbling blocks" to the goal of multilateral freeing of trade. In this regard, the following recommendations are made:

- RTA members should reduce external trade barriers while participating in regional initiatives. Both theory and empirical evidence suggest that the lower the external trade barriers, the lesser the possibility of trade diversion.
- Solving the systemic problem represented by the

"spaghetti bowl" is a rather urgent problem for global RTAs. The complex rules of origin, used beyond what is necessary to prevent trade deflection or the transhipment of goods from third countries through a member for the purpose of obtaining preferential RTA tariffs, have indeed been evolving toward protectionism. While it is unrealistic to abolish the rules of origin in RTAs, it is highly advisable to harmonise them, although the process is doomed to be difficult. At the minimum, in the interest of regional integration, Asian countries, while negotiating RTAs, should reach an informal common understanding on adopting same or similar rules of origin.

- Apart from rules of origin, other trade institutions, including national policies, should also be harmonised or coordinated at the regional level to further economic integration, provided that the harmonisation is beneficial. This would involve domestic competition policies, product standards, regulatory regimes, investment laws, service rules, environmental polices, and so on.46 Policymakers should however be careful about this as, in some situations, "there are good reasons for diversity in domestic policies across nations and that harmonization is not a welfare-enhancing proposition". [29]
- In any event, a RTA should be WTO-plus and should adopt the common trade rules already established by the WTO.
- Open regionalism is integral to the success of RTAs which is building blocks of the multilateral trading system. "Open regionalism" is defined as having the following characteristics: (i) open membership, with membership extended to non- members on a mutually reciprocal basis; (ii) commitment of members to lower external trade barriers while trade is liberalised internally on an MFN basis; (iii) encouragement of unilateral liberalisation by members to other members or non-members. Although Asian countries are encouraged to conduct unilateral

liberalisation in any event, it is however doubtful that, in the interest of Asian economic integration, an Asian FTA or East Asian Economic Community should extend its membership to countries outside the region.

The comparison across regions and over time suggests several observations.

First, the overall association between institutionalization and the regional orientation of trade appears tenuous, as underscored by the fact that Asia ranks above North America despite lacking the regional equivalent of NAFTA.

Second, while regional institutions can strongly facilitate regional trade and investment, which they appear to have done in Europe and North America, they are not strictly necessary for robust regional markets, as evidenced by East Asia.

Third, market integration is an ambiguous predictor of regional cooperation in related areas, such as monetary and financial matters. If the integration of goods markets were the leading factor, East Asia could be expected to seriously pursue exchange-rate stabilization and monetary cooperation, as did Europe in the 1970s. So, the relationship between market integration and institutionalization of regional cooperation is likely to hinge substantially on factors residing in the broader context.

Notes

1. Alan Winters, "Regionalism versus Multilateralism" World Bank Policy Research Working Paper 1687 (Washington D.C.: The World Bank, 1996).
2. Mario B. Lamberte, "An Overview of Economic Cooperation and Integration in Asia" in Asian Development Bank, Asian Economic Cooperation and Integration: Progress, Prospects, and Challenges (Manila: Asian Development Bank, 2005) at 4.
3. Ibid.
4. WTO Secretariat, "Scope of RTAs", online: <http://www.wto.org/english/tratop_e/region_e/scope_rta_e.htm.
5. Bela Balassa, The Theory of Economic Integration (Homewood, Illinois: Richard D. Irwin Inc., 1961) pp 1.
6. The Single European Act, OJ L 169 of 29.06.1987.

7. The text of the Bali Concord II is available online at <http://www.aseansec.org/15159.htm>.
8. Peter Lloyd, "What is a Single Market. An Application to the Case of ASEAN" (2005) 22:3 ASEAN Economic Bulletin 251 at 252 and 254.
9. Peter Lloyd & Penny Smith, "Global Economic Challenges to ASEAN Integration and Competitiveness: A Prospective Look" REPSF Project 03/006a, at 11, online: <http://www.aadcp-repsf.org/cgi/axs/ax.pl.http://www.aadcp-repsf.org/docs/03-006a Final Report.pdf>
10. Ibid.
11. Jagdish Bhagwati has suggested the use of "preferential trade agreements" instead of free trade agreements and custom unions because the latter two phrases can mislead the public to equate them with non-preferential free trade. See Jagdish Bhagwati, Pravin Krishna & Arvind Panagariya, eds., Trading Blocs: Alternative Approaches to Analying Preferential Trade Agreements (Cambridge, Massachusetts: The MIT Press, 1999) pp 33.
12. F. Machlup, "Economic Integration" in Miroslav N. Jovanovic, ed., International Economic Integration: Critical Perspectives on the World Economy, Volume I: Theory and Measurement (London and New York: Routledge,1998) at 142.
13. Eisuke Sakakibara & Sharon Yamakawa, "Market-driven Regional Integration in East Asia" in Julie McKay, Maria Oliva Armengol & Georges Pineau, eds., Regional Economic Integration in a Global Framework 35-78 (Proceedings of the G20 Workshop, 22-23 September 2004, Beijing, China) (Frankfurt: European Central Bank, 2005) pp 35-38.
14. Julie McKay, Maria Oliva Armengol & Georges Pineau, eds., Regional Economic Integration in a Global Framework (Proceedings of the G20 Workshop held in Beijing, China, 22-23 September 2004) (Frankfurt: European Central Bank, 2005) pp 12-14.
15. C. Randall Henning, "Regional Economic Integration and Institution Building" in Julie McKay, Maria Oliva Armengol & Georges Pineau, eds., Regional Economic Integration in a Global Framework (Proceedings of the G20 Workshop held in Beijing, China, 22-23 September 2004) (Frankfurt: European Central Bank, 2005) pp 79-80.

16. The word 'juggernaut' – defined as "any massive inexorable force that advances crushing whatever is in the path" – stems from a British mispronunciation of the Hindu diety of the Puri shrine, Jagannath. A festival is held in Puri involving the 'chariot of Jagannath', an enormous and unwieldy construction that requires thousands of people to get it rolling. Once started, however, it rolls over anything in its path.
17. J. Viner, "The Economics of Customs Unions", in Miroslav N. Jovanovic, ed., International Economic Integration: Critical Perspectives on the World Economy, Volume I: Theory and Measurement (London and New York: Routledge, 1998) at 169.
18. Ibid.
19. 24 Asian Development Bank (ADB), Asian Development Outlook 2002 (Manila: Asian Development Bank 2002) at 176; World Bank, Global Economic Prospects 2005 (Washington DC: World Bank, 2005) at 57-65.
20. World Bank, Trade Blocs (Oxford: Oxford University Press, 2000) at 30-31.
21. ADB, supra note 24 at 175-176.
22. Jagdish Bhagwati, The World Trading System at Risk (Princeton, New Jersey: Princeton University Press, 1991) at 59.
23. Jiangyu Wang, "China's Regional Trade Agreements: The Law, Geopolitics, and Impact on the Multilateral Trading System." (2004) S.Y.B.I.L. 119 at 143.
24. Lawrence H. Summers, "Regionalism and World Trading System" in Policy Implications of Trade and Currency Zones (Kansas City: Federal Reserve Bank, 1991) 299, online:<http://www.kansascityfed.org/publicat/Sympos/1991/SYM91.HTM>.
25. International Monetary Fund, Asia and Pacific Regional Economic Outlook (Washington D.C.: IMF, 2006) pp 75, online: <http://www.imf.org/external/pubs/ft/reo/2006/eng/01/areo0506.htm> .
26. Bernard Hoekman & Maurice Schiff, "Benefiting from Regional Integration" in Bernard Hoekman, Aaditya Mattoo & Philip English, eds., Development, Trade, and the WTO (Washington D.C.: the World Bank, 2002) pp 552.
27. Marrakesh Agreement Establishing the World Trade Organization, 15 April 1994, 1867 U.N.T.S. 3 at Annex 1B, Art. V [Thereinafter WTO Agreement].

28. Regarding the domino effect of regionalism, see e.g., Richard Baldwin, "A Domino Theory of Regionalism", National Bureau of Economic Research (NBER) Working Paper No. 4465 (Cambridge, MA: NBER, 1993).
29. Arvind Panagaria, "The Regionalism Debate: An Overview" (1999) 22(4) World Economy 477 pp 506.

References

Albertin, G. (2001) "Will regional blocs expand?" LSE (mimeo).

Artis, M. and Nixson, F. (2001). The Economics of the European Union, Oxford University Press.

Balassa, B. (1974), "Trade creation and trade diversion to the European Common Market" in B. Balassa, European Economic Integration, North-Holland, Amsterdam.

Baldwin, Forsild, Martin, Ottaviano and Robert-Nicoud (2003) Economic Geography and Public Policy, Princeton University Press, London.

Baldwin, R.E. (1994), Towards an integrated Europe, CEPR, London. Manuscript freely downloadable from http://heiwww.unige.ch/~baldwin.

Baldwin, R.E. (2002), "Asian Regionalism: Promises and Pitfalls," paper presented at KIEP Seminar on East Asia Free Trade Agreement, held in Seoul Korea, 27 September 2002.

Baldwin, R.E. (2003), "The Spoke Trap," paper presented at KIEP in Seoul Korea, December 2003.

Baldwin, R.E. and C. Wyplosz (2003), The Economics of European Integration, McGraw-Hill, London.

Baldwin, R.E., R. Forslid and J. Haaland (1996). "Investment Creation and Diversion in Europe", The World Economy, Vol. 19, No. 6, pp 635-659.

Baldwin, Richard and A. Venables, (1995), 'Regional economic integration,' in Grossman and Rogoff (eds), Handbook of international economics: (Amsterdam: North Holland).

Baldwin, Richard E (1997). "The causes of regionalism", The World Economy, Vol. 20, No, 7, pp 865-888.

Baldwin, Richard E. (1987). "Politically Realistic Objective Functions and Trade Policy: PROFs and Tariffs", Economic Letters, 24, pp 287-290, 1987.

Baldwin, Richard E. (1993), "A domino theory of regionalism", NBER WP 4465 (Cambridge). Published as: Baldwin, Richard

E. (1995), "The domino theory of regionalism", in Baldwin, Haaparanta and Kiander (eds.), Expanding membership of the European Union (Cambridge: Cambridge University Press).

Baldwin, Richard E. (1993), "A domino theory of regionalism", NBER WP 4465 (Cambridge).

Baldwin, Richard E. (1994). Towards an Integrated Europe. CEPR, London.

Stepping stones or building blocs? Regional and multilateral integration 129 Baldwin, Richard E. and A. Venables (1995), "Regional Economic Integration", in Handbook of International Economics: Volume III, G. Grossman and K. Rogoff (eds.), North-Holland, Amsterdam.

Baldwin, Robert E., and Richard E. Baldwin (1996), "Alternative approaches to the political economy of endogenous trade liberalisation", European Economic Review, 40, 7775-782.

Barbieri, Katherine and Gerald Schneider. 1999. "Globalization and Peace: Assessing New Directions in the Study of Trade and Conflict." Journal of Peace Research, 36: 387-404.

Bergsten, F. (1996), "Competitive liberalisation and global free trade: A vision for the early 21st century", (Washington DC: Institute for International Economics).

Bergsten, F. (1996), "Open Regionalism", (Washington: Institute for International Economics).

Bhagwati, J (1993), "Regionalism and multilateralism: An overview", in Anderson, K and Blackhurst, R. (eds), Regional integration and the global trading system, (London: Harvester-Wheatsheaf).

Bhagwati, J and A. Krueger (1995), The dangerous drift to preferential trade agreements, (Washington: American Enterprise Institute).

Blomstrom, M. and A. Kokko (1997), "Regional integration and foreign direct investment", CEPR DP 1659 (London).

Brander, J. and P. Krugman (1983) "A reciprocal dumping model of international trade", Journal of International Economics 15, 313-321.

Brenton, Paul and M. Manchin (2002), "Making EU trade agreements work: the role of rules of origin", CEPS Working Document No. 183. www.ceps.be Cable, V. (1994), "Overview", in Cable, V. and D. Henderson (1994), Trade Blocs?

The future of regional integration, (London: Royal Institute of International Affairs).

CEA (1991), Economic report of the President, (Washington: Council of Economic Advisors).

CEPR (1992), Is bigger better: The economics of EC enlargement, CEPR, (London).

Commonwealth Secretariat (1995), "Impact of Uruguay Round and Nafta on Commonwealth Caribbean Countries", (London).

Cooper, C. and D. Massell (1965), "Towards a general theory of customs unions in developing countries", Journal of Political Economy.

Baldwin Davis, D. and D. Weinstein, 2002, "Market access, economic geography and comparative advantage: An empirical assessment," Journal of International Economics.

De Melo, J. and Panagariya, A. (1993), "Introduction", in De Melo, J. and Panagariya, A. (eds), New dimensions in regional integration, (Cambridge: Cambridge University Press for CEPR).

De Torre, A. and M. Kelly (1992), "Regional trade arrangements", IMF Occasional papers, No. 93 (Washington).

Deutsch, Karl W. 1968. The Analysis of International Relations. Englewood Cliffs, NJ: Prentice Hall.

Dixit, A., G. Grossman and E. Helpman (1997), "Common agency and coordination: General theory and application to government policy making", Journal of Political Economy, 105, 4, 752-770.

Either, W. (1996), "Multilateral roads to regionalism", CIES DP, (University of Adelaide).

Fernandez, R. (1997), "Returns to regionalism: An evaluation of non-traditional gains from RTAs", CEPR DP 1634 (London).

Freund, C. (1998) "Regionalism and permanent diversion", Board of Governors of the Federal Reserve System International Finance Discussion Papers Number 602.

Fujita M., Krugman P. and A. Venables (1999) The Spatial Economy: Cities, Regions and International Trade (Cambridge (Mass.): MIT Press).

Galal, A. and B. Hoekman (1997), Regional partners in global markets: Limits and possibilities in the Euro-Med agreements, CEPR (London).

GATT (1993c), GATT/1596, Press Communiqué, 16 September (Geneva).

Grossman and Helpman (1996), "Rent dissipation, free riding and trade policy", European Economic Review, 40, 795-803.

Grossman, Gene and Elhanan Helpman, (1994) "Protection for Sale," American Economic Review, 84, 833-850.

Harrison, G., T. Rutherford, and D. Tarr (1996), "The economic implications for Turkey of a customs union with the EU," Policy Research Paper, 1599, World Bank. http://econ.worldbank.org/files/589_wps1599.pdf

Hillman, A. (1982), "Declining industries and political-support protectionist motives", American Economic Review.

Stepping stones or building blocs? Regional and multilateral integration.

Hillman, A. (1989), The political economy of protection, (London: Harwood Academic Publishers).

Hufbauer, H and Schott, J.(1992), North American Free Trade: Issues and Recommendations, (Washington: Institute for International Economics).

Hufbauer, H and Schott, J.(1993), NAFTA: An Assessment, (Washington: Institute for International Economics).

Hufbauer, H, J. Schott, and D. Clark (1994), Western Hemisphere Economic Integration, (Washington: Institute for International Economics).

Irwin, D. (1996). Against the tide: An intellectual history of free trade. Princeton: Princeton University Press.

Kemp, M. and H. Wan (1976) "An elementary proposition concerning the formation of customs unions", Economic Journal.

Kowalcyz, C. and R. Wonnacott (1992). "Hubs and Spokes, and Free Trade in the Americas", NBER WP 4198.

Krishna , K. (2003), "Understanding Rules of Origin", Pennsylvania State University mimeo.

Krishna, K and A. Krueger (1995), "Implementing Free Trade Areas: Rules of Origin and Hidden Protection", NBER WP4983.

Krishna, P. (1998) "Regionalism and multilateralism: A political economy approach", Quarterly Journal of Economics 113(1), 227-251.

Krueger, A. (1993), "Free trade agreements as protectionist devices: Rules of origin", NBER WP 4352, (Cambridge MA).

Krugman, Paul (1980) Scale economies, product differentiation, and the pattern of trade, American Economic Review 70, 950-9.

Krugman, Paul (1993) "The Hub Effect: or Threeness in Interregional Trade", in W. Ethier, E. Helpman and J. Neary (eds), Theory, Policy and Dynamics in International Trade, Cambridge University Press, Cambridge.

Krugman, Paul (1993) "The Hub Effect: or Threeness in Interregional Trade", in W. Ethier, E. Helpman and J. Neary (eds), Theory, Policy and Dynamics in International Trade, Cambridge University Press, Cambridge.

Krugman, Paul (1993), "Regionalism versus multilateralism: Analytic notes", in De Melo, J. and Panagariya, A. (eds), New dimensions in regional integration, (Cambridge: Cambridge University Press for CEPR).

Baldwin Lawrence, R. (1996), Regionalism, multilateralism and deeper integration, (Washington: Brookings Institute).

Levy, P. (1997) "A political-economic analysis of free-trade agreements", American Economic Review 87(4), 506-519.

Mansfield, E. and H. Milner (1999). "The New Wave of Regionalism", International Organization 53, 3, pp. 589–627.

Mansfield, Edward D. and Jon C. Pevehouse. 2000. "Trade Blocs, Trade Flows, International Conflict." International Organization 54: 775-808.

Martin, P. and G. Ottaviano (1996), "The geography of multi-speed Europe", Economic International 67, 45-65. In English: CEPR discussion paper 1292.

McCallum, John (1995), "National borders matter: Canada-U.S. regional trade patterns', American Economic Review 85, 615-23.

Meade, James (1955), The theory of customs unions, Oxford.

Milward, A. (1992). The European rescue of the nation-state, Cambridge University Press, Cambridge.

Oneal, John R., Bruce Russett, and Michael L. Berbaum 2003 "Causes of Peace: Democracy, Interdependence, and International Organizations, 1885-1992" International Studies Quarterly 46 (1), March 2003.

Panagariya (1996), "APEC and the United States", CIES DP, (University of Adelaide).

Panagariya, A (1999), "Preferential trade liberalisation: The traditional theory and new developments", University of Maryland mimeo. (download form www.bsos.umd.edu/econ/panagariya/song/surveypt.pdf).

Puga, Diego and A. Venables (1997). "Preferential trading arrangements and industrial location", Journal of International Economics, 43, pp 347-368.

Robert-Nicoud, F. (2001) "A simple model of agglomeration with vertical linkages and capital mobility", LSE (mimeo).

Sapir, A. (1992), "Regional integration in Europe", Economic Journal.

Sapir, A. (1997), "Domino effects in Western European Trade, 1960-1992", CEPR DP (London).

Schiff, M. and L. Alan Winters (2003). Regional Integration and Development. New York: Oxford University Press for the World Bank.

Stepping stones or building blocs? Regional and multilateral integration 133.

Schott, J. (1988), "The free trade agreement: A US assessment" in J. Schott and M. Smith (eds), The Canada-US free trade agreement: The global impact, (Washington: Institute for International Economics).

Schott, J. (1989), "More free trade areas?" in J. Schott (ed.), Free trade areas and US trade policy, (Washington: Institute for International Economics).

Schott, J. and G. Hufbauer (1992), "NAFTA: Questions of form and substance", in Waverman, L. (ed.), Negotiating and implementing a North American free trade agreement, (Vancouver: The Fraser Institute).

Serra et al. (1997), Reflections on regionalism: Report of the study group on international trade, (New York: Carnegie Endowment for International Peace).

Smith, M. (1988), "The free trade agreement in context: A Canadian perspective", in The Canada-United States free trade agreement: The global impact (Washington: Institute for International Economics).

Summers, L. (1991), "Regionalism and the world trading system", in L. Summers (ed.) Policy implications of trade and currency zones, Federal Reserve Bank of Kansas City.

USTR (1981), North American Trade Agreements, (Washington: Office of the US Trade Representative).

Viner, J. (1950), The Customs Union Issue, Carnegie Endowment for International Peace, NY.

Weinberg, G. (1996). Germany, Hitler and World War II. Cambridge

University Press.

Whalley, J. (1993), "Regional trade arrangements in North America: CUSTA and NAFTA", in De Melo, J. and Panagariya, A. (eds), New dimensions in regional integration, (Cambridge: Cambridge University Press for CEPR).

Whalley, J. (1996), "Why do countries seek regional trade agreements?", NBER WP 5552 (Cambridge MA).

Whalley, J. (1996), "Why do countries seek regional trade agreements?", NBER WP 5552 (Cambridge MA).

Winters, A. (1996), "Regionalism versus multilateralism", World Bank Policy Research Working Paper 1687, (Washington).

Wolf, M. (1994), The Resistible Appeal of Fortress Europe (Washington: American Enterprise Institute).

Wonnacott, P. (1987), The United States and Canada: The quest for free trade, (Washington: Institute for International Economics).

134 Baldwin Wonnacott, R. (1990) "U.S. Hub-and-Spoke Bilaterals and the Multilateral Trading System", C.D. Howe Institute Commentary, No. 23, October 1990, pp. 1-22.

WTO (1995), Regionalism and the world trading system (Geneva: WTO Secretariat).

WTO (2003), "The changing landscape of RTAs", Regional Trade Agreements.

Section of the Trade Policies Review Division, WTO Secretariat; paper prepared for 14 November 2003 seminar in Geneva.

Yeats, S. (1997), "Does Mercosur's trade performance raise concerns about the effects of regional trade arrangements" World Bank Policy Research WP 1729 (Washington).

Yi, S. (1996), "Endogenous formation of customs unions under imperfect competition: Open regionalism is good", Journal of International Economics, 41, 151-175.

2

Prospects and Challenges of Asian Economic Integration: Lessons from European Union

2.1 Introduction

The History of the formation on the European Union takes us back around 1951, with the formation of European Coal and Steel Community (ECSC) between France, West Germany, Belgium, Luxembourg and the Netherlands to pool the steel and coal resources of its member-states. This treaty was sign at Paris. This was a fulfilment of a plan developed by a French economist Jean Monnet, publicized by the French foreign minister Robert Schuman, which was also strongly supported by the United States. The "Treaty of Pars" entered in force by 1952 and was time limited to 50 years. This coalition was very important because steel had played an important part in arms production in World War II and was a fundamental resource of the western European states.

The goal was a common program of post-war production and consumption of steel and coal that will unite in cooperation and reconciliation between the two countries: France and Germany by controlling steel and coal which were fundamental to war industries. The ECSC was the promoter for the later development of the European Community who became latter the European Union. The 9 May was chosen as The "European day" as a celebration of the creation of the European Union as Schuman presented the proposal on May 9, 1950 known as the "Schuman Declaration" that is considered to be the beginning of the creation of the Union. Encouraged by the United States, an attempt was made to create a European Defence Community (EDC) and a European Political Community (EPC) to allow troops to be raised from

Germany to face the Soviet threat but these attempts proved overambitious.

The European Union will have a European Commission that was formally the Commission of the European Communities as the executive body and alongside with the European Parliament and the Council of the European Union where the three main institutions governing the Union. The Enlargement Europe's integration project has now been running for half a century, a period spanning the post-war birth of economic cooperation and the more recent enlargements and deepening of the union. The project has been enormously successful in both political and economic terms, although there have been frequent tensions and undoubted failures. This paper draws out some of the main messages from the European experience of integration. We look at both the political and institutional development of the European Union, and at its economic development. What have been the driving forces behind the integration process? What institutions have developed to manage integration? What has been the impact of integration on trade flows and income levels across European countries? We then endeavour to draw out some of the lessons that the European experience may have for integration in Asia. Evidently, the two continents are very different in both political and economic terms. On the economic side, integration has had a large impact on European trade and incomes, both through trade creation and through intensifying competition. One might argue that the heterogeneity of countries in Asia offers an even greater potential for trade creation, and also for using integration as a force to facilitate the development of production networks.

On the political level, European experience suggests that achieving the economic gains has required continuing and far reaching policy measures. These, in turn, require a deep political commitment to integration and the existence of institutions to promote integration and protect it from the inevitable inter-member frictions and preoccupations with national goals. In Europe progress has been driven largely by the Franco-German partnership and by the Brussels institutions. It is hard to see what their equivalents in Asia might be. Therefore, for Asia, the economic arguments are compelling but the lack of political commitment suggests that trade integration will not necessarily be followed by deeper economic integration.

2.2 European Integration and Institutions with Asia

This section reviews the history of European integration and institutions to see what lessons they contain for Asia. It will become plain that the two exercises are fundamentally different and that the casual drawing of parallels could be very misleading.

2.2.1 EU: Apolitical Ideological Phenomenon: European integration is has a long history .It is an ancient aspiration, although its current manifestation arises from the geo-politics of the mid-twentieth century: the desperate need, following World War II, to find a way of preventing future Franco-German conflict, coupled with a strong sense of internationalism that saw the future in terms of institutionalized co-operation between countries. [1] Perhaps the most important factor in understanding the history of post-war European integration is to see that it was essentially apolitical-ideological phenomenon. It was not driven by the careful calculation of economic costs and benefits, still less by trade negotiators, but by a grand vision which had fortunate economic side effects. This fact has had fundamental effects on Europe's evolution, for the grand vision which helps to move internal debates beyond mercantilism and the calculation of benefits issue-by-issue. It induces a generalized reciprocity, whereby every party gains in the end, but where every one recognizes the value of the system as a whole and is prepared to accept losses on some deals. The day-to-day compromises necessary to achieve co-operative outcomes become easier to make, or, which is basically the same thing, easier to sell at home.

2.2.2 Framework of European Institutions: The first major step in modern European integration was the European Coal and Steel Community (ECSC), founded in 1951, whose origins illustrate the political motivation for integration. Its purpose was to stimulate the recovery of heavy industries in (West) Germany while making it impossible for their output ever to be used to wage war again. The proposal-due to Jean Monnet and Robert Schuman-was that, by establishing a truly common European market in coal, iron and steel, countries would become so interdependent that war would be not only 'unthinkable, but materially impossible'. The customs union was supplemented by a 'High Authority', which had the power to dictate national output quotas, establish maximum and minimum prices, and enforce competition. The High Authority was an administrative body, controlled in policy but not day-to-day matters by a Council of the Community on which the separate governments were represented, and also by a European Parliament. A Court of Justice was established to oversee the legal aspects of the Community. Following the ECSC, attempts were made to establish both a defence community (the EDC) and a political community (the EPC).

Both failed, so the 'integrationists' were thrown back onto economic integration in the form of the European Economic Community (EEC), and the atomic energy community (Euratom), which were created in the Treaties of Rome in 1957. At first, the EEC and Euratom existed separately but parallel to the ECSC, but in 1967 the three bodies were merged, to from the European Communities (EC) with one Commission (successor to the High Authority), one Council, one Parliament and one Court. The Maastricht treaty, in 1992, turned the EC into the European Union (EU), creating European citizenship, some cooperation in foreign and security affairs, and paving the way for monetary union. These institutions of integration have evolved and expanded, but the basic structures remain as they always were. Thus although the

EU now has a common currency (introduced for the 'Eurozone' countries in 2002) and (limited) powers to make common political and foreign policies, it is in essence just a continuation of the old EEC, with institutions designed primarily for deep micro-economic integration. Its governance is shared between a Commission, a Council, a Parliament and a Court. The Commission comprises commissioners appointed by member states for four-year terms, two from each of the larger members and one from the others. It initiates Union policy and executes it, but it cannot actually make policy - that falls to the *Council.*

The Commission is explicitly supranational, and is charged with preserving and promoting the European ideal. The *Council* formally comprises the foreign ministers of all member states, although much business is conducted by ministers concerned with specific issues, e.g., agriculture ministers discuss the Common Agricultural Policy (CAP). [2] The Council shares executive power with the Commission. It may adopt the latter's policy proposals, in which case they become law, but it may not generally amend them. Decisions are theoretically taken by qualified majority vote, where votes are allocated to member states according to size.

Until the 1990s, however, all countries informally had a right of veto on issues of alleged fundamental national interest (under the "Luxembourg Compromise"). As a result decisions had to be reached by trading compromises (often on unrelated issues) to obtain a unanimously acceptable package. Recently strong efforts have been made to re-establish majority voting in most spheres (but not, for example, fiscal policy and various 'pet areas' such as audio-visual policy) and there is hope that this will reduce the horse-trading. Nonetheless, the tradition of consensus remains strong within the EU. The Court of Justice interprets Union law. Its findings are binding even on member governments. The judges are appointed by member states, but they are required to be quite independent of national interests and cannot be removed by member governments. The

European Parliament has a small but growing role in the Union. It must be consulted by the Commission and the Council before they decide many issues, and it has some power over the Union budget. Its greatest power is to dismiss the Commission *en masse,* although this is such an unwieldy weapon that it is of little practical use. [3] These institutions form a constitutional structure just as complex and delicately balanced as the US Constitution, but without, of course, its democratic legitimacy. Like the latter, they have to balance "states' rights" against the centre and rely on powerful legal bodies for enforcement. Arguably such balances are necessary to create the confidence that allows member governments to proceed with deeper aspects of integration that impinge directly on issues of sovereignty and internal distributions of income.

2.2.3 Success and Failure Go Together: European integration has always been a rather 'on and off' affair with periods of enthusiasm and rapid advance followed by periods of doubt and retrenchment. The former are, understandably, associated with economic booms and the latter with recessions. Thus he early 1980s found the EU very much down in the dumps. After the severe anti-inflationary policies at the beginning of the decade, the US and Japanese economies began to recover, but those of the EU seemed firmly stuck in the mire. Moreover, the rapid increase in intra-EU trade that had characterized the early stages of integration seemed to have halted or even gone into reverse. The cry was frequently heard that 'the steam had gone out of integration' and doubts were expressed about the viability of the EU as an institution, let alone any further progress.

During such 'depressions', the Commission's role as the guardian and champion of the European ideal has been vital to the goal of integration. While member governments, and thus the Council of Ministers, are focusing on their local problems, the Commission is constitutionally required to take a broader, longer, and more European view. In the mid-1980s its response to the lethargy of the European economy was dramatic and imaginative. It had long been recognized that the actual integration of the EU economies fell short of the aspirations of the Treaty of Rome. Recalling the stimulus that the initial creation of the EEC had induced, and following the prevailing intellectual trend towards economic liberalism, the Commission proposed a bold step towards complete economic integration with the launch in 1986 of the Single Market Initiative.

Similarly, the Commission was the driving force behind the Maastricht Treaty of 1992, which formally created the EU and extended the competences of the Union to foreign affairs and justice. This was far from popular, being rejected by a referendum in Denmark and very nearly so in France. It illustrates a further cycle in the dynamics between the Commission and the states: flushed with one success (in this case the Single Market), the Commission attempts to follow it by further deep integration and centralization, only to find it rejected by governments and electorates. A further cycle followed, with the adoption of monetary union (2002), and then the rejection of the proposed EU constitution by the voters of France and the Netherlands (2005). These rejections, however, do not threaten the basic fabric of the common market: tribute to its deep foundation in European perceptions, and to its pragmatic and non-confrontational mode of progress.

2.2.4 Balance of Power in EU and Asia: The preceding section showed the importance to EU development of political will, and following from that, institutional depth. A key driver of both has been, and continues to be, the Franco-German relationship. It is at this fundamental level that Asia looks most different from the EU. Not only is the post-war political imperative absent, but so too is the balance of power that obtains within the EU. Table 2.1 gives income shares and population shares of countries in the Asia and in the EU. The motivating force in Europe has been the need for two roughly equal-sized powers to co-operate and create something new that is different from either of them. The third power, the UK, is large enough to be taken seriously but not to derail the whole enterprise.

Table 2.1: GDP Shares of Countries in Asia and EU

Europe (EU 15)				Asia (ASEAN + 3)	
	1958	1973	1998	-	2003
Germany	20.1	26.6	25.1	Japan	62.8
France	21.2	19.7	17	China	19.9
UK	23.2	14.1	16.7	South Korea	7.5
Italy	11	12.9	14	ASEAN	9.8
Other EU	7.3	11.7	27.2	-	-
Other Non-EU (future members of EU 15)	17.2	15	0	-	-

ASEAN: Brunei, Cambodia, Indonesia, Lao PDR, Malaysia, Myanmar, Philippines, Singapore, Thailand, Vietnam.

As Table 2.1 shows, France, Germany and the UK accounted for 19.7 percent, 26.6 percent and 14.1 percent of EU output in 1973. The Asian predicament, on the other hand, is that China and Japan together would account for 82.7 percent of output in an ASEAN+3 blocs, dominating its output. And of course, these two countries are at different stages of development. The rise of China is viewed with suspicion in Japan and there is not yet a recognition that the two economies may one day become roughly equivalent in size and should cooperate. The third power, Korea, is not nearly the size of Japan and China, and would not necessarily have the influence of the UK. As China's economy expands at nearly 10 percent per annum, it and Japan will be the key to the success of an ASEAN+3 FTA. The same is true when population is taken into account as China alone is more than double the population size of the 10 countries of ASEAN. Overall, the different size distributions of members in Asia and the EU make it difficult to perceive strong parallels in the two groups' political dynamics.

2.2.5 Decision-taking in the EU: We have seen that institutional reform in the EU has proved difficult, but day to day decision taking has been broadly successful. The key features have been the initial and continuing European vision, the balance of power, and the role of the commission. To this must be added the fact that it has generally proved possible to buy off dissent. This is partly because the broad agenda of EU competencies creates scope for deal-making.

There is a 'generalised reciprocity' - losses on some issues can be accepted in expectation of gains on other issues. It is also because direct, if limited, fiscal transfers are available. The role of fiscal transfers increased greatly from the 19890s onwards. The original 'Six' EEC members were fairly homogenous in terms of income levels, but later enlargements began to introduce a wider spread, especially the 'Southern Enlargement' to Greece (1981), Spain and Portugal (1986) and more recent enlargements to Eastern Europe (2004, the Czech Republic, Estonia, Hungary, Latvia, Lithuania, Poland, Slovakia and Slovenia, as well as Cyprus and Malta). This widening membership raised serious issues of intra-EU distribution, not only in helping the new poorer members to catch up, but also within existing members. Regional policy of one form or another–the 'structural funds' and 'cohesion funds' now account for more than one-third of the budget of the EU and 0.37 percent of total EU income.

In fact, distribution is a major factor in much EU decision making, and the existence of institutions to address it helps to prevent it from becoming a barrier to progress and an impediment to efficiency enhancing decisions. The transfer mechanism-small as it is compared with those in federal and unitary states has been essential to the running of the EU since the southern accession. As a direct consequence of its relatively consensual nature, policy making in the EU is patchy, inconsistent and ragged. Compromise and pragmatism have been the watch-words, rather than efficiency and elegance, with particular members being granted derogations from some measures and the enforcement of others relying heavily on turning a blind eye. One might regret this, but it is notable that despite a number of shocks, European integration has avoided serious set-backs for half a century.

2.2.6 Progress of Economic Integration in Asia: We have argued that key features underlying the success of the EU are a vision; the development of central institutions; a balance of power; and, arising from these aspects, a general ability to reach compromise agreements. How does Asia square up against these features? It is interesting that statements of the motivation driving Asian integration are almost entirely defensive. For example, an overview of cooperation in Asia (Lamberte 2005) gives five driving forces: a defensive response to the rise of regionalism elsewhere; the slow progress in multilateral trade liberalisation; competition with other regions of the world for FDI; concern to tidy up bilateral agreements; and institutionalising the de facto increase in economic interactions. The leading countries in the region do not present integration as a means to heal historical conflict – on the contrary, discussions of integration tend to inflame old wounds and highlight political tensions. As for institutional development, there is no impetus for a pan-Asian framework, along the lines of Europe in the post-War period.

The largest economy in the region, Japan, was closely tied to the United States after World War II and its development was accordingly western-oriented. China in the post War period turned inward when political turmoil and Communism kept its doors closed until the 1980s and 1990s. The ASEAN countries first established their regional alliance in 1967. The Association of Southeast Asian Nations was started by Indonesia, Malaysia, Philippines, Singapore, and Thailand. Later on, Brunei joined in 1984, Vietnam in 1995, Laos and Myanmar in 1997, and Cambodia in 1999. The original five members joined together to secure themselves against communist expansion in Vietnam. In 1976, it increased its scope to economic cooperation and in 1991 embarked on developing a free trade area known as the ASEAN FTA (AFTA). However, the extent of trade among ASEAN countries has always been limited despite the intent to create a FTA. Approximately 23 percent of exports from ASEAN countries are sold to other ASEAN countries. This is in contrast to intra-Europe trade which accounts for three-quarters of all exports. There is also little institutional framework in the ASEAN trade bloc. ASEAN has made some headway in developing a dispute settlement system, but the system is considered to lack transparency.

In general, there is no supra-national institutional structure to bring together the ASEAN+3 nations. The nations have vastly different political and legal systems, and two of the countries (China and Vietnam) are transition economies which have mixed state/market economies. The structures found in the EU–including a court and parliament-are fundamentally lacking in Asia. Moreover, the institutional and political differences among these nations make it unlikely that there is a premise for deep integration.

The balance of power has already been discussed. The major economies of Japan and increasingly China make the region appear more similar to the dominance of the United States in discussions of the FTAA. The next largest economy is South Korea, which is considerably smaller than the two major economies, while the total GDP of ASEAN only just exceeds that of Korea. The highly unbalanced size of the economies in Asia will make the role of China and Japan critical in any FTA, and by the same reasoning means that their agreement will be essential in any successful regional economic agreement. However, these two nations have considerable political differences, manifested in public rebukes over the Japanese prime minister's visits to the controversial Yasukuni shrine among others.

2.2.7 Messages for Asian Economic Integration: What are the implications of this for the day-to-day decision taking that has to take place in a regional integration agreement? The current ASEAN arrangements are rife with exemptions and exceptions. Without vision, or institutions, or breadth of agenda or transfer mechanisms, this is unsurprising. The challenge for ASEAN+3 will be to overcome political differences and adopt a pro-active stance toward a FTA. At the moment, the ASEAN-China discussions are underway to establish a FTA by 2010. This is causing Japan to act to establish an ASEAN-Japan FTA, and accordingly South Korea. This defensive stance does not hold the potential of the EU to compromise and work toward an integrationist agenda. Instead, Asia looks more likely to be characterised by multiple bilateral agreements among these nations driven by an economic agenda; to realise gains from trade from rising intra-regional trade in Asia which currently accounts for 50 percent of all trade and is increasing due to China's fast growth.

Therefore, in contrast to Europe, Asia lacks the successful features that have shaped regional integration in the EU. There is no grand vision, no impetus to develop central institutions, there exists a disparate set of economic powers and no evidence of an ability to reach compromise agreements. Asian integration is characterised by a defensive motive in reaction to regionalism elsewhere and the slowness of multilateral trade agreements as well as recognition of the rapid development of regional trade. The moves toward integration are thus motivated by economic gains without a corresponding set of political will and institutional vision. The balance of power further suggests that one or two countries will dominate any arrangement, moving Asia more toward a hub and spoke system than an integrated region.

2.3 Economic Integration through Trade and Production Networks

Since Asian integration is focussed around free trade, as opposed to an attempt at deeper political integration, we now turn to the economics of integration. The EU is far from being a perfect parallel, being more compact geographically, more homogenous in income levels, and more intent on deeper integration, but it provides our best view of the long-run economic effects of regional integration.

2.3.1 Basic Economic Principles of European Integration: Enshrined in the Treaty of Rome are the four basic economic principles underlying European economic integration; freedom of trade in goods; freedom of trade in services; free mobility of capital; and free mobility of labour. We discuss progress in these areas (leaving labour mobility to one side), highlighting both the obstacles that have been encountered and the outcomes that have been attained. We look first at trade, where several quite distinct mechanisms have been at work. The first is that integration causes reorganisation *between* sectors of the economy; sectors expand or contract in line with efficiency differences between countries, although there are also concerns about trade diversion. The second is that trade changes the nature of competition between firms and induces an industrial reorganisation *within* sectors of the economy; this is often associated with foreign direct investment. Trade may also cause large changes *within firms*, as production networks develop; we postpone discussion of this aspect of trade until section 3.2, on Asia. Following discussion of these issues we turn to looking at outcomes, in particular the extent to which there has been convergence of incomes within the EU, and then to some of the policy questions that have arisen.

2.3.2 EU and the Growth of Trade: European integration had a dramatic effect on the geographical patterns of members' trade. Every member has seen a strong re-orientation of its trade towards other members following accession or the formation of the EEC. Moreover this is as true of manufacturing (and probably services) as of the grotesquely distorted agricultural trade. As an original member, Germany experienced increasing integration with the remaining five from 1957, with duty-free and quota-free access from 1968.

The UK acceded on January 1, 1973 and Spain on January 1, 1986. The pattern is very clear: starting slightly before the formal date of the integration, the trade share starts to rise. It rises for 10-12 years and then stabilises. For Spain the growth is still continuing at the end of the period. Freund and McLaren (1999) have explored the dynamics of regionalism more formally using both trade shares and trade intensity indices. [4] For the latter-the more appropriate measure analytically-they find some evidence of anticipation effects-starting on average 2½ years before formal integration-followed by 9½ years of higher growth before achieving a new steady-state. [5] On average EU countries increased their intra-bloc trade intensity by 53 percentage points over this process.

The growth of trade can lead to economic gains through increased specialisation. The specialisation may arise in response to technological or factor endowment differences between countries, or may occur because of the benefits of clustering related activities in one place. In either case, market integration should promote an increase in specialisation, as the cost of trade is reduced. There is evidence that EU integration has been associated with a rather modest increase in manufacturing specialisation. Measures of the difference between the industrial structures of EU countries have been computed (at the level of 36 industrial sectors, Midelfart-Knarvik et al. 1999). All EU countries except the Netherlands have, since the late 1970s, seen their industrial structure becoming more dissimilar from that of other EU countries. For the initial six members of the EU there is a more or less steady increase in specialisation throughout the period. Later entrants experienced increasing specialisation starting from around their date of entry.

However, despite this, EU countries and regions remain very much less specialised than comparable size geographical units in the US. So far at least, integration has not caused specialization and clustering of activity to go as far as the US experience suggests would be expected in a single country.

Econometric analysis of these changing patterns of specialization indicates that it is largely in line with intra-union comparative advantage. For example, skilled labour intensive activities have tended to relocate towards skilled labour abundant countries, and R&D intensive activities have relocated towards scientist abundant countries (Midelfart-Knarvik and Overman 2002). However, reallocations in line with intra-union comparative advantage are not necessarily welfare increasing as they could be at variance with countries' comparative advantage with the rest of the world. This is the phenomenon of trade diversion.

2.3.4 Trade Creation and Trade Diversion: Increased intra-bloc trade is frequently taken as indicating successful economic integration, especially in popular debate, but, of course, it shows no such thing. The traditional economic question hinges around whether the share increases as a result of trade creation or trade diversion. There is no doubt that European integration has been accompanied by a good deal of trade creation, both internally as well as so-called external trade creation, in which imports from outside the bloc displace members' domestic production and/or expand consumption. Thus, Truman's (1975) decomposition of apparent consumption of manufactures into shares due to imports from partners, imports from non-partners and domestic supplies, shows both sources of imports growing strongly at the expense of the domestic share. Truman finds that out of 53 country-sector combinations observed over 1960-68, 31 display such 'double trade creation' while a further 13 display internal creation and external diversion.

Over 1975-82 Jacquemin and Sapir (1989) find roughly similar proportions of 'double trade creation' and less evidence of trade diversion, while Sapir (1992) finds 'double creation' for aggregate EC-9 trade over 1980-91. The predominant pattern of 'double trade creation' does not imply absence of trade diversion, as external trade should be compared with what it would have been in the absence of integration. There is an unavoidable need to specify the *anti-monde* when estimating integration effects. Two approaches exist to modelling the *anti-monde* more explicitly. First, one can model trade flows in terms of prices and incomes and explicitly allow for the different tariffs faced by different suppliers. This requires considerable information and some effort to model the determinants of trade flows through time in a theoretically coherent fashion. Winters (1983) takes this approach to UK manufacturing trade following its accession to the EEC in 1973. He finds relatively little trade diversion, but certainly some evidence of it.

The second approach is to use a gravity model, which essentially uses trade between other (unrelated) countries to identify the *anti-monde* for partners' trade. The gravity model explains trade between two countries in terms of their incomes, populations, location and geographical characteristics, plus at least two sets of dummy variables to capture the effects of each regional arrangement: one on intra-bloc trade and one on trade between partners and non-partners. The coefficients on such dummy variables reflect a huge variety of effects and can be highly significantly different from zero at any point in time. Hence to measure integration effects one needs to observe not their levels but their changes over periods when regional integration has occurred. Within Europe, Bayoumi and Eichengreen (1997) find strong signs of EEC-EFTA trade falling below expected values as the EEC was formed, and some evidence of the acceding countries' trade with non-members similarly falling below par as they joined. [6]

Sapir (1998) similarly finds EU-EFTA trade penalised by EEC formation and enlargement. Soloaga and Winters (2001) use a much wider range of countries than just Europe to define their *anti-monde*, but at the expense of considering only the period 1980-96. They use three dummies to capture trade effects, breaking the extra-bloc trade effect into an export and an import effect. In 1980 the EU shows unusually strong trade with non-partners and lower than expected trade within the bloc. (This is a common result in gravity models based on large samples of countries.) As integration deepens and Iberia enters the Union, however, these effects decline absolutely-that is, intra-trade grows relative to expected and extra-trade falls. Moreover, Soloaga and Winters show that these changes are statistically significant, suggesting the presence of trade diversion. The overall message from these studies is then that there has been rapid trade growth and trade creation, but there is some evidence of trade diversion occurring as well. Of course, the extent of trade diversion varies across sectors, and the grossly distorting Common Agricultural Policy has certainly been trade diverting for members who would otherwise have had a more liberal agricultural trade regime.

2.3.5 Industrial Reorganization, Competition, Scale, and Market Integration: A central feature of EU trade is that a large part of it has been intra-industry, rather than inter-industry. Such trade is not (necessarily) based on cost or comparative advantage differences between countries, but can instead arise simply from competition between firms in imperfectly competitive markets. Small, national, segmented markets are liable to be dominated by a few national producers, possibly operating at sub-national scale and exploiting considerable monopoly power. Market integration should remove this segmentation, allowing firms to compete more effectively in other national markets and permitting expansion of relatively efficient firms. Market integration permits firms to be larger (and better exploit economies of scale) *and* competition to be more intense. EU experience has indicated that, in some sectors at least, achieving truly integrated markets can be quite difficult. Even when tariffs have been eliminated, markets appear to remain segmented, with substantial price differentials between countries, and borders still having a strongly negative effect on trade flows. These observations were amongst the motivations for the Single Market Initiative, launched in 1986.

The Single Market Initiative (SMI) was launched in 1986

for completion in 1992, with the objective of eliminating market segmentation and 'completing the internal market'. The economic policy measures introduced fall into four main categories: (1) the simplification or removal of frontier formalities, facilitating and speeding the flow of goods across borders; (2) the simplification of product standards, in particular the adoption of the 'mutual recognition principle', whereby goods approved for sale in any member state are deemed acceptable in all; (3) the deregulation of transport sectors, allowing for improved efficiency in the internal distribution of goods; and (4) the opening up of public procurement to supply from all member states. Although individually small, these measures were estimated collectively to reduce the costs of trade across borders by an amount equal to several percent of the value of goods traded. More importantly, their indirect effects were predicted to lead to gains equivalent to several percent of EU GDP, as markets became more competitive *and* firms reorganised, increasing their scale to that of the larger integrated market. Evidence on actual gains is patchy. The SMI was accompanied by a burst of merger activity, and there is some evidence of further trade creation (Pelkmans 2001). Griffith (2001) in a study of UK manufacturing finds a significant increase in both labour productivity and total factor productivity in establishments in sectors that were particularly affected the SMI.

Increased scales of operation have been attributed to the SMI, particularly in sectors where liberalization of public procurement was important, although the size of firms in the EU remains generally smaller than their US counterparts. The Single Market Initiative left countries with different national currencies, until monetary union was introduced for 12 core (Eurozone) currencies in 2002. Part of the motivation of this initiative was to promote price transparency and achieve further market integration, although most of the analysis has surrounded its macro-economic impact. What messages come from this experience of market integration for Asia?

The European experience points to the importance of 'deep integration'. The pro-competitive and scale economy gains of market integration can be impeded by frontier frictions that individually appear quite minor, but collectively allow firms to retain dominant positions in their home markets. The list of such frictions is long. A free trade area, as opposed to a customs union is bound to retain border formalities as well as rules of origin. Contingent protection has been widely used both by the US and within Asia, and its 'trade chilling' effects are well known (ADB 2005). Meeting national product standards is costly, and harmonisation of standards almost impossible. Europe took the mutual recognition route, but this involves a level of acceptance of foreign standards and a willingness to delegate product approval to foreign institutions that is inconceivable in Asia. Despite the success of the Single Market Initiative, it has not reached all–or even many of the largest–areas of economic activity. Opening up of service sectors to competition was one of the objectives of the Single Market Programme, imposing on member states the obligation to abolish restrictions on the free movement of services and extend mutual recognition to professional qualifications. However, progress remains slow, with differing legal standards and regulatory regimes still impeding cross border investments and competition. This remains an area where the European Commission is still performing its role of trying to secure further market integration, while encountering stiff opposition from a number of member states.

2.3.6 Rapid Expansion of Foreign Direct Investment: Accompanying the rapid growth of trade in the EU there has been expansion of foreign direct investment (FDI). World FDI stocks have grown faster than both income and trade in recent decades, and the EU-15 holds around one-third of the stock of inwards FDI. This share surged to over 40 percent at the time of the Single Market Initiative driven by a cross-border merger wave. The importance of FDI for EU economies is illustrated by the fact that 47 percent of Irish manufacturing employment is in foreign owned firms, and this share is substantial even the larger EU countries (France 26 percent, UK 16 percent). Much of the growth of FDI within the EU has been intra-EU investments, which accounts for a majority of the total. Investments from outside the region have also been important as economic integration has allowed outside firms to supply the entire European market from a single plant. Indeed, for many suppliers FDI is a much more important means of reaching the European market than is foreign trade. For manufacturing as a whole, sales of goods by US subsidiaries in the EU were, in 1998, 3.75 times larger than EU manufacturing imports from the US. There is also considerable evidence that some of the inwards Japanese investments of the 1980s were driven largely by EU tariff and non-tariff barriers.

These investments are perceived to have important positive effects. Productivity is generally higher in firms that are multinational than in firms that supply only the domestic market (Martin, R. and C. Criscuolo 2001). Particular importance attaches to FDI in services, as this may be the only means through which foreign competition can enter the domestic market. Consequently both the entrenched interests of incumbent firms and the potential economic gains from liberalisation are large. Opening up of service sectors to competition was one of the objectives of the Single Market Programme, imposing on member states the obligation to abolish restrictions on the free movement of services and extend mutual recognition to professional qualifications. However, progress remains slow, with differing legal standards and regulatory regimes still impeding cross border investments and competition.

2.3.7 Case for Convergence: Some of the most important economic questions concern the effects of regional integration on growth. Is regional integration likely to be good for growth in the region as a whole, and for poorer countries in particular? Standard neo-classical trade theory gives the presumption that integration should lead to convergence of factor prices and incomes–with the limit being factor price equalisation. However, a number of qualifications need to be made to this benchmark case. Even if integration brings convergence of per-capita income, it need not bring steady convergence of all factor prices. Feenstra and Hanson (1997) show how the relocation of production activities to low wage countries can reduce wages of unskilled labour in these countries. The argument is that the activity that relocates may be unskilled labour intensive relative to other activities in the high-wage country, but skilled labour intensive relative to activities in the low-wage host country. In a more general model in which comparative advantage stems both from endowments and from location (with remote regions having a comparative disadvantage in high transport costs goods), reducing trade barriers brings peripheral countries into the trading system and raises their real incomes. However, changes in the prices of individual factors can go either way, depending on both the location and the endowments of individual countries (Venables and Limao 2002).

Some analyses of wage differences across Europe have focussed less on factor endowment differences across countries, and morc on the relationship between locations with good market access (the centre) relative to those with worse access (the periphery). Empirically, European cross-country wage differentials follow a strong 'centre-periphery' wage gradient, and there has been concern about the possibility that integration might draw activity out of peripheral regions and into the centre. Theory suggests that this gives rise to a U shaped relationship between the ratios of wages in the periphery to those in the centre as the degree of integration changes (Krugman and Venables 1990). When trade barriers are high local manufacturing is protected, allowing higher wages to be maintained; at the other extreme, perfectly free trade brings factor price equalisation. It is at intermediate levels of trade barriers that firms are drawn into 'central' regions which offer large markets and from which they can supply the periphery. Peripheral regions are poor locations for manufacturing, and as a consequence have lower wages in equilibrium. In the European context it has generally been argued that barriers are low enough that countries are on the upward sloping section of the U.

Further reductions in trade barriers cause firms to relocate to lower wage peripheral regions, this flattening wage gradients. Empirically, the evidence on convergence suggests that this has—to a limited extent—happened. Turning to the evidence, the EU has experienced significant, although by no means steady, convergence of per capita income across member states. The outstanding features are the rapid catch up of Ireland, Spain and Portugal, and at the same time the continuing poor performance of Greece. The overall experience of convergence has been analysed by many authors and can be summarised in many different ways. Summary measures of the cross-country dispersion of per capita income in the EU indicate significant convergence through the 1960s and 1970s, although no further aggregate change during the 1980s. There was some resumption of convergence between countries from the late 1980s, although this was accompanied by divergence at the sub-national level (Puga 2002).

2.3.8 Role of EU Policy: A continuing message is that the economic benefits outlined above have not been achieved simply by removing tariffs, but have required continuing leadership from the EU institutions and from some of the member states. The best examples are the Single Market Initiative and monetary union, as discussed above. However, in addition to these positive interventions, there have also been repeated interventions by the EC to prevent the use of national policies to distort competition. While increased mobility of firms can reduce the incentives to use burdensome regulation, it can also increase incentives to use distortionary subsidy policies, and this has been an issue in the EU. National interventions can take many different forms. At one extreme are direct state aids to industry, which amounted to some 4 percent of EU manufacturing value added in 1986-88, a figure that had declined to below 3 percent by the late 1990s. The bulk of this goes to R&D support and to meet regional policy objectives. Of the part that goes to specific industries, aid is highly concentrated on a few sectors, particularly shipbuilding and steel. Other national policies include general infrastructure and training schemes and use of corporate taxation; low corporate taxes in Ireland have been viewed as highly effective in attracting mobile FDI projects to Ireland from other potential locations in the EU.

Aware of the possible distortions to competition that would arise if countries were free to subsidise industry, articles 92 and 93 of the Treaty of Rome explicitly prohibit such subsidies. These articles are policed by active monitoring and intervention. For example, between 1998 and 2000 more than 1500 cases were reviewed by the Commission and in 7 percent of these cases negative decisions were reached requiring recovery of aid (European Commission, 2001). As for corporate taxation, Ireland has had several instances of conflict with the EU. Negotiations with the Commission led to termination of a complete corporate tax holiday on profits related to export sales and to an increase of the basic rate of corporate income tax from 10 percent to 12.5 percent. The weakness of these policies lies in the number of loopholes. For example, state aids are allowed in order to reduce regional disparities, and can take the form of regional incentives to enterprises in selected (but large) regions. Total expenditures to an enterprise are capped, and aids to new investments are preferred to ongoing subsidies.

While policy in these areas is still developing, the broad conclusion of the research literature is that these policies have done little to distort the location of industry. Midelfart-Knarvik and Overman (2002) show that specialisation is taking place according to comparative advantage, despite the use of state aids. Braunerhjelm et al (2000) conclude that competition for activity generally takes the form of measures that count as good economic management, rather than wasteful tax or subsidy competition.

2.3.9 Scenario in Asia Countries: We have argued that the EU has received gains from trade creation and specialisation, and perhaps more important gains from market integration and the associated pro-competitive effects and industrial reorganisation. However, achieving market integration has required continuing policy effort from the EC to secure liberalisation. What might the experience of Asia look like compared to this? The share of emerging Asia in world trade has doubled, to nearly 20 percent, over the last 20 years, and trends in Asian trade and investment are widely documented elsewhere (IMF 2002; Ng and Yeats 2003; Zebregs 2004). Two points are particularly noteworthy. First, there has been particularly rapid growth of intra-regional trade, with the share of emerging Asia as a destination for exports from other countries in emerging Asia doubling to 40 percent over a 20 year period. And second, much of the growth is in intra-industry trade. The rise in intra-industry trade in Asia can be seen in Table 2.2 which gives the estimates since the 1980s (IMF 2002). It shows that for East Asia, three-quarters of total trade growth can be accounted for a rise in intra-industry trade.

Table 2.2: Intra-industry Trade as a Percentage of Total Trade Growth

Averaged over 5 years

	1986-1990	1991-1995	1996-2000
East Asia	42.5	46.9	75.0
South Asia	31.2	21.8	34.5

Source: IMF 2002.

Superficially, this looks similar to experience in the EU, but there are important points of difference. The first is that the greater heterogeneity of Asian economies creates more scope for gains from comparative advantage than was the case in EU, particularly with its initial membership. Second, in Asia much of the growth in trade is through vertical specialisation, so intra-industry and intra-regional trade both reflect a rise in cross-border production chains and supply chains. Whereas in Europe high levels of intra-industry trade reflected 'horizontal' trade in similar products, in Asia it reflects high levels of 'vertical' trade in products at different stages of the production process in a particular sector. Similar comments apply to FDI. In the EU most FDI is 'horizontal,' while much Asian FDI is 'vertical'.

The former occurs mainly in order to serve the local market, and involves making investments that duplicate investments in the home country, as when an assembly plant is built in each market. The latter are made to minimize production costs, and involve moving stages of the production process to lowest cost locations, such as the relocation of unskilled labour intensive stages of production to low wage economies. A measure of the extent of vertical specialisation is the ratio of merchandise trade to merchandise value-added. Increasing numbers of parts and components that travel across borders for further processing would result in a higher trade-to-value added ratio. In spite of the difficulty of distinguishing final from intermediate goods, the rising ratios of total merchandise to value-added indicate the growing presence of cross-border production chains in Asia, as seen in Table 2.3. This evidence is also consistent with the export-oriented growth strategy undertaken by Asian nations. Local capacity building would be much slower than plugging into an existing global production chain of a multinational firm.

If much of the growth in Asian trade has been of a different sort of trade from that in the EU–'vertical' rather than 'horizontal' intra-industry trade–what implications does this have for policy making? The first point is that trade frictions and trade costs are particularly important, as vertical specialisation means that products cross borders multiple times during the various stages of the production process. The second point is that reducing these costs may require much less institutional effort in Asia than in the EU. Horizontal intra-industry trade involves existing firms in each country becoming more exposed to import competition (as well as having more export opportunities). There is therefore always a constituency of incumbent firms that will seek to retain import barriers, and it is this that has made market integration in the EU so difficult, and required repeated policy interventions, such as the SMI. By contrast, vertical intra-industry trade involves much of a plant's output being exported. It therefore poses no threat to existing firms in the same line of business–indeed, there may not be any such firms.

Table 2.3: Ratio of Merchandise Trade to Merchandise Value-Added

(in percentage)

	1980	1990	2000
Asian region	93.8	115.6	168.5
China	12.1	23.7	32.9
Taiwan, Singapore, Hong Kong, South Korea	216.5	259.3	365.5
Pakistan, Bangladesh, Malaysia, the Philippines, Thailand, Indonesia	39.4	52.4	84.3

Source: IMF 2002.

Thus, while the institutional mechanisms that Europe has needed to secure 'deep integration' are absent in Asia, their absence may be relatively unimportant, at least for the development of production networks. The historical record already indicates that the lack of deeper integration has seemingly not hampered the growth of intra-industry trade in Asia. It would however be incorrect to see trade and FDI in Asia as entirely 'vertical' in nature. For example, the opening of the Chinese economy is attracting 'horizontal' investment in China, given the current higher costs of accessing the Chinese market through trade. As China itself is a large market potentially 2-3 times larger than the US and EU, the economies of ASEAN would benefit from integration with such a market given their small domestic economies. In other words, the opening of China's market has attracted FDI for production reasons on account of its low cost labour but also increasingly due to the high trade barriers in China's domestic markets (Table 2.4). For ASEAN in particular, the trend of inward FDI moving to China raises questions and concerns about the location of industry. Economic integration, rather than just reduction in tariffs, would allow Asia to benefit not only from trade creation and specialisation, but also the pro-competitive effects of market integration and industrial reorganisation.

Table 2.4: Foreign Direct Investment Inflow, 1998-2004

(in billions US$)

	1998	1999	2000	2001	2002	2003	2004
China	45.5	40.3	40.7	46.9	52.7	53.6	60.6
ASEAN	22.2	27.3	23.4	19.4	13.5	19.4	25.6

Sources: China Statistical Yearbook, various years;
ASEAN Statistical Yearbook, various years.

However, the benefits from integration are likely to be uneven, given the difference in size and income of the ASEAN+3 countries. With the EU institutional framework, there is scope for redistribution and transfers, particularly seen with the accession of 10 new countries mainly from Central and Eastern Europe in 2005. In Asia, there would no similar framework and less room for bargaining and trades. Therefore, although the heterogeneity in income levels and endowments of Asia suggests that traditional comparative advantages can be exploited with the lowering of tariffs, the lack of deeper integration could limit the gains from trade. The shift of FDI to China and the development of a potentially large domestic market which is beginning to transform the nature of investment suggest that an integrated market would be potentially beneficial. However, the lack of a vision or a supra-national body to implement economic policies as well as the historical rifts among these nations makes such deep integration unlikely. The lessons from Europe should well be heeded, though, including the evidence on trade diversion and the entrenchment of special cases such as agriculture which is a concern for Japan and South Korea.

2.4 Basis of Integration

2.4.1 Successful Integration of Europe: The refrain throughout this paper is that European integration has been successful because it has been a continuing process of steps to achieve deeper integration, going far beyond the removal of tariffs. In addition to this internal dynamic, the development of a large regional trading arrangement also creates powerful incentives for non-members. The point is essentially that in addition to benefiting insiders, regional integration may well harm countries left outside. Trade diversion is one mechanism. Countries come to source their imports from other countries in the bloc rather than from outsiders, this reducing the demand for outsiders' exports and depressing their terms of trade. Another mechanism arises from firms' location decisions. It will be profitable to relocate plants inside the bloc, in order to get the benefits of duty free access to a large market. These forces create 'domino effects' (Baldwin 1993), whereby a free trade area creates incentives for outsiders to either join the free trade area, or to create an alternative competing area. In Europe these forces played out in two ways. First, the European Free Trade Area (EFTA) was established as an alternative to the EC in 1960, with a membership including the UK and Scandinavian countries. But second, the attraction forces created by the larger EC meant that a stream of countries left EFTA to join the EC, with the residual EFTA countries (Norway, Switzerland, Iceland and Lichtenstein) forming the European Economic Area with the EU in 1994. In addition, countries that were in neither EFTA nor the EU sought to join the EU, taking it to its current membership of 25 countries, with further applications for membership being negotiated.

2.4.2 Challenges in Asia: There has not been a political will behind a free trade area in East Asia. The major economies in the region also have a history of avoiding preferential trade agreements, namely, Japan and China. Even bilateral trade agreements are rare. South Korea signed its first ever FTA with Chile in 2003. The driving force behind integration in Asia is therefore considerably different from Europe. The economic motives are the predominant ones. The dynamics would thus predict that countries will enter into FTAs to secure trade relationships, which could generate a 'domino effect.' This can result in a proliferation of bilateral trade agreements or a regional FTA (characterized by a hub and spoke system) that captured these bilaterals, but not necessarily a FTA that is characterized by deeper economic integration. Countries would aim to join a FTA if others did, but there is no mechanism (political or institutional) that would push the FTA to become more economically integrated. The rise of China has the potential of transforming the dynamics toward more economic integration in a way that is not dissimilar to the U.S. in the proposed FTA, but the same concerns about the dominance of the U.S. would apply to China/Japan. Moreover, having two dominant and historically diffident countries would add a further dimension of tension.

Thus, unlike the European experience, the recent momentum behind the development of regional trade in Asia is based on defensive motivations rather than clear aims and objectives. The development of regional agreements elsewhere in the world, such as EU, NAFTA, alongside the slow progress of the development of the multilateral WTO framework provided some of the impetus behind the drive to form ASEAN+3. The fragility felt in the region after the Asian financial crisis of 1997-98 also contributed to a desire to increase the gains from trade.

However, the remarkable growth of China in the past 14 years since it implemented its "open door" policy undoubtedly has contributed to the momentum behind ASEAN+3. China since 1992 has increased its market share of global manufactured exports to an impressive 6 percent from just over 1 percent and joined the WTO in 2001, becoming a part of the global trading system. It has also become the world's third largest exporter and importer, as well as its fourth largest economy. The initial reaction in the Asian region was dominated by the perception that China would adversely affect the trade position of its neighbours. However, the evidence suggests that China is a magnet for foreign direct investment and has integrated into Asian production chains. Intra-industry trade during the 1990s increased to account for 75 percent of intra-regional trade growth in Asia (IMF, 2002). China's abundant, low cost labour and considerable domestic market are behind the increase. In 2002, China accounted for 14 percent of all exports from developing countries in Asia, of which approximately 80 percent was intermediate and capital goods for production and the remainder was goods for consumption (Zebregs, 2004). This figure is set to grow as trade barriers such as the Multi-Fibre Agreement are removed, which would allow China to sell more textiles and clothing with the elimination of the worldwide quota system in 2005.

A free trade agreement between an ASEAN country and China could fuel the impetus for other ASEAN countries to pursue a FTA. A FTA between Japan and South Korea, or between China, Japan and South Korea could similarly start a domino movement among ASEAN countries whose firms would not wish to lose their trade positions in these large economies. Baldwin (2005) believes that a Northeast Asian FTA (NEFTA) comprised of China, Japan and South Korea could provide a trigger since their collective size would jeopardize between 35-45 percent of ASEAN exports. These bilateral trade agreements or a NEFTA could generate a momentum toward ASEAN+3. However, the lack of will for deeper integration among Asian countries as well as existing divisive political relationships make the prospects for regional integration less likely than in Europe. The development of bilateral agreements could, however, result in a "hub and spoke" system where the large economies of China and Japan are the main hubs while the others form spokes (Baldwin 2005). Baldwin (2005) argues that though this arrangement exists in Europe, it can have the effect of marginalizing the spoke economies because industrial firms tend to locate in the hub economies. In this system, the first best gains from trade are unlikely to be realized. If Asia, on the other hand, does adopt a regional free trade area, then the effects on the economic performance of the region would be positive and indeed considerable.

The Asian economies have different endowments and historically different specializations, which allow for considerable gains from trade. Most of the ASEAN countries are small in size; in fact, the sum of their GDP equals that of South Korea. They are economies without sizeable domestic markets and tend to be economies which are affected by cycles in the global economy, and particularly slowdowns in developed markets such as the U.S., EU, and Japan which are major export destinations. With the rise of China in the region, the patterns of trade could potentially be dramatically affected. Although aggregate consumption is comparatively low in China, it has a population in urban areas that dwarves that of the U.S. and EU. With economic growth exceeding 9 percent per annum, incomes are expected to double approximately every 8 years. Economic integration with an economy the size of China's would generate considerable gains from trade for ASEAN, increasing the consumption/production possibilities of these economies as well as increasing efficiency. Moreover, China and Japan are major trading partners who are at different stages of development, and the gains from accessing this integrated market would again be notable. Including South Korea would extend this market considerably, particularly given its industrial development. East Asia has the potential of becoming a formidable economic region.

The gains from a FTA are significant for the developing countries in ASEAN as well as for the developed countries of

Japan and South Korea. For ASEAN, economic integration would provide the market that they would individually lack. For Japan and South Korea, utilizing the different endowments of ASEAN and China would allow their economies to sustain economic performance. For China, economic integration would improve the efficiency of the proliferating production chains which already exist and are growing in the region, which would complement its economic development. In short, the potential gains from a FTA are considerable in Asia. However, the political will and institutional structures in ASEAN+3 are much less favourable than in Europe. There have been discussions of creating an Asian Monetary Fund, but the lack of a historical perception of Asia as a viable political goal and the tensions in the region make economic integration more remote than in Europe.

2.5 Conclusions

The refrain throughout this chapter is that European integration has been successful because it has been a continuing process of steps to achieve deeper integration, going far beyond the removal of tariffs. The EU experience shows how these stresses can be handled and points to the importance of deep integration in achieving the full potential of a regional agreement. However, the EU performance is grounded in the deep political commitment of its members and in the creation of a political and institutional framework that can pursue integration and regional reform independently of national governments.

It is in these dimensions that Asia is most fundamentally different from the European Union, and the possibility of following the European model is limited. While complementarities between Asian economies mean that there are benefits from regional integration, if 'deep integration' cannot be achieved, then the benefits of multilateral liberalization exceed those of regional integration, and should perhaps be the focus of trade reform in Asia. This paper observed limitedly that the Asian economic integration is more driven by the market and liberalization generated auto forces than State initiated institutionalized frameworks. It is also observed that market-driven financial integration has also been underway as a result of the increased deregulation of the financial system, opening of financial services to foreign institutions and liberalization of the capital account. It has also observed that regional financial cooperation, through the Chiang Mai Initiative (CMI), the ASEAN+3 economic surveillance processes, and the Asian Bond Markets Initiative along with other recent developments, has been taking root firmly in Asia.

These efforts are not only undertaken in East Asia, but South Asian countries have also started regional policy dialogue on financial cooperation. It is noted that sub-regional cooperation on infrastructure is a key part of the economic integration process in Asia. In this regard, it can be argued that connecting Asian countries through roads, ports, bridges, power and telecommunication networks is fundamentally important for another wave of income and growth and employment creation in Asia. One of the remarkable achievements in this regard is the Greater Mekong Sub-region Programme (GMS). Involving Cambodia, China, Laos, Myanmar, Thailand and Vietnam, the GMS has achieved international recognition with regard to the development of infrastructure to enable the development and sharing of the resource base, and promote the freer flow of goods and people in the sub-region. It has also been found that in the process of this integration, China and India, given their size and population, as well as their central strategic position in international and regional economic relations, will inevitably play fundamentally important and sometimes even dominating roles.

China's rapid and massive rise as an economic power has an enormous impact on the global and regional economy. India's Involvement in Regional Integration in South Asia as a prominent member of SAARC, SAPTA, SAFTA, and BIMSTEC is also very significant.

Notes

1. The same kind of internationalism which created UN, IMF, World Bank and GATT (WTO).
2. The meeting of heads of government is known as the European Council. It has regular bi-annual meetings.
3. In 1999 the entire commission resigned, under parliamentary pressure, over allegations of fraud and mismanagement.
4. The trade intensity index for i's trade with j is (Tij/Tiw)/[(Twj-Tij)/Tww], where T represents trade in both directions and where subscript w represents the world
5. Anticipation effects have been noted previously - e.g. in Winters (1983) for the UK.
6. Just as with the apparent consumption exercise, these exercises are coloured by the reduction in the accidents' tariffs on other countries as they adopted the common external tariff. In this case, however, the external trade changes may reasonably be attributed to integration.

References

Asian Development Bank (2005) *Asian Development Outlook.* Baldwin, R. E. (1993), "A Domino Theory of Regionalism," in Baldwin, Haaparanta and Kiander (eds.) *Expanding Membership of the European Union*. Cambridge: Cambridge University Press.

Baldwin, R. E. (1997), "The Causes of Regionalism," *The World Economy*, vol. 20, no. 7, pp. 865-888.

Baldwin, R. E. (2005), "Asian Regionalism: Promises and Pitfalls," in Choong Yong Ahn, Richard E. Baldwin, Inkyo Cheong (eds.) *East Asian Economic Regionalism:Feasibilities and Challenges*. Berlin: Springer.

Baldwin, R. E. and A.J. Venables (1997), "International Economic Integration," in G. Grossman and K. Rogoff (eds.) *Handbook of International Economics, vol. 3*. Amsterdam: North Holland.

Bayoumi, T. and B. Eichengreen (1997), "Is Regionalism Simply a Diversion: Evidence from the Evolution of the EC and EFTA", in Ito, T. and Krueger, A. O. NBER East Asia Seminar on Economics, vol. 6, *Regionalism versus Multilateral Trade*

Arrangements, Chicago, The University of Chicago Press.

Braunerhjelm P. et al (2000) 'Integration and the regions of Europe: how the right policies can prevent polarization', Centre for Economic Policy Research, London.

Feenstra, R. and G. Hanson (1997), "Foreign Direct Investment and Relative Wages: Evidence from Mexico's Maquiladoras", *Journal of International Economics*, 42, 371-93.

Freund, C. and J. McLaren (1999) 'On the dynamics of trade diversion; evidence from four trade blocks', International Finance discussion paper no 637, Board of Governors of the Federal Reserve System, Washington D.C.

Fujita, M., P. Krugman and A.J. Venables (1999), *The Spatial Economy: Cities, Regions, and International Trade*, MIT press, Cambridge MA.

Griffith, R. (2001) 'Product market competition, efficiency and agency costs: an empirical analysis' working paper 01/12. Institute for Fiscal Studies, London.

International Monetary Fund (IMF) (2002), *World Economic Outlook*, September 2002.

Jacquemin, A. and A. Sapir (1988) "International Trade and Integration of the European Community: An Econometric Analysis", *The European internal market: Trade and competition Selected readings.* Oxford; New York; Toronto and Melbourne: Oxford University Press . 202-12.

Krugman, P. and A.J. Venables, (1990) 'Integration and the competitiveness of peripheral industry' in C. Bliss and J. de Macedo, (es) *Unity with diversity in the European Community*, CUP, Cambridge.

Lamberte, M.B. (2005) 'An overview of economic cooperation and integration in Asia', in *Asian Economic Cooperation and Integration: Progress, Prospects, and Challenges, Manila: Asian Development Bank.*

Martin, R. and C. Criscuolo (2001) 'A note on ownership and productivity in UK businesses', mimeo Centre for Economic Performance, LSE.

Midelfart-Knarvik, K-H., H.G. Overman, S. Redding and A.J. Venables (1999), "The location of industry in Europe", CEPR, London.

Midelfart-Knarvik, K-H. and H.G. Overman, (2002) 'Delocation and European integration; is structural spending justified?' *Economic*

Policy, 35, 321-359.

OECD (1999) *Measuring Globalisation*, OECD, Paris.

Pelkmans, J. (2001), *European Integration: methods and economic analysis*, Pearson, London.

Political and Economic Planning, (1962), '*Atlantic Tariffs and trade*' Chatham House, London.

Puga, D. (2002) 'European regional policy in the light of recent location theories, *Journal of Economic Geography* 2(4), 372-406.

Sapir, A. (1992) 'Regional integration in Europe', *Economic Journal*, 102, 1491-1506.

Sapir, A. (1998) 'The political economy of EC regionalism', *European Economic Review*, 42, 717-32.

Shatz, H. and A.J. Venables (2001) 'The geography of international investment' in *The Oxford Handbook of Economic Geography*, eds G.L. Clark, M.P. Feldman and M.S. Gertler, OUP, Oxford.

Soloaga, I. and L. A. Winters (2001), "Regionalism in the Nineties: What Effect on Trade?", Centre for Economic Policy Research, Discussion Paper Series, no. 2183.

Truman, E.M. (1975) 'The effects of European economic integration on the production and trade of manufactured products' in B. Balassa (ed) *European Economic Integration* North Holland, Amsterdam.

Venables, A.J, (2003) "Gainers and losers from regional integration agreements', *Economic Journal*, forthcoming.

Venables, A.J, and N. Limao (2002) "Geographical disadvantage: a Heckscher-Ohlin-von Thunen model of international specialisation', *Journal of International Economics,* 58, 239-263.

Venables, A.J, L.A Winters and Linda, Y (2006) ' Economic Integration in Asia; European Perspective', in Regional Integration in East Asia from the point view of Spatial Economics, JRP Series No. 138, IDE-JETRO.

Winters, L.A. (1983) "British Imports of Manufactures and the Common Market", *Oxford Economic Papers*, vol. 36, 1983, pp. 103-118.

World Trade Organisation (2005) *International trade statistics 2005*, Geneva: WTO.

Zebregs, H. (2004) "Intraregional Trade in Emerging Asia," *IMF Policy Discussion Paper No. PDP/01/1,* pp. 1-23.

3

Towards Asian Monetary and Financial Integration

3.1 Introduction

Trade regionalism, through regional cooperation and integration and in the form of regional trade agreements (RTAs), is rising globally, although Asia has jumped on the bandwagon only recently. It is argued that the Asian economic integration is more driven by the market and liberalization generated auto forces than State initiated institutionalized frameworks. It is also observed that market-driven financial integration has also been underway as a result of the increased deregulation of the financial system, opening of financial services to foreign institutions and liberalization of the capital account.

What are the pre-conditions to ensure a successful monetary and financial integration process? Are better developed financial markets, deeper trade and factor market integration, liberalized capital markets among the pre-conditions? Traditional literature suggests a set of criteria for optimum currency area. Among the criteria are factor mobility (Mundell, 1961) trade integration (McKinnon, 1963), regional production patterns (Kenen, 1969), policy preference, high correlation of shocks among members, and so on. Generally speaking, countries with strong trade and financial ties are identified as candidates for optimum currency area (OCA). When applying the above-mentioned criteria, some studies found that even Euroland is not an Optimum currency area. One reason is that at present there is neither a high degree of factor mobility within Euroland nor factor immobility outside Euoland. Some other studies found that Asian countries can form a monetary union without incurring so much opportunity costs of losing monetary independence and policy autonomy.

This argument is based on the progress made by Asian countries in the area of trade, production networks, floating arrangements of currency etc. Similarly ,some initiatives like Asian Bond Fund, Chiang Mai Initiative (CMI), the ASEAN+3 economic surveillance processes, Asian Bond Market initiatives, cross boarder mergers and acquit ions, growing intra-regional foreign direct investment, increasing intra-industry trade flows in the region, emerging role of China and India etc. are the positive developments towards financial integration. This paper explored various issues related to trade, financial and monetary integration in Asia. This chapter discussed that the trade integration has progressed significantly in Asia, driven mainly by market forces, the emergence of cross-boarder production networks and rise of India and China as a manufacturing and export base of goods and services. It is examined in this chapter that financial integration in Asia remained relatively weak. The Asian economies have developed closer linkages with developed financial markets, rather than among themselves. This chapter suggested the role of national authorities and multinational institutions for strengthening the financial markets and harmonizing regulations and steps to mitigate the vulnerability that might arise from greater cross boarder capital flows. With the deepening of integration, the economies move towards a common exchange rate. Though, Asia is still away from this. Therefore, Asia could not be considered an optimal currency area, and it is premature for the region to embrace a common exchange rate framework, or monetary union

3.2 Increasing Globalization of Production and Financial Integration in Asia

3.2.1 Growth and Integration in Asian Trade: Asia has made significant progress in trade and production integration in recent years. Between 1991 and 2006, intra-regional exports among the 11 Asian economies of China, Hong Kong, India,

Indonesia, Japan, Korea, Malaysia, the Philippines, Singapore, Taiwan and Thailand (Asia11) expanded more than fourfold, from US$287 billion to US$1.6 trillion. (Table 3.1) This represents annual growth averaging 12 percent, exceeding that for the European Union (EU15, 6 percent) [1] and the North American Free Trade Agreement economies (NAFTA; 9 percent). Intra-Asia11 exports as a share of the region's total exports also rose from 40 percent in 1990 to 49 percent in 2006.

Asia's trade integration has not merely focused on lowering internal barriers to trade and investment but has proceeded alongside an enhancement of the region's links with the rest of the world. Thus, the growth in Asian intra-regional trade has not come at the expense of trade with the rest of the world. Asia11 has enlarged its share of global trade and now accounts for 27 percent of the world's total exports, up from 22 percent in 1990.

Table 3.1: Intra-regional Exports

(US$ billion)

	1990	1995	2000	2006	Average annual growth, 1991-2006 (%)
Asia1 1	287	648	794	1,605	12
ASEAN 5	25	70	87	137	12
EU 15	985	1,260	1,415	2,458	6
NAFTA	226	394	676	881	9

Sources: IMF, *Direction of Trade*; IMF, *International Financial Statistics*; and CEIC.

Significantly, Asia11's exports to economies outside the region quadrupled over the period 1991 to 2006, rising from US$434 billion to US$1.7 trillion, or 14 percent of the world's exports. (Table 3.2) Hence, whilst intra-regional trade flourished in Asia, trade with the rest of the world has also grown rapidly; over the last 15 years, the ratio of the growth in extra-regional exports to the growth in intra-regional exports has been about 0.6 for Asia11 and 0.9 for ASEAN 5. [2] (Table 3.3)

Table 3.2: Exports of Selected Asian Economies

(US$ billion)

	1990	1 995	2000	2006
Asia11	721	1,345	1,703	3,289
of which extra-regional	434	697	909	1,684
China	62	149	249	969
India	18	31	42	121
Japan	288	443	479	647
ASEAN5	139	312	406	686
of which extra-regional	114	242	319	549

Sources: IMF, *Direction of Trade*; IMF, *International Financial Statistics*; and CEIC.

Table 3.3: Growth in Extra-regional Exports to Growth in Intra-regional Exports Ratio

	1991-2000	2001-2006	1991-2006
Asia11	0.6	0.8	0.6
ASEAN 5	0.7	1.2	0.9
EU15	1.4	1.3	1.4
NAFTA	0.3	1.5	0.5

Sources: Calculations based on data from IMF, *Direction of Trade*; IMF, *International Financial Statistics*; and CEIC.

Within the ASEAN 5 grouping, trade has also risen dramatically. Intra-ASEAN 5 exports grew at an average rate of 12 percent annually between 1991 and 2006. (Table 3.1) Furthermore, the intra-regional trade intensity [3] for ASEAN 5 far exceeds that for the EU 15 and NAFTA (Table 3.4). Over the last decade, intra-ASEAN 5 exports almost doubled in value terms, from US$ 70 billion in 1995 to US$ 137 billion in 2006. (Table 3.5) However, the share of intra-regional exports in ASEAN 5's total exports has remained stable at around 20 percent over the last five years, as the region's exports have gained an increasing foothold in the global marketplace.

In addition, although Singapore and Malaysia have tended in the past to dominate intra-ASEAN 5 trade, there is evidence that integration has become more broad-based, as country shares in intra-ASEAN 5 exports have become more evenly distributed. (Table 3.5)

Table 3.4: Intra-regional Trade Intensity*

	1990	1995	2000	2006
Asia 11	2.0	1.9	2.0	2.0
ASEAN 5	3.7	3.0	3.6	3.8
EU 15	1.4	1.5	1.7	1.7
NAFTA	2.0	2.3	2.1	2.4

*Defined as the ratio of intra-regional trade to the region's total trade, normalised by the region's share of global trading activity.
Sources: Calculations based on data from IMF, *Direction of Trade*; IMF, *International Financial Statistics*; and CEIC.

Table 3.5: Share of Intra-ASEAN 5 Exports

(Percent)

	1990	1995	2000	2006
Indonesia	10	9	12	13
Malaysia	34	28	29	29
Philippines	2	3	7	6
Singapore	44	45	39	38
Thailand	10	15	13	15
Total	100	100	100	100

Sources: Calculations based on data from IMF, *Direction of Trade*; IMF, *International Financial Statistics*; and CEIC.

While intra-regional trade in Asia has grown rapidly, comparisons with Europe and NAFTA suggest that there is room for even further expansion. Intra-regional exports as a share of total exports for both Asia 11 and ASEAN 5 are still lower, at 49 percent and 20 percent in 2006 respectively, than in the EU 15 (60 percent) and NAFTA (52 percent).

3.2.2 Trade Integration Driven by Cross-border Production Networks: The emergence of cross-border production networks has played a crucial role in forging trade linkages among the Asian countries, although a large portion of final demand (for instance, for electronics products) resides outside the region. These networks take advantage of countries' specializations within industries, weaving together greater economic interdependence among countries with complementary capabilities. Competitive forces have thus spurred an increase in intra-industry trade around specific industry clusters, notably, electronics, automobiles and oil.

Increased complementarily among countries follows from the shift in organizational focus from the firm to the "contractual network of firms tied together by mutual long-term interest" (Stopford, 1994). The prevalence of these networks is demonstrated by the growing trend towards the outsourcing of core manufacturing functions-not just to subsidiaries based in foreign countries, but also to third party contractual suppliers indigenous to those countries. In sectors such as electronics and automobiles, firms are becoming linked by a complex architecture of networks that extend outside the firm to span across the entire value chain: from logistics, to components, to final products.

The establishment of production networks in the region has, in turn, significantly boosted trade flows in intermediate parts and components, and led to a deepening of the trade links among Asian countries. Further, the proliferation of these networks highlights the importance of tariff and non-tariff barriers to trade in intermediate goods; as a product advances along the regional production chain, the multiple tariffs (and other barriers to trade) levied by the different economies at each stage of processing cascade down, and could add significantly to the overall cost of the final good. Conversely, removing intra-regional tariffs and other barriers should have a multiplier effect on trade by lowering the cost of intermediate goods exports, and thus, final exports from Asia become more competitive in world markets.

Unequivocally, there are significant gains from trade (in final products), as consumers get to enjoy more types of goods in greater quantity. Yet, trade in intermediate goods forms a substantial portion of intra-Asian trade, and recent research findings suggest that intermediate goods trade could yield significant additional gains; it makes intermediate production processes more efficient, improves the allocation of productive inputs and lowers the prices of final goods. For example, Feltenstein and Plassmann (2005) find that liberalizing trade in intermediate goods increases the value of imports and generates significant welfare gains within the region. In particular, they estimate that the admission of China and Korea into the ASEAN Free Trade Area, and the corresponding removal of all mutual tariffs among the economies involved (China, Korea and ASEAN 5), will raise the values of Chinese and Korean imports of final goods by about 74 percent and 13 percent respectively, and by between 1.1 percent for Malaysia and 3.7 percent for the Philippines among ASEAN 5. Furthermore, ASEAN 5 could see welfare gains of about US$0.7 billion initially, extending to about US$ 36 billion over 75 years. The welfare gains for China and Korea are even greater, at about US$ 365 billion over 75 years.

3.2.3 China's Role in Trade Integration: In the last two decades, China has been the principal catalyst of regional production and trade integration. China's share of Asia11's intra-regional exports surged from just 14 percent in 1990 to 24 percent in 2006. At the same time, China has become an increasingly important destination for Asia's exports, as the share bound for the developed markets fell. Between 1990 and 2006, the proportion of Asian (Asia11 excluding China) exports bound for China rose from less than 5 percent to 19 percent, while the combined proportion of goods exported directly to the US and the EU15 fell from 46 percent to 30 percent over the same period. China has also been the major contributor to Asia's enlarged share of global trade. China alone accounted for a third of the increase in Asia11's exports to the world between 1990 and 2006. Not surprisingly, China's share of Asia11's total exports tripled, from just 9 percent to 29 percent, over this period.

The region's trade with China is underpinned by industry-specific production networks, notably in electronics. China's growing share of Asia's exports is largely attributed to the shifting dynamics of manufacturing within the region and China's increased importance as a regional processing hub for products finally exported to developed markets. Hence, despite the G3's (the US, the EU and Japan) falling share of Asia's direct exports, these developed markets remain important locations of end-demand. For example, the Asian Development Bank (2007) estimates that the G3 ultimately accounts for 61 percent of total final demand underlying exports from East Asia. [4]

While the G3 markets remain important for Asia, China has also become an important source of end-demand for the region. MAS (2003) estimates that some two-thirds of China's imports from East Asian economies are destined for domestic consumption. [5] Over the longer term, as the Chinese economy grows, the strength and importance of its domestic demand is expected to increase.

3.2.4 Financial Integration in Asia: Compared to trade integration, financial integration is still limited in Asia (excluding Japan). To begin with, Asia's financial markets are shallow relative to developed economies; Asia's bond markets, for example, constitute only 115 percent of GDP, compared to 203 percent in the US and 170 percent in the EU. Excluding Japan, Asia's percentage falls to only 56 percent (IMF, 2007). Further, the region exhibits a higher degree of financial integration with developed country markets than within itself. In banking, for example, major foreign lenders comprise mainly American and European institutions, while cross-border banking flows among Asian economies are relatively limited (Cowen *et al.*, 2006). Regional stock markets show little participation from investors in other Asian economies, and foreign shareholding, while significant, is dominated by non-Asian advanced economies. For example, although foreigners account for 41 percent of trading activity on the Hong Kong Stock Exchange, only one-fifth of this is accounted for by other Asian economies (Hong Kong Exchanges and Clearing Limited, 2006).

The developed markets of Europe and the US account for significant shares of portfolio investment in Asia. In 2005, the EU15 and the US accounted for 32 and 38 percent respectively of the foreign portfolio assets invested in 10 Asian economies, while Asian economies accounted for only 15 percent. (Table 3.6a) Likewise, the bulk of Asia's foreign portfolio assets is invested in the developed markets; in 2005, 30 percent of Asian source economies' foreign portfolio assets was invested in the EU15, compared to 20 percent invested within the region. (Table 3.6b)

Compared to Europe, the lesser degree of financial integration within Asia could be partly attributed to the generally lower level of economic development and other pre-determined factors reflecting regional circumstances, such as relatively greater distances between countries, the lack of a common language and fewer shared land borders (Eichengreen and Park, 2004). Eichengreen and Park also argue that financial integration is less advanced in Asia than in Europe because Asia has not gone as far in promoting intra-regional trade—Europe has a fully-fledged single market in goods and services, but the formation of an Asian free trade area is incomplete. Financial integration in Asia has also been hindered by restrictions on capital mobility and relatively underdeveloped capital markets and institutions.

3.2.5 Linkages between Trade and Financial Integration: Empirical research provides some support for the view that greater trade integration could lead to increased financial integration (Eichengreen and Park, 2004; Lane and Milesi-Ferretti, 2003). Increased intra-regional trade and investment can generate greater demand for cross-border trade-financing activities and capital flows. Greater trade openness also increases the effective cost of restrictions on capital flows, creating the impetus for further financial openness and integration. For example, trade openness may encourage capital flight through over-invoicing of imports and under-invoicing of exports, thus undermining capital controls (Aizenman, 2003).

Table 3.6a: Foreign Portfolio Investment in Asia10*

(Percent share)

Source	2001	2002	2003	2004	2005
Asia8	14	17	16	17	15
EU15	35	27	33	33	32
US	37	38	37	35	38
Japan	6	6	4	4	4
Others	8	12	11	10	11
Total	100	100	100	100	100

Table 3.6b: Asia 8 Foreign Portfolio Investment**

(Percent share)

Destination	2001	2002	2003	2004	2005
Asia10	15	14	17	18	20
EU15	27	32	31	31	30
US	20	18	17	17	16
Japan	6	3	3	3	4
Others	32	33	32	31	30
Total	100	100	100	100	100

*Asia10 comprises China, Hong Kong, India, Indonesia, Korea, Malaysia, the Philippines, Singapore, Taiwan and Thailand;
**Asia8 excludes China and Taiwan due to data unavailability.
Source: IMF, *Coordinated Portfolio Investment Survey*, July 2007.

Conversely, financial integration may also enhance trade integration and growth. Deeper financial integration should help to channel Asia's large pool of savings towards financing investment within the region. The pooling of liquidity could reduce financing costs for Asian firms and encourage investment, the expansion of regional production networks, and, therefore, trade integration.

Financial integration could bring other benefits as well. The deepening and integration of regional capital markets could help to reduce excessive dependence on bank financing, short-term borrowing and financing from outside the region. This could reduce the volatility of capital flows and the vulnerability of Asian economies to capital reversals. Increased competition resulting from financial integration could also improve the efficiency by which financial resources are allocated, raise the incentives for transparency and better corporate governance, and impose greater market discipline on macroeconomic policies. Enhanced competition would also catalyse market development and innovation, thus creating the potential to lower the cost of capital further and stimulate more investment. Further, financial integration provides opportunities for risk-sharing and diversification within the region.

Increased investment due to financial deepening and integration could also help to reduce Asia's saving glut, which is especially important as Asia's current account surpluses are likely to persist, led by China's growing trade surpluses. China's current account surplus, for example, is expected to reach US$ 274 billion, or 6.2 percent of GDP, in 2011 (IMF, 2006b).

Further, a more developed financial sector in Asia could encourage capital flow from rich to less wealthy economies in the region. This appears to be the case in Europe, where increasing financial integration corresponds with capital flowing "downhill" from rich to poor (or less rich) countries within the Union, with poorer countries that are financially integrated running larger current account deficits, and the richer countries running surpluses (Abiad *et al.*, 2007). Likewise, deeper financial integration among Asian countries could induce a similar reversal of the Lucas paradox [6] and faster income convergence within the region.

The linkages between trade and financial integration imply that Asia's increasing trade integration with China and India could facilitate more progress in regional financial integration. For example, China's largest trading partners and foreign direct investors, particularly Hong Kong, Japan and the US, have the largest number of bank branches in the country as well. (Table 3.7) The majority of foreign banks' business in China is related to multinational corporations from the same home country, with a significant proportion in trade-financing. As Chinese and Indian corporations expand, they could turn increasingly to regional capital markets for financing, for example, by listing on regional stock exchanges, especially those of Hong Kong and Singapore. Already, over 40 percent of all foreign companies listed on the Singapore Exchange are from China (Singapore Exchange Limited, 2007).

Table 3.7: Foreign Business Activity in China, 2005

US$ billion	No. of bank branches	Volume of trade* with China	Direct investment in China
Hong Kong	94	137	20.2
Japan	75	185	4.6
US	42	212	2.9
UK	27	25	0.7
France	23	21	0.4
Germany	23	63	2.0
Korea	23	112	3.9
Singapore	18	33	2.3
Italy	18	19	0.3
Netherlands	15	29	0.8

*Exports plus imports.

Sources: Almanac of China's Finance and Banking, 2006; and CEIC.

While trade integration is important for deeper financial integration, it is not the only driving factor. Financial integration could be deepened through the removal of capital controls and other administrative barriers to cross-border capital flows. While a country may open up to trade, it may still choose to restrict capital flows due to concern about the volatility of capital flows or strong opposition from local financial institutions and industry incumbents. China, for example, is deeply integrated via trade links with global and regional markets, but its financial sector remains relatively closed to external participants. As Eichengreen and Park (2004) point out, the removal of controls on capital account transactions is linked to deeper financial integration. China and India's progressive capital account liberalisation should thus expand the region's pool of liquidity and contribute even further to regional financial integration.

3.2.6 Vulnerabilities Associated with Financial Integration: Although financial integration brings numerous benefits, there are attendant risks. In particular, capital account liberalisation could induce destabilising capital flows. While integration could facilitate the flow of capital to capital-scarce economies with positive output effects, integration could also induce capital outflow from capital-scarce economies with weaker institutions and policies to capital-abundant economies with stronger institutions. Recent global economic recession has strengthened the doubts.

Some studies have found that free capital mobility invites speculative "hot" money and increases the likelihood of financial crises, with no discernible positive effects on investment and output (Rodrik, 1998; Stiglitz, 2002). Thus, the benefits of further financial sector reforms and deeper regional integration may not be evenly distributed. Greater integration could leave economies more vulnerable to abrupt changes in capital flows and heighten the transmission of regional shocks through contagion effects. Moreover, as Kaminsky *et al.* (2004) point out, capital flows tend to be pro-cyclical. Periods of capital inflows are associated with expansionary macroeconomic policies, while periods of capital outflows are associated with contractionary policies. This means that the direction of capital flows can exacerbate economic or financial distress "when it rains, it pours".

Financial integration is also likely to affect the structure of the financial system, which in turn, may have implications for financial stability. For example, the development of cross-border infrastructure to facilitate trading, payments, clearing and settlement could form the channels for, and increase the risk of, cross-border contagion. Furthermore, the proliferation of cross-border ownership, mergers and acquisitions, and the entry of foreign financial institutions could create vulnerabilities for domestic financial sectors. The international nature of capital movements also makes it difficult to exercise prudential regulation and put in place other safeguards, such as deposit insurance and lender-of-last-resort facilities, for imparting stability to domestic credit markets. Given these risks, regulatory frameworks and domestic institutions would need to be strengthened in tandem with liberalisation measures.

3.3 Role of Institutions in Fostering Financial Integration

3.3.1 Financial Liberalisation and Reforms: Since the 1997-98 Asian Financial Crisis, a number of countries in the region have implemented various financial sector reform and liberalisation measures. Some countries have eased their restrictions on foreign ownership of financial assets, particularly in banking. Further, regional economies now recognise that the development of competitive capital markets could be an important way of increasing the efficiency of the overall financial system, which, prior to 1997, had been dominated by banks.

It is important, however, that the pace and sequence of financial liberalisation and reform be contingent on having in place sound macroeconomic policies, good governance and strong financial supervision as key underlying supports. Following the Asian Financial Crisis, there is now greater recognition in the region that a sound institutional framework is critical to maintaining a robust financial system. As countries liberalise their financial sectors, they have strengthened financial supervision and put in place more prudential safeguards. Some countries have also made efforts to improve their legal infrastructure and establish more effective corporate governance frameworks, albeit with varying degrees of success.

3.3.2 Asian Energy Dialogue: Among the other priorities would be creation of an Asian Energy Dialogue to pursue proposals of Asian strategic energy reserve, gas grids and development of Asian energy market (Nagesh Kumar 2005). They could also begin creating institutional infrastructure for scientific and technological cooperation in Asia to exploit the synergies for mutual benefit. Nagesh Kumar has also estimated the relative welfare gains from Economic Integration in JACIK (Japan, ASEAN, China, India and Korea).He further compared JACIK with EU and NAFTA in terms of GDP and exports and found that JACIK is ahead of both. Therefore, the potential gains for Asian integration are very significant.

3.3.3 Need for Official Coordination and Cooperation: The progress made in European integration has much to do with explicit governmental initiatives that complement private sector development, through a top-down approach. [7] In contrast, Asian integration has largely been driven by the private sector, especially global multinational corporations. The European experience suggests that there is scope for greater policy coordination and political impetus to propel the integration process in Asia forward.

Closer economic integration is not simply the assimilation of markets and economic systems; it is also increased cooperation and coordination among economies in the region. Given Asia's growing economic weight, deeper integration provides a means for the region to project its voice in the global arena. Coordination among economies is also necessary to address issues that transcend national borders. These include the orderly adjustment of international savings-investment imbalances, the development of a regional safety net to minimise or even pre-empt financial crises and contagion, the mutual recognition and harmonisation of regulations, and the development of cross-border financial infrastructure.

3.3.4 Some Progress in Financial Integration: Some of the progress made in Asian financial integration over the past few years may be attributed to concerted efforts by governments in the region to develop markets and build regional financial infrastructure. Such initiatives include the Asian Bond Market Initiatives and the Asian Bond Fund. These efforts have borne some results. Although developed markets still account for a larger share of Asia's foreign portfolio investments and the share due to intra-regional investments continue to lag that observed in Europe, the proportion has shown encouraging growth over the last few years. Furthermore, cross-border mergers and acquisitions in the financial sector have increased, in line with growing intra-regional foreign direct investment (FDI) flows in the financial sector. For example, between 2002 and 2006, the value of financial sector cross-border mergers and acquisitions within the region reached US$ 16 billion, twice the amount during the preceding five-year period. These FDI flows represent an important development that complements the rising importance of intra-industry trade flows in the region.

3.3.5 Agenda for Institutional Reforms: Many economists agree that deeper financial integration is probably needed to support the rapid growth of intra-regional trade and investment. Asia still exhibits a heavy dependence on financing from outside the region, not only for investment, but also for international and intra-regional trade. Effective financial linkages between lenders and borrowers appear to be lacking within the region. To illustrate, even today, swaps between certain Asian currencies cannot be carried out directly, thus raising transaction costs for businesses and investors. Business costs could be lowered if there was a more effective intermediation infrastructure directly linking borrowers and lenders across countries.

One option considered was for Asia to develop its own infrastructure for the payment and settlement of regional financial flows, or some form of an Asian dollar clearing system. The trade-financing business would benefit from this move. Regionally-active banks already provide US dollar trade-financing on a regular basis, but most of the secondary trading of trade-finance instruments remains outside Asia. An efficient payment and settlement system would attract banks to do more business in this region and help to foster a more active secondary market for the discounting of trade-finance paper. Over time, the market for trade-finance instruments denominated in major regional currencies could also grow.

Another area could be the promotion of cross-border investment and strategic partnerships among Asian financial institutions, as exemplified by the activities of Singaporean banks in other Asian financial markets. This could enable Asian banks to carve out their niche in financing the region's multinational corporations or small-and medium-sized enterprises, and help improve Asian businesses' access to financial services.

Besides bank funding, regional capital markets and portfolio investment flows could also play a greater role in financing regional production and trade. Cross-border capital flows have not benefited fully from the expanding economic linkages in the region; the development of domestic and regional capital markets needs to be expedited to provide more channels for long-term funding through equity and debt instruments. Participants concurred that Asian economies should aim to create a deeper and more efficient secondary market for bonds in the region, and that more needs to be done to create deeper linkages between the banking and securities sectors. It was also observed that the emphasis should lie in broadening the demand and supply of debt and equity instruments, building up infrastructure, and reducing cross-country restrictions to capital flows.

It has been noted that a number of initiatives to boost financial exchanges and deepen integration within the region have already been implemented. For example, the Chiang Mai Initiative was established to provide emergency liquidity through swap agreements, and efforts have been made to catalyse the development of a regional bond market, including the Asian Bond Market Initiative and the Asian Bond Fund.

There is a need of the measures required to promote regional financial liberalisation and integration. First is to have in place adequate legal, regulatory, and institutional arrangements. This might include, for example, regional rating agencies, regional credit guarantee mechanisms, and a regional settlement framework to facilitate cross-border transactions. This, in turn, should be reinforced by tax reforms and other regulatory enhancements that would strengthen corporate governance and transparency standards.

Second is the progressive removal of impediments to cross-border financial transactions. Some measure of progress has been achieved through the ASEAN Roadmap on capital account liberalisation.

Third is the harmonisation of rules, and making them consistent with international best practices. If tax regulations, for example, are not coordinated, there could be biases or unintentional shifts in capital flows (regulatory arbitrage). There is thus a need for more regional policy coordination as countries modernise and enhance their tax and regulatory systems.

One inevitable consequence of financial integration is the increased risk of cross-border spillovers and contagion. Therefore, in deepening financial integration, reforms of the financial system, such as the adoption of risk-based assessment and supervision, are needed to maintain financial stability.

The integration of Asian financial markets will likely be an evolutionary process and the sequencing of necessary reforms needs to be properly determined. While it ca be argued that

that all the above-mentioned measures are essential, there was greater uncertainty as to how best to sequence specific reforms. Nevertheless, unlike trade and production integration, which has been largely driven by the private sector, financial integration will require the authorities to play an important role, to provide the required public goods and foster the necessary conditions for financial integration to proceed. The public sector's role will be especially important in areas such as the development of financial market infrastructure and the creation of the mechanisms and institutional arrangements for crisis prevention, management, and resolution.

3.4 Monetary Policy and Exchange Rate Framework

3.4.1 Post-crisis Exchange Rate Regimes: Significant changes to the monetary and exchange rate frameworks in Asia have occurred since the Asian Financial Crisis of 1997-98, as countries searched for a new nominal anchor in place of informal tight exchange rate pegs to the US dollar. Paradoxically, the Crisis increased economic disparities in the region, thus making monetary integration more difficult, but rekindled political interest in Asian monetary and exchange rate cooperation. The crisis demonstrated, amongst other things, that unilateral exchange rate regimes (including *de facto* dollar pegging) did not cope very well in the early 1990s when confronted with massive capital inflows into the region. Some countries eventually succumbed to Mundell's "Impossible Trinity", namely the difficulty, if not impossibility, of juggling three economic policy objectives in the air at once: managing the currency (in effect dollar pegging), retaining some autonomy in domestic monetary policy, and being integrated with international capital markets (free capital mobility).

In the aftermath of the Asian Financial Crisis, a number of commentators suggested that perhaps a "corner" solution might be better, i.e. either keep convertibility and a stable currency but abandon monetary independence and fix the currency, preferably backed by a currency board, or keep monetary policy and convertibility but abandon currency management and adopt a free float. However, as Wilson (2006) observes, a hard peg is perceived to be too rigid for most countries in Asia; with the notable exception of Hong Kong, Asian economies have not been in a hurry to give up monetary policy independence. In comparison, the potential costs of a clean float are seen to be too great for emerging economies with weak financial infrastructure. There would be a risk of serious currency misalignment with real consequences for exports and inflation targets, and continued volatility in capital flows and foreign exchange markets, characterised by manipulation and herd behaviour, could heighten the risk of destabilising speculation.

3.4.2 Return of the Middle Way: Recognition that the "corner" solutions may be unattractive or unfeasible for many countries in Asia, therefore, puts the emphasis back on intermediate exchange rate regimes, such as managed floating, some mixture of inflation targeting and exchange rate management, and unilateral basket regimes. In the post-crisis period, average currency volatility, both in effective terms and bilaterally against the US dollar, dropped substantially compared to the crisis period, but was still higher than in the pre-crisis period. To some extent, this has been a consequence of the move towards greater exchange rate flexibility, which is likely to be increasingly important as the saving-investment imbalances in the region are projected to be sustained, and exchange rate adjustments would eventually be required to restore equilibrium.

It has been suggested that Asian economies should consider moving towards a common exchange rate framework. Among others, an underlying problem is that the diversity of exchange rate regimes in the region transmits fluctuations in major currencies into fluctuations in bilateral regional exchange rates, thus affecting relative competitiveness. In particular, a country with a tighter *de facto* peg with the US dollar compared to its export competitors might find itself unable to compete when the dollar appreciates strongly against the yen and the euro.

Rose (2000) finds that a currency union has a large, positive impact on international trade; he estimates that two countries that share the same currency trade three times as much as they would with different currencies. Rose postulates a few possible reasons for such a phenomenon—a common currency signals a serious commitment by governments to long-term integration, facilitates trade by conferring greater price transparency, and helps to overcome foreign exchange hedging costs in the absence of derivatives markets. A common currency could also lead to deeper financial integration, which in turn spurs trade in goods and services.

These benefits of a common currency naturally raise the question of whether Asia constitutes an optimum currency area (OCA). A group of economies may form an OCA if they are closely linked by factor mobility and trade in goods and services, or if there is evidence of convergence in the levels and behaviour of key macroeconomic indicators relevant to a common monetary policy, such as inflation, unemployment, budget deficits (indicating fiscal sustainability), interest rates and exchange rates. Other OCA criteria include evidence of small and synchronised supply and demand shocks among the potential members, common business cycles, flexibility to adjust quickly to shocks, and a system of non-distortionary fiscal transfers to redistribute gains within the region.

Empirical work on whether Asia constitutes an OCA has largely revolved around *ad hoc* application of single OCA criteria, as well as more formal modelling of the magnitude and characteristics of the supply and demand shocks affecting countries over time. This includes analysing the intensity of intra-regional trade, the speed of adjustment to shocks, and whether supply and demand disturbances are correlated. Earlier work by Bayoumi and Eichengreen (1994), Bayoumi and Mauro (1999) and Eichengreen and Bayoumi (1996) indicate that Asian economies satisfy various economic conditions for forming an OCA. Later empirical work, however, has been less supportive (Chow and Kim, 2000; Zhang *et al.*, 2004).

Nevertheless, OCA criteria may not be strictly necessary as pre-conditions for monetary integration as these criteria could be endogenous (Frankel and Rose, 1996). Countries could satisfy the OCA criteria *ex-post* and historical extrapolation could therefore be misleading. High inflation countries, for example, may be more willing to join a monetary union precisely because it will enable them to bypass domestic political constraints and gain the credibility of the common central bank.

The potential endogeneity of the OCA criteria led Eichengreen (2004) to modify the original criteria for a successful monetary union to the following: (i) the capacity to delegate monetary policy to an international institution; (ii) a culture of monetary transparency; (iii) open capital accounts; and (iv) a common transmission mechanism. Eichengreen believes that Asia could fulfil these criteria over the medium-term. At the moment, however, Asia is still some way from satisfying them.

Hence, notwithstanding some evidence that Asia satisfies *economic* criteria for forming an OCA, it is broadly recognized that Asia lacks the requisite *institutions* and *socio-political* forces to meet the modified OCA criteria, and to achieve the same level of integration that was achieved in Europe prior to the creation of the euro.

Further, notwithstanding Rose's (2000) finding, other empirical studies have questioned the link between the reduction of exchange rate volatility and the boosting of trade between partner economies. For comprehensive surveys, see Côté (1994), McKenzie (1999) and Clark *et al.* (2004). In her survey, Côté reports that while many studies have found that exchange rate volatility has a negative impact on trade, the magnitude tends to be small. Likewise, Clark *et al.* (2004)

found no robust negative relationship between exchange rate volatility and trade flows in their empirical analysis. Various reasons have been proffered for the weak link between exchange rate volatility and trade. For example, the proliferation of derivative instruments could have lowered the costs of hedging against exchange rate fluctuations. Furthermore, exchange rate movements across various currencies could provide offsetting effects on the profitability of multinational firms, or even create profitable opportunities for trade and investment.

3.4.3 A Regional Currency Arrangement: Despite uncertainty about Asia's suitability as an OCA and ambiguity over the effects of currency volatility on trade, there are those—such as (Ogawa and Ito, 2002) and (Williamson, 1998, 2005)—who argue for establishing a regional common currency basket arrangement. Using both common weights and a basket would minimise the effects of fluctuations in major currencies on Asian currencies, and, at the same time, reduce intra-Asian exchange rate instability.

Others, in particular McKinnon, have argued that Asia is already a *de facto* dollar bloc (McKinnon, 2001; McKinnon and Schnabl, 2004). Asian economies could thus consider pegging unilaterally or collectively to the dollar, or attach a large weight to it in their currency baskets. This could help stabilise intra-bloc exchange rates and long-run exchange rate expectations, as well as to anchor regional price levels and gain the benefits of a larger dollar-trading zone among close trading partners. The appeal of such a proposal depends on whether there is sufficient evidence of a natural "dollar area" in the Asian region. Notwithstanding the US dollar's predominance in the invoicing of Asia's trade, the suspicion remains that Asia, with its diversified trade patterns, does not constitute a "*sufficiently* optimum" currency area with respect to the US, in the way that many Latin American countries may be, by virtue of their strong bilateral trade and investment links. The emergence of China as a major regional trade partner, and the expected increase in the flexibility of the Yuan in currency markets, may also weaken Asia's link with the dollar (Wilson, 2006).

In terms of the evolution towards a common currency area, one can envisage a process whereby exchange rates in the region are first managed on a consistent basis, for example, by potential OCA members unilaterally shifting to a managed float regime based on a basket of currencies. Initially the composition of the basket and its currency weights could differ among countries according to each country's trade pattern and capital movements. Currency regimes that are presently either tightly pegged to the US dollar or floating freely could be shifted gradually towards a basket-based managed floating system. Over time, the composition and weights of the currencies in the unilateral baskets could be standardized in preparation for a common currency.

3.5 The Parallel Currency Approach

Barry Eichengreen (2006) [8] has discussed the parallel currency approach to Asian Monetary Integration. He suggested that Asian countries should collectively peg their currencies to the dollar, the yen, or a dollar-yen-euro basket or establish a multilateral currency grid like the European Monetary System. The resulting exchange rate stability would promote intra-regional trade, simplify investment planning, and encourage cross-border participation in local bond markets. Experience with establishing and maintaining a system of stable exchange rates would help to ready the region for the introduction of a single currency. Asia, in this view, should emulate Europe's approach to regional monetary integration.

But, along with the attractions of the European example, there are also dangers. Defending a system of currency pegs in the presence of high capital mobility requires the close convergence of policies and the maintenance of confidence. If either pre-condition is disturbed, a country will require extensive financial support in order to defend its peg or to undertake an orderly realignment. The Chiang Mai Initiative announced in 2000 is just such a system of swap lines and credits but, revealingly, Asian countries have been reluctant to actually utilise it.

Eichengreen mentioned in his paper that he is not the first one to develop this idea. Mori *et al.* (2002) have proposed the creation of an Asian Currency Unit as a way of creating an environment in which the private sector can participate in the discussion of monetary integration. Agarwala (2003) has proposed the creation of a parallel currency as an initial step toward a single currency for South Asia.

In practice, Asian countries possess neither the willingness to subordinate other policies to these imperatives nor the solidarity needed to offer extensive financial supports. Absent an appetite for political integration, there is little readiness to create a regional central bank like the European Central Bank, since there is no counterpart to the European Parliament to hold it accountable for its actions. Hence, there is little prospect of early monetary union to tie down expectations. A system of Asian currency pegs would consequently be fragile and crisis prone. As a road to monetary unification it would be a dead end.

Better would be for governments to create an Asian Currency Unit, or ACU, constituted as a weighted average of Asian currencies, and allow it to circulate alongside their national currencies. This would have three advantages. First, it would not be necessary to stabilise exchange rates between the currencies comprising the basket; hence, fragility would be less. Second, the parallel currency would be more stable than any one national currency in terms of aggregate Asian production and exports; it would thus be a vehicle for encouraging intra-regional trade and investment. Third, the decision to move to a single currency could be driven by economics rather than politics. Only when a critical mass of producers, exporters and investors had adopted the parallel currency would it be clear that Asian economies were ready for monetary unification.

3.5.1 Mechanics: Eichengreen further explained that the building on experience with the ECU, the ACU would be defined as a fixed number of units of each constituent currency—including, for example, the 10 ASEAN currencies plus the Japanese yen, Chinese yuan, and South Korean won. While the quantity of each component currency would remain fixed, its contribution to the value of the ACU thus would vary with its exchange rate; as currencies depreciated, their weight in the ACU would decline. The composition of the basket might be revised periodically to reflect the changing weights of the participating countries. Weights could be determined by the share of the country in regional GDP or exports.

Official ACUs would be created in exchange for swaps of a fraction of the international reserves of participating central banks. The amount of these swaps could change periodically to reflect changes in the quantity and value of those gold and dollar reserves. Participating central banks would agree to accept ACUs in transactions among themselves. Governments would agree to experiment with the issuance of ACU-denominated bonds.

The existence of these benchmarks would make it more attractive for financial and non-financial firms to issue and accept ACU-denominated liabilities and assets, subject to standard prudential regulations. Bond or deposit documentation would specify that when the composition of the official ACU basket changed, the value of private ACU assets and liabilities would change accordingly. The value of the private ACU would be guaranteed by the commitment of the issuer (such as a bank accepting a deposit) to convert the instrument into its underlying components. Arbitrage would in any case prevent significant divergences from opening up between the value of the private ACU and the constituent currencies.

3.5.2 Pegs and Dollars: There exist at least two

motivations for monetary cooperation in Asia. One is to limit exchange rate variability within the region in order to promote intra-regional trade and investment. The other, manifest in calls for a common basket peg against the dollar and the euro, is to buttress exchange rate stability *vis-à-vis* the rest of the world. But, as Williamson (2005) notes, there is no incompatibility between the two objectives. Nothing prevents a group of countries adopting a basket of outside currencies as their peg from also basing a parallel regional currency on a basket of their own currencies.

But not only is the rationale for the two strategies different, the effects are different as well. Pegging Asian currencies to the dollar, the euro or a basket of which they comprise a part would heighten the attractions of these outside currencies for transactions within Asia. In contrast, allowing Asian currencies to float against the euro and the dollar would make it more attractive to transact in a stable regional composite.

To gain widespread use, the ACU must out-compete not just existing Asian currencies but also the dollar, which is widely used for cross-border transactions in the region, as noted above. This observation has led authors like Mundell (2002) to advocate that Asian countries should adopt the dollar as a "common parallel currency" that is, as an officially-recognised currency for use in invoicing and settling trade. But, as intra-Asian trade continues to grow, invoicing and settling in a common Asian currency will become more attractive relative to invoicing and settling in dollars. In any case, Asian countries are reluctant to give the currency of an outside power legal tender status for domestic transactions. As a result, the residents of an Asian country must still convert dollars into the national currency when making tax payments or engaging in other domestic transactions requiring a unit with legal tender status.

Under the parallel currency approach, Asian governments would give the ACU full legal tender status for domestic use, which would make it more attractive. There are also reasons to think that the dollar will grow more volatile relative to Asian currencies as Asian countries relax and abandon their pegs to the greenback in the interest of greater flexibility and to the extent that America's twin deficits lead to a weaker dollar. This will make using ACUs rather than dollars more attractive. Finally, the hold of network externalities and therefore the advantages of incumbency may be less in our financially-sophisticated age than was the case in the past. Given the proliferation of instruments in financial markets and the decline in bid-ask spreads, it is easier for market participants to contemplate alternatives.

Eichengreen further argued that the appeal of this approach is that the pace of progress would be dictated by economics rather than politics. This is consistent with the emphasis of Asian governments on market-led rather than politically-led growth since the crisis of 1997-98. It accommodates the fact that the context is different than in Europe, where the transition to monetary union was supported by a commitment to political integration. That this commitment is less in Asia renders it questionable that a politically-led process could lead smoothly to monetary union.

Officials can help to prepare the way for the parallel currency. Constructing a true free trade area and promoting the further expansion of supply-chain networks in Asia can make it attractive for the private sector to transact using the parallel currency. By issuing debt denominated in the parallel currency, governments can help to create a benchmark asset and more liquid secondary markets, encouraging ACU issuance by banks and firms. They can make markets in the parallel currency more attractive by investing in the establishment of an efficient regional clearing and settlement system.

Even if regional integration heightens the attractions of the parallel currency as a unit of account, store of value, and medium of exchange, the inertia favouring national currencies is strong. History suggests that they will not be quickly out-competed by a parallel regional currency. Prudential policies to limit the risks to financial stability created by currency mismatches will also slow adoption of the parallel currency. But if this means that the process culminating in a single Asian currency will take time to unfold, this is not necessarily a bad thing, especially since years will have to pass before the entire range of supportive conditions is in place for Asian monetary unification.

3.6 Relevance of Europe's Experience for Asian Integration

The Europe's experience in integration-a mammoth enterprise extending over the last 60 years and involving 25 countries and more than 450 million people-could shed some light on the way forward for Asia.

In the case of Europe, financial integration was initially propelled by a customs union, which stimulated internal trade. In the mid-1980s, steps were taken to promote further integration through the creation of an internal market with free movement of goods, services, capital and persons. This objective of creating an internal market as the basis for trade integration opened the way for the introduction of a single currency, which in turn accelerated the pace of regional financial integration. In Asia as well, closer integration in the real sector—in trade and production—has preceded further deepening of financial integration.

While Europe's integration story is characterized by unique elements that might not be entirely applicable to Asia, it was felt that Europe's success and experience could still hold some important lessons for this region. First, Europe's integration has demonstrated that the benefits of financial integration are real and tangible—financial integration has helped to enhance capital productivity and output growth, and has served as a powerful instrument of economic reform, particularly by facilitating corporate restructuring and fostering innovation.

Second, Europe has shown that financial integration is a complex and multifaceted affair. In order to link the different sectors and activities in a modern financial system, the blueprint for integration must be both comprehensive and detailed. Europe's experience has illustrated that financial integration poses major technical challenges and requires careful preparation and consistent implementation.

Third, Europe has demonstrated that the process of financial integration needs to take into account the particular characteristics and requirements of the member countries. European national financial systems have typically evolved over time to reflect specific socio-economic preferences. Hence, any effort to integrate these various national systems has important social and cultural implications. It is thus evident that successful financial integration requires sufficient political will to reach often difficult compromises among the countries concerned. Without this political will and the relevant institutions to translate such will into practice, the process of integration may encounter formidable roadblocks.

Finally, Europe has recognised that the interests of ordinary citizens should be upheld as a key objective of financial integration. The efficiency gained in financial integration comes mainly through measures to improve the supply-side functioning of institutions and markets. However, these measures will not be fully reflected in economic performance unless the benefits filter down to the end-users of financial services. To this end, it is important to ensure that integration enhances, rather than diminishes, competition in the financial system, and that investor and consumer interests are adequately protected. Further, the authorities should recognize that financial markets function not just for the benefit of industry, but also for households and individuals.

In comparing Europe's and Asia's approaches to integration, there was agreement that Asian financial integration is likely to evolve as a bottom-up, market-driven process through the collective interactions of individual market participants. The process in Asia is likely to be propelled less by politics than has been the case in Europe, where integration was thrust forward via government directives and overarching institutions. In other words, the Asian process could be better characterised as "evolutionary", while the European model, especially in its later stages, could be described as "revolutionary". Asia's path is likely to proceed from the integration of trade, to the development of multinational production networks, to the integration of finance, and finally, perhaps, to monetary integration.

3.7 Summing Up

This chapter explored various issues related to trade, financial and monetary integration in Asia. Trade integration has progressed significantly in Asia, driven mainly by market forces, the emergence of cross-border production networks and China's rise as a manufacturing and export base. In contrast, financial integration in Asia remains relatively weak, with Asian economies developing closer linkages with developed financial markets, rather than among themselves. There is hence scope for deepening financial integration to better reap its various benefits. In this respect, national authorities and multilateral institutions have important roles to play, not just in strengthening domestic financial markets and liberalising capital flows, but also in developing intra- regional financial infrastructure, harmonising regulations and taking steps to mitigate the vulnerabilities that might arise from greater cross-border capital flows.

As integration within Asia deepens, it has been suggested that the region's economies move towards a common exchange rate framework. However, current conditions suggest that Asia could not yet be considered an optimum currency area (OCA), and it is hence premature for the region to embrace a common exchange rate framework, or monetary union. In particular, political factors inhibit such a development. Nonetheless, alternative variations of a regional currency arrangement have been proposed. These include a scheme whereby potential OCA members unilaterally shift to a managed float regime based on a basket of currencies, with the composition and weights of the baskets gradually standardised over time. Alternatively, a multi-speed approach could be considered, whereby countries that are ready move to integrate their currencies first. grow into a broader Asian Economic Community.

Notes

1. This grouping includes the initial 15 members of the European Union.
2. ASEAN5 comprises Indonesia, Malaysia, the Philippines, Singapore and Thailand.
3. This is defined as the ratio of intra-regional trade to the region's total trade, normalised by the region's share of global trading activity.
4. For this estimate, East Asia comprises Cambodia, China, Hong Kong, Indonesia, Korea, Laos, Malaysia, Mongolia, Myanmar, the Philippines, Singapore, Taiwan, Thailand and Vietnam.
5. For this estimate, the exporters comprise Indonesia, Korea, Malaysia, the Philippines, Singapore, Taiwan and Thailand.
6. This refers to Robert Lucas' (1990) observation that capital flows from rich to poor countries remain limited despite the higher marginal product of capital in poorer countries.
7. For some background on the relevance of European integration to Asia, see Wyplosz (2002), Wilson (2006), and Eichengreen and Park (2004).
8. This paper was published in The American Economic Review, Vol. 96, No. 2, May 2006.

References

Abiad, A, Leigh, D, and Mody, A (2007), "International Finance and Income Convergence: Europe is Different", *IMF Working Paper* No.07/64.

Agarwala, R (2003), "Road to a Single Currency for South Asia", *RIS Policy Brief* No. 9 (December), pp. 1-4.

Aizenman, J (2003), "On the Hidden Links Between Financial and Trade Opening", *NBER Working Paper* No. 9906.

Asian Development Bank (2007), "Uncoupling Asia: Myth and Reality", *Asian Development Outlook 2007*, p. 69.

Bayoumi, T and Eichengreen, B (1994), "One Money or Many? Analyzing the Prospects for Monetary Unification in Various Parts of the World", *Princeton Studies in International Finance*, No. 76.

Bayoumi, T and Mauro, P (1999), "The Suitability of ASEAN for a Regional Currency Arrangement", *IMF Working Paper* No. 99/162.

Chow, HK and Kim, Y (2000), "Exchange Rate Policy in Singapore: Prospects for a Common Currency Peg in East Asia", *The Singapore Economic Review*, Vol. 45, No. 2, pp. 139-164.

Clark, P, Tamirisa, N, Wei, SJ, Sadikov, A and Li, Z (2004), "A New Look at Exchange Rate Volatility and Trade Flows", *IMF Occasional Paper* No. 235.

Côté, A (1994), "Exchange Rate Volatility and Trade: A Survey", *Bank of Canada Working Paper* No. 94-5.

Cowen, D, Salgado, R, Shah, H, Teo, L and Zanello, A (2006), "Financial Integration in Asia: Recent Developments and Next Steps", *IMF Working Paper* No. 06/196.

Eichengreen, B (2004), "Real and Pseudo Preconditions for an Asian Monetary Union", presented at Asian Development Bank High-Level Conference on Asia's Economic Cooperation and Integration, Manila, 1-2 July, 2004.

Eichengreen, B and Bayoumi, T (1996), "Is Asia an Optimum Currency Area? Can It Become One? Regional, Global and Historical Perspectives on Asian Monetary Relations", in Collignon, S, Pisani-Ferry, J and Park, YC (eds.), *Exchange Rate Policies in Emerging Asian Countries,* Routledge, New York, pp. 347-364.

Eichengreen, B and Park, YC (2004), "Why Has There Been Less Financial Integration in Asia than in Europe?", *Monetary Authority of Singapore Staff Paper* No. 28.

Feltenstein, A and Plassmann, F (2005), "The Welfare Analysis of a Free Trade Zone: Intermediate Goods and the Asian Tigers", *Monetary Authority of Singapore Staff Paper* No. 41.

Ferry, J and Park, YC (eds.), *Exchange Rate Policies in Emerging Asian Countries,* Routledge, New York, pp. 327-340.

Frankel, J and Rose, A (1996), "The Endogeneity of the Optimum Currency Area Criteria", *NBER Working Paper* No. 5700

Ho, C and McCauley, R (2003), "Living with Flexible Exchange Rates: Issues and Recent Experience in Inflation Targeting in Emerging Economies", *BIS Working Paper* No. 130.

Hong Kong Exchanges and Clearing Limited (2006), "HKEx Fact Book 2006", http://www.hkex.com.hk/data/factbook/2006/e/30.pdf .

IMF (2006a), "Classification of Exchange Rate Arrangements and Monetary Frameworks", <http://www.imf.org/external/np/mfd/er/ 2006/eng/0706.htm>.

IMF (2006b), "People's Republic of China: Staff Report for the 2006 Article IV Consultation".

IMF (2006c), "Regional Integration and Macroeconomic Policies", Background Paper for the Second High-level Seminar on Asian Integration, May.

IMF (2007), "Financial Market Turbulence: Causes, Consequences, and Policies", *Global Financial Stability Report,* September 2007.

Kaminsky, G L, Reinhardt, C M and Vegh, C A (2004), "When it Rains, it Pours: Pro-cyclical Capital Flows and Macroeconomic Policies", *NBER Working Paper* No. 10780.

Kumar, Nagesh (2005), "Towards a Broader Asia Community: Agenda for the East Asian Summit", RIS Discussion Papers, RIS- DP# 100, http://www.ris.org.in

Mundell and A. Swoboda (eds). 1969, Monetary Problems of The International Economy. Chicago: University of Chicago Press.

Khor, HE, Robinson, E S and Lee, J (2004), "Managed Floating and Intermediate Exchange Rate Systems: The Singapore Experience", *Monetary Authority of Singapore Staff Paper* No. 37.

Lane, P R and Milesi-Ferretti, G M (2003), "International Financial Integration", *IMF Working Paper* No. 03/86.

Lucas, R (1990), "Why Doesn't Capital Flow from Rich to Poor Countries?", *The American Economic Review*, Vol. 80, No. 2, Papers and Proceedings of the Hundred and Second Annual Meeting of the American Economic Association, (May, 1990), pp. 92-96.

McKenzie, M (1999), "The Impact of Exchange Rate Volatility on International Trade Flows", *Journal of International Surveys*, Vol. 13, pp. 71-103.

Mckinnon, R.I. 1963. *"Optimum currency areas"*, American

Economic Review, Vol. 53, September. 717-725.

McKinnon, R (2001), "After the Crisis, the East Asian Dollar Standard Resurrected: An Interpretation of High-Frequency Exchange-Rate Pegging", in Stiglitz, J E and Yusuf, S (eds.), *Rethinking the East Asian Miracle*, Oxford University Press, New York, pp. 197-247.

McKinnon, R and Schnabl, G (2004), "The East Asian Dollar Standard, Fear of Floating, and Original Sin", *Review of Development Economics*, Vol. 8, No. 3, pp. 331-360.

Monetary Authority of Singapore (2003), *Macroeconomic Review*, Vol. II, Issue 1, January.

Mori, J, Kinukawa, M, Nukaya, H and Hashimoto, M (2002), "Integration of East Asian Economics and a Step by Step Approach Towards a Currency Basket Regime", *IIMA Research Report* No. 2 (November).

Mundell, R (2002), "Does Asia Need a Common Currency?", *Pacific Economic Review,* Vol. 7, No. 1, pp. 3-12.

Reinhart, Mundell, R. 1961. "A Theory of Optimum Currency Areas." *American Economic Review* 51:657-64.

Ogawa, E and Ito, T (2002), "On the Desirability of a Regional Basket Currency Arrangement", *Journal of the Japanese and International Economies*, Vol. 16, No. 3, pp. 317-334.

Rodrik, D (1998), "Who Needs Capital-Account Convertibility?", A paper for a Princeton International Finance Section Symposium.

Rose, A (2000), "One Money, One Market: the Effect of Common Currencies on Trade", *Economic Policy*, Vol. 15, No. 30, pp. 7-46.

Singapore Exchange Limited (2007), "Annual Report 2007", <http://www.sgx.com/sgx_ar2007/index.html>. *Monetary Authority of Singapore 92.*

Stiglitz, J (2002), "Capital Market Liberalization and Exchange Rate Regimes: Risk without Reward", *The Annals of the American Academy of Political and Social Science*, Vol. 579, pp. 219-248.

Stopford, J (ed.) (1994), *Rejuvenating the Mature Business: The Competitive Challenge*, Harvard Business School Press, Boston.

Williamson, J (1998), "The Case for a Common Basket Peg", in Collignon, S, Pisani- Williamson, J (2005), "A Currency Basket for East Asia, Not Just China", *Policy Briefs in International Economics*, No. PB05-1.

Williamson, J (2005), "A Basket Peg for Asia?", unpublished

manuscript, Institute for International Economics.

Wilson, P (2006), "Prospects for Asian Exchange Rate Cooperation: Why an ERM Solution Might be the Most Palatable", *Journal of the Asia Pacific Economy*, Vol. 11, No. 1, pp. 1-34.

Wyplosz, C (2002), *Regional Exchange Rate Arrangements: Lessons from Europe for East Asia*, Mimeo, Graduate Institute for International Studies, Geneva and CEPR.

Zhang, Z, Sato, K and McAleer, M (2004), "Is a Monetary Union Feasible for East Asia?", *Applied Economics*, Vol. 36, No. 10, pp. 1031-1043.

4

Market-driven Regional Integration in Asia

4.1 Introduction

Regional integration can take many forms, and nowhere is this more evident than in the vastly different integration processes taking place in the regions of Europe and Asia. The subject of this chapter is regional integration as it has developed in Asia with a focus on the drivers of that integration. While the study is not intended as a direct comparison of integration in Asia and Europe, it will include some comparisons between the two regions.

Integration in Asia has progressed very slowly and is still in an early stage despite that the process has continued for decades. In fact, it could be said that the process began centuries ago–even as far back as the 15th century. By comparison, European integration has progressed steadily and has gradually deepened over the last 50 years to reach an advanced stage today with a common currency and well-developed regional institutions. Thus, the speed of progression and the level of integration attained in the two regions are quite dissimilar. In addition to these differences, the drivers behind the integration process in each region are different. In Europe, the origins of integration have been institutional in nature, and the development of institutions has been prominent throughout the process.

Thus, regional institutions have been the driving force behind integration in Europe. In Asia, the development of regional institutions has also occurred; however, progress in this area has been slow and the few existing institutions are fairly weak and ineffective. Nevertheless, regional integration is taking place in Asia, but the driving force is the market rather than policy or institutions. Corporations and the production networks they have established· are driving integration in Asia.

The chapter is organized as follows. We begin by reviewing the early stages of regional integration in both Europe and Asia, and in so doing, identify the initial motivations for integration to be political in both cases. Then we examine two elements of policy driven regional integration–regional institutions and regional agreements–in an effort to assess the degree to which policy has played a role in the integration of each of these regions. In this assessment we compare the well-developed institutions of the European Union (EU) with the much weaker regional institutions in Asia, and we determine the level of each region's participation in regional agreements. We then evaluate market driven integration in East Asia by exploring the development of cross-border production networks beginning with a review of the region's trade and foreign direct investment (FDI) patterns as the key elements of these networks. Next, we use data on parts-and components trade to assess the level of production sharing in the region, noting the special roles of Japan and China, and argue that production sharing in East Asia has grown not only on a regional basis but also on a global basis.

4.2 Motivations for Regional Integration

The motivations for regional integration in both Europe and Asia were initially similar in that they were both political in nature. In Europe, economic interdependence was thought to be the most effective means to promote the political cooperation that was highly desired in the region after World War II. Therefore, economic means would be used to achieve a political goal. The early catalysts for the formation of the European Community included Hitler and the fear of Germany, the United States and its aid under the Marshall Plan, and fear of the Soviet Union and its spread of communism. [1] The Frenchman, Jean Monnet, first president of the European Coal and Steel Community (ECSC) and generally accepted principal architect of European unity, believed that unification would be best achieved through economic rather than military coordination. His proposal for a single high-level authority to supervise the development of the coal and steel industries in West Germany and in France led to reconciliation between those two countries, and this reconciliation was the basis for the European integration that followed. In Asia, political cooperation was also a motivating factor in early regional integration efforts, particularly in the formation of the Association of Southeast Asian Nations (ASEAN), which is the earliest (still existing) regional forum in East Asia today.

When ASEAN was formed in 1967, Southeast Asian nations recognized that the political environment in the region was changing, so they moved to align themselves in a way that would enable them to deal with it in a unified manner but at the same time would preserve their respective national interests. In fact, although the aims of ASEAN were created to focus on economic, social, and cultural development, the association played a significant role in fulfilling the political needs of Southeast Asian nations at that time. These political accomplishments included the restoration of amicable relations between Malaysia and Indonesia and the forging of an alliance among the non-communist members of the region. Although integration in both Europe and East Asia began for political reasons, thereafter the driving force for integration differed in each case. The drivers were governments and regional institutions (both political and economic) in Europe's case, and corporations and markets in East Asia's case.

4.2.1 Policy-driven Regional Integration: The degree of regional integration that is driven by policy or government initiative can be estimated in part by examining two elements of regional cooperation: regional institutions and regional agreements. The examination of these elements for Europe and Asia reveals that Europe has proceeded further in the development of regional institutions and in the adoption of regional agreements than has Asia. These findings lead us to conclude that Europe's integration is driven by policy to a much greater extent than is Asia's integration.

4.3 Europe's Regional Institutions

While European corporations have undeniably played an important role in furthering Europe's integration through their trade and foreign direct investment, the origins of integration in Europe were institutional in nature, and the regional institutions that were created have become a driving force for the deepening of that integration. Member states have delegated some of their decision-making power to these regional institutions so that decisions on specific matters of joint interest can be made through a democratic process at the regional level. [2]

The institutional origins of Europe's integration began in the early 1950s. Jean Monnet, often viewed as an institution builder, has been credited with nearly single-handed creation of Europe's first institution for integration, the European Coal and Steel Community. He was also the driving force behind the creation of the European Defence Community (EDC) and the European Atomic Energy Commission (EURATOM).

The European Union's decision-making process involves primarily the first three institutions (the European Parliament, the Council of the European Union, and the European Commission). This so-called "institutional triangle" is responsible for producing the policies and laws that apply throughout the European Union. The next two institutions, the Court of Justice and the Court of Auditors, also play important roles in this process. All European law is currently treaty based, and the three primary procedures for enacting new European Union laws are called co-decision, consultation, and assent. Of these three procedures, the co-decision procedure is the most common procedure for passing European Union legislation, and it places the European parliament and the Council on an equal footing so that the laws they pass are in fact joint acts of the Council and Parliament. Under the consultation procedure Parliament merely gives its opinion.

The European Commission chooses which procedure to follow when it proposes a new law, and this choice is dependent on which treaty-article the proposal is based. Europe's institutions developed early in the integration process and their decision-making authority now covers a wide swath of European society, including labour and employment, [3] education, health, crime, taxes, economic policy, transportation, and others. In addition, the integration of Europe has been recently widened with the addition of 10 Eastern European countries, and it has been further institutionalized with the agreement among European leaders on a European constitution, which if approved will provide a single set of rules to replace the various treaties that have governed the union since the 1950s. Of course, the constitution was agreed after many compromises were made, and before it can take effect it must be ratified by all 25 countries, some of whose voters have displayed considerable apathy and disaffection with the union in recent elections. Nevertheless, the fact that an agreement among the leaders of so many heterogeneous states could be reached at all is a momentous achievement and reflects the strong political will and importance of policy in Europe's integration process. [4]

4.4 Asia's Regional Institutions

Asia's efforts to formalize regional cooperation into a workable arrangement for the promotion of trade, investment, and security in the region have been varied but not very successful. In spite of the fact that the first attempts at regional cooperation in Asia date back to the 1950s, the same decade the European Union's institutions originated, regional institutions particularly in East Asia have been slow to develop, and even after almost five decades they are not highly advanced or very influential. The region's early efforts at institutional development were complicated by (1) the heterogeneity of many political, economic, and social aspects of the region, (2) political tensions between certain countries historically, (3) the desire to protect national interests and specific industries (for example, agriculture and automobiles), and (4) Asia's historical openness in trade and FDI and its long-standing relationships with the United States and the European Union. Consequently, many of the regional cooperative arrangements that were formed at that time no longer exist. Nevertheless, there are several regional groups that currently represent the region, including the Association of Southeast Asian Nations, Asia-Pacific Economic Cooperation (APEC), Asia-Europe Meeting (ASEM), and the Bangkok Agreement.

Although the regional groups in East Asia are often referred to as "regional institutions," they are in fact dissimilar in a number of ways from the institutions of the European Union. East Asia's regional institutions include some member countries that are actually located outside of East Asia. Examples are APEC, which includes countries in North and South America, and the Asia-Europe Meeting, which is in reality an interregional group comprising countries in Europe and Asia. In addition, unlike the European Union's institutions, which exist within one regional group (the European Union) and serve separately defined functions within that regional group, Asia's institutions are separate groups of countries with members often belonging to more than one group. In addition, some of these groups may have broadly similar goals and objectives, such as the reduction of tariffs for members, but they often have different agendas for achieving these goals, which can result in confusion and duplication of effort among members and also presents a non-unified face to the rest of the world.

ASEAN, which includes 10 nations, is probably the best known and most active regional institution in East Asia. ASEAN's initial purpose as stated in its founding document, the Bangkok Declaration, is "to accelerate the economic growth, social progress and cultural development in the region." Nevertheless, it is widely acknowledged that the main impetus for ASEAN's formation was political.1However, in order to fulfil its stated objective of economic cooperation, ASEAN attempted to implement a number of economic initiatives, most of which were industrial cooperation initiatives. Through these initiatives ASEAN aspired to facilitate economic cooperation by developing region wide industrial capacity as an alternative to national industrialization in order to harness the power of the region's huge population.

However, the early economic plans initiated by ASEAN (in 1976 to 1988), such as the ASEAN Industrial Projects (AIP), the Preferential Trading Arrangement (PTA), and the ASEAN Industrial Complementation (AIC), were generally ineffective. The intent of these industrial-type cooperative efforts was to involve resource pooling and market sharing and thus allow the ASEAN economies to take advantage of economies of scale and a large combined market. These schemes were supposed to enable individual countries to specialize in manufacturing specific components as a means of developing large-scale industries (for example, automobiles). This would then increase complementarities among regional economies and eventually increase intra-regional trade and investment. Finally, industrial cooperation was intended to shift the focus of industrialization from a national level to a regional level. As regional industrialization would grow, regional cooperation would increase and lead to further industrialization. Theoretically, this plan should have worked, but in reality it did not. The various industrial cooperative efforts were largely unsuccessful because of problems related to implementation, financing, and private sector involvement. ASEAN's early attempts at economic cooperation did not contribute to the remarkable economic performance of the ASEAN countries at the time.

The good performance at that time was rather the result of

their trade and investment links with each other and the rest of the world. Europe's decision-making process, discussed above, is institutionalized. In other words, the process is set forth in its founding treaties and carried out by its three main institutions: the European Parliament, the Council of the European Union, and the European Commission. In East Asia, there is a similar process called consensus decision-making, but its usage is not stipulated by any particular authority or policy. It exists as a feature of Asian relationship culture. Consensus decision-making, along with the accommodation of the interests of others and non-interference in the internal affairs of neighbouring nations, is the basis for the concept called the "ASEAN Way". [5] Although the "ASEAN Way" has been credited with enhancing political stability in the region, it has also been faulted for inhibiting rather than promoting economic cooperation within ASEAN.

4.5 Regional Agreements

In addition to the broad regional integration frameworks like the European Union and NAFTA, there are narrower regional arrangements formed between two or more countries that are another form of government-led cooperation. Regional agreements have existed for more than 50 years, and even though they are usually referred to as "regional *trade* agreements or arrangements" (RTAs) or "free *trade* areas" (FTAs), they often include articles or clauses dealing with areas such as foreign direct investment and services in addition to those dealing with trade.

During the last decade the move to regionalism has become a headlong rush. Of the 194 agreements notified at the beginning of 1999, 87 were notified since 1990. The last 10 years have witnessed qualitative, as well as quantitative, changes in regional integration schemes. There have been three major developments.

The first is the recognition that effective integration requires more than reducing tariffs and quotas. Many other barriers have the effect of segmenting markets and impeding the free flow of goods, services, investments, and ideas, and wide ranging policy measures—going well beyond traditional trade policies—are needed to remove these barriers. This so-called deep integration was first actively pursed in the Single Market Program of the European Union (EU), and elements of this program are now finding their way into the debate in other regional agreements. The second is the move from "closed regionalism" to a more open model. Many of the trading blocs that were formed between developing countries in the 1960s and 1970s were based on a model of import substituting development, and regional agreements—with high external trade barriers—were used as a way of implementing this model. The new wave of regional agreements—including resurrection of some old agreements—have generally been more outward-looking, and more committed to boosting, rather than controlling, international commerce.

The third development is the advent of trade blocs in which both high-income industrial countries and developing countries are equal partners in agreements designed to bolster the economies of all the member countries. Perhaps the most important example of this is the North American Free Trade Area (NAFTA), formed in 1994 when the Canada-U.S. Free Trade Agreement was extended to Mexico. EU has linked with the transition economies of Eastern Europe through the Europe Agreements, and has developed the EU-Turkey customs union and a Mediterranean policy potentially incorporating agreements with nearly every Mediterranean country. There has been discussion of replacing the EU's trade preferences of the Lomé agreements with reciprocal trade agreements with these developing countries.

These developments have occurred against the backdrop of globalization. New technologies and more liberal trading regimes have led to increased trade volumes, larger investment flows, and increasingly footloose production. All these considerations point to the need for a new analysis of regional integration agreements—one that takes into account political as well as economic effects, that assesses the opportunities for deep integration, and captures the new potentials created by North-South agreements.

Between 1948 and 2006, a total of 194 primary regional instruments dealing with trade and FDI were adopted worldwide. Of these 160 regional instruments only 16 instruments (bilateral, regional, and interregional) involved Asian countries, and they were formed (but not adopted in all cases) more recently—between 1980 and 2006. The relatively small number of such instruments involving Asia indicates that the region is a newcomer to cooperative arrangements of this type. In comparison, Europe has in force 22 such instruments that are bilateral, regional, or interregional, plus 71 bilateral association, cooperation, framework, and partnership agreements that include investment-related provisions (56 for the European Community and 15 for EFTA).

In 1992, ASEAN responded to an environment of increasing regionalism in the world and an uncertain multilateral trading system by creating the ASEAN Free Trade Area (AFTA). AFTA is the earliest major regional trade arrangement in East Asia. It has been successful in reducing regional tariffs, for which it was initially conceived, and has also worked to remove no tariff barriers. While AFTA is best known for its trade measures, it also promotes FDI although this area is primarily dealt with through the ASEAN Investment Area (AIA), which was formed in 1998.

In recent years, interest in forming regional arrangements has accelerated in East Asia. Since 2000, six trade-FDI instruments involving East Asia have been adopted with 14 more currently (as of 2003) under consultation or negotiation.. Most of these are bilateral, and nearly half of them include Japan as one of the bilateral partners. However, ASEAN is also rapidly pursuing comprehensive arrangements with other Asian partners, the most prominent of which is the ASEAN China Free Trade Agreement (ACFTA) adopted in 2002.

Which can be seen from the foregoing discussion that Europe's integration has been driven by governments and their policies through the creation of powerful regional institutions that have in their own right further deepened integration in the region. East Asia, however, has not been able or willing to establish such strong institutions despite a long history of trying to do so. Nor has East Asia participated to the extent that Europe has in the adoption of regional agreements, which have increased markedly on a global scale in recent years. In the next section, we will take a closer look the development of East Asia's integration and the forces that are driving it.

4.6 Market-driven Regional Integration in Asia

Given the undeveloped condition of East Asia's institutions, the region's historical preference for maintaining national control and sovereignty, and the weak political will for making the tough decisions necessary to advance regional cooperation, one could ask whether regional integration is taking place at all in East Asia, and if it is taking place, what is driving it. The remainder of this paper will address these questions and in the process show that regional integration is indeed proceeding in East Asia and that it is driven by market forces. In fact, the main driving force for regional integration in East Asia has been and continues to be the trade and FDI carried out by multinational corporations (MNCs) and the consequent development of cross-border production networks. We will reveal how the growth of assembly trade (or trade in parts and components) in the region is evidence of the growth of production networks or production sharing. We will also show that East Asia's involvement in production sharing has promoted its regional integration but not at the expense of its participation in production networks on a global scale.

While U.S. multinational corporations were the initiators of international production networks, MNCs in Japan and Europe quickly followed their lead, and MNCs in the Asian NIEs also became involved later on. Furthermore, China is playing an increasingly significant role in these networks. Before proceeding to a discussion of East Asia's involvement in production networks, however, we will examine trends in the development of East Asia's integration as reflected in its trade and FDI patterns.

4.6.1 East Asian Trade and Foreign Direct Investment: Trade and foreign direct investment are closely linked as important elements in cross border production networks, which are the foundation of market-led integration in East Asia. An examination of trade and FDI trends provides valuable information about the development and geographic distribution of production networks and the progression of integration in the region. On a global basis, trade and FDI have grown rapidly over the past two decades. East Asia has not only shared in that growth, but its performance has been distinguished among that of developing countries worldwide.

4.6.2 Trading Patterns: From 1978 to 2006, global exports of goods and services rose by 5.5 percent annually in real terms. Developing countries' exports of goods and services increased at nearly the same rate, slightly less than 6 percent annually in real terms, during the same period while their aggregate exports-to-GDP ratio rose by more than half. During the second decade of this period (the 1990s), the merchandise exports (not including services) of developing countries rose 8.5 percent per year, considerably more than the trends of less than 2 percent in the 1980s.

All the developing countries of East Asia have experienced significant growth in exports since the East Asian crisis in 1997-98, except in 2001 when many of them suffered a decline in exports. Merchandise export growth in developing East Asia was 12.1 percent in 2002 and 22.6 percent in 2003, and growth in Southeast Asia was 4.7 percent in 2002 and 12.8 percent in 2003. China's export growth has been exceptional, 22.4 percent in 2002 and 34.6 percent in 2003, due to its growing production capacity and good competitive position.

Developing East Asia and Southeast Asia's merchandise

import growth followed the same general trend as their export growth—10.4 percent (2002) and 24.3 percent (2003) for East Asia and 4.2 percent (2002) and 10.6 percent (2003) for Southeast Asia. Here again, China had the highest growth rate of all developing East Asian countries in those two years, with the rate in 2003 (41 percent) nearly double the rate in 2002 (21.3 percent). China's exceptional import growth was the result of its "strong domestic demand, higher oil prices, and lower tariffs," and this growth caused China's trade surplus to decline from US$ 44.2 billion in 2002 to US$ 41.4 billion in 2003.

The rapid growth in developing country exports has been attributed in large part to the change in the composition of their exports from traditional agriculture and resource products to manufactured goods. Low and middle-income groups have increased the share of manufactured products to 80 percent and 70 percent, respectively, of their exports. Reportedly, this increase is not just the result of price declines for agricultural and resource commodities relative to manufactured goods, neither is it attributable to the impact of large, high-growth exporters such as China and India. Even excluding China and India from the calculation, the share of manufactured goods in total exports of developing countries rose significantly – from 10 percent in 1980 to 60 percent in 2001. In East Asia and the Pacific (including China but not India) the share rose from just over 50 percent in 1981 to nearly 90 percent in 2001.The World Bank (2003c, p. 41) attributes this growth in manufactured product exports to "a combination of policy reforms, structural changes in global production processes, and general economic trends related to continuous increases in real per capita incomes." For developing countries, not only labour-intensive goods but also (and even more so) high-technology goods, in particular electronics, contributed to the gain in manufactured exports.

For low-income countries the growth rate in all three levels of technology manufactures (low, medium, and high) was well above the world average in 1981 to 2001. This is true whether or not China and India, which together have very high growth rates, are included. Particularly noteworthy is the 26 percent growth rate in low-income countries' exports of electronic manufactures, such as computers, televisions, and components. This rate drops by 5 percentage points if China and India (with a combined growth rate of 36 percent) are excluded.

A major contributing factor to the change in the export patterns of developing countries, especially the increase in high-technology exports, is global production sharing.38 Electronic products, in particular, can be readily broken down into parts and components that can be manufactured and then assembled in different locations. This capability facilitates the formation of cross-border production networks for these and similar products. Later in our discussion we will reveal that there has been an increase Worldwide in the trade of parts and components and that East Asia has a significant and rising share of that trade. This growth in parts-and-components trade is an indication of East Asia's increased participation in production networks.

4.6.3 Intra-regional Trade: For centuries, East Asia's trade has been characterized as both global and regional. Reflecting the global aspect, all ASEAN countries reported over 10 percent of their trade (imports, exports, or both) to be with the European Union and the United States in 2001. However, nearly all East Asian countries also have significant trade with one or more regional partners, with Japan being a major partner for most, followed by Singapore, China, and a few other larger regional countries.

Over the past two decades, East Asia's intra-regional merchandise exports have increased as a share of total world exports from 4.6 percent in 1980 to 11.8 percent in 2001 and as a share of total East Asian exports from 33.7 percent in 1980 to 47.7 percent in 2001. These increases are consistent generally with the increases in NAFTA's intra-regional shares in world exports (from 5.4 percent in 1980 to 10.4 percent in 2001) and in total NAFTA exports (from 33.6 percent to 55.5 percent in those years, respectively). The trend for the European Union, however, is different in that its intra-regional exports as a share of world exports declined from 29.5 percent to 22.9 percent between 1990 and 2001, and they declined as a share of total European Union exports from 65.9 percent to 61.3 percent in the same period. However, the European Union's shares since 1980 have been at a much higher level than those of either East Asia or NAFTA, and they have remained fairly stable for the past few years.

Nevertheless, this decline is noteworthy considering that Europe is the region that has become the most integrated during that time. Overall, it is revealed that over the past 10 to 20 years East Asia's intra-regional trade has increased significantly in importance in terms of world trade and its own trade, and that it is quite intense, particularly when compared with the intra-regional trade of other regions.

4.6.4 Patterns of FDI Flows: Spurred by significant liberalization in East Asia during the 1980s and early 1990s, foreign direct investment inflows to the region increased about 2.6 times from an annual average of US$ 55 billion in 1991-96 to US$ 144 billion in 2000. Although inflows then declined to US$93 billion by 2002, this figure still represents a 69 percent increase since the beginning of the 1990s. In 2002, China attracted US$ 53 billion in FDI, the largest share of FDI inflows in the region as well as in the developing world. This level of inflows represents a new high for China whose inflows were an annual average of only half that amount (US$ 25.5 billion) in 1991-96. China's advantage in attracting FDI lies in its huge domestic market, sustained rapid growth, improved export competitiveness, and recent accession to the WTO. Also contributing to its flows is the large overseas network of Chinese workers.

The largest foreign direct investor in ASEAN from 1995 to 2001 (except in 1997) was the European Union, which accounted for 19-40 percent of investment.The next largest investor is the United States, with a share of 20-30 percent in the past few years. Although the value of direct investment from the European Union and the United States in ASEAN was down significantly in 2001 from that in 1999 (by 41 percent and 37 percent, respectively), disinvestment (primarily in Indonesia and Malaysia) by Australia, Hong Kong (China), and Korea, and other unspecified countries in 2001 pushed up the share for the European Union and the United States. The share of ASEAN's FDI that comes from Japan dropped significantly from 23 percent in 1997 to only 9 percent in 2005. This was in part due to Japan's disinvestment in Indonesia of US$ 1.7 billion in 2000 and US$ 1.1 billion in 2001, and its disinvestment in Malaysia of US$ 1.2 billion in 2001.

Japan's investment in China has been increasing since 1999. Before that, Japan invested far more in ASEAN-4 (Indonesia, Malaysia, the Philippines, and Thailand) than in China, but that investment began to decline sharply in 1997. By 2002, the share of Japan's outward FDI to China was 8.1 percent, whereas that to ASEAN-4 was lower, at 6.8 percent. Although FDI outflows from Japan to East Asia rose by 2.8 percent in 2002, this finding reflects primarily increased flows to the Asian NIEs (by 20.3 percent) and to China (by 20.8 percent). Outflows to ASEAN-4 declined by 25.3 percent in 2002.

The specific industries targeted by Japanese investment in China have changed over time. In the mid-1980s, it was the food industry; in the early 1990s, it was the textiles industry; and since the end of the 1990s, it has been the chemical, electrical machinery, and transport machinery industries.

4.6.5 Intra-regional FDI: Compared with those of the European Union, Asia's intra-regional flows make up a smaller, but increasing, share of total flows. In 2001, 49 percent of the European Union's FDI outflows stayed within the European Union, and that share rose even higher to 66 percent in 2002. By comparison, the developing East Asian group comprising ASEAN, China, and Hong Kong (China) as host economies and ASEAN, China, Hong Kong (China), Korea, and Taiwan (China) as source economies had a somewhat smaller intra-regional share of 37 percent in 1999, increasing to 40 percent in 2001. The Asian region has been at the forefront of a movement that began in the 1980s when MNCs located in developing countries began to increase their outward investment, mostly in other developing countries. South, East, and Southeast Asian firms have accounted for the major portion of these outflows—between 51 and 81 percent of developing-country outflows since 1997. This position can be attributed to the export-oriented growth in these countries, which led to the growth of their MNCs; the MNCs then invested intra-regionally as well as in industrial countries.

There has been a noticeable shift intra-regionally in flows away from the ASEAN countries to China. This shift was partly due to the Asian crisis, but recently, it has been caused more by the increase in China's attractiveness as a host country—an attractiveness generated largely by its lower wage costs and its highly skilled labour, as well as its increasingly liberalized trade and FDI environment. Not only Japan, but also other major regional investors, including Hong Kong (China), Korea, and Taiwan (China), are focusing on China. Between 1999 and 2001, Taiwan (China) reduced its investment in ASEAN by 67 percent while increasing its investment in China by 15 percent. Korea disinvested in ASEAN in 2001 and raised its investment in China by a remarkable 69 percent. And China raised its investment in ASEAN by 94 percent.

4.6.6 Trade and FDI in East Asia: We can draw some general conclusions about East Asia's trade and FDI patterns:

- East Asia still does a great deal of trade with, and receives a large amount of direct investment from, the United States and the European Union, albeit from some European Union countries more than others.

- Although the United States and certain European countries are still Japan's primary trade and investment partners, there are signs of a shift in both Japan's trade and its FDI from outside to inside the region, and there are shifts within the region as well, such that Japan's shares of trade with and investment in China are beginning to surpass those with ASEAN.
- ASEAN's trade with Japan is declining, while its trade with China and Korea is rising, and ASEAN is receiving less investment from Japan as well.
- The rise of China is having a major effect on the region's trade and FDI patterns as MNCs both inside and outside the region shift operations to that country, often from other countries within the region.

From these observations, we can discern the continuation of the highly liberalized nature of East Asia's trade and direct investment and the importance of maintaining its extra-regional relationships. At the same time, intra-regional relationships are strengthening as individual countries struggle to find a way to prosper and grow in the shadow of a rising China. Trade and FDI are closely linked as major elements in the broader phenomenon of cross-border production networks. These networks and their role in the integration of East Asia are the focus of the discussion in the remainder of this paper.

4.6.7 Cross-border Production Networks and Regional Integration in East Asia: Cross-border production networks are the focus of much analysis and discussion in economic literature today. Although this phenomenon is identified in the literature by various names with sometimes different definitions, [6] Borrus, Ernst, and Haggard (2000, p. 2) describe it in its broadest sense.

By a lead firm's "cross-border production network" (CPN) we mean the inter- and intra-firm relationships through which the firm organizes the entire range of its business activities: from research and development, product definition and design, to supply of inputs, manufacturing (or production of a service), distribution, and support services. We thus include the entire network of cross-border relationships between a lead firm and its own affiliates and subsidiaries, but also its subcontractors, suppliers, service providers, or other firms participating in cooperative relationships, such as standard setting or R&D [research and development] analysis.

Multinational corporations (MNCs) are attributed with initiating the phenomenon of cross-border production networks through their establishment of subsidiaries in other countries to handle certain stages of production. While MNCs are still at the centre of most production networks, local firms in host countries are becoming increasingly involved in networks as subcontractors that are not directly part of an MNC. Also emerging from the production network phenomenon are global contract suppliers who serve a large and diverse set of purchasers. In East Asia the concept of "third-party logistics" is emerging. This concept involves the outsourcing of logistics by international manufacturers to specialized service providers who can handle the efficient transport of components through "multimodal transport systems packaged with simplified trade documentation and clearances valid across modes" (Yusuf 2003, p. 278).

In recent years, production networks have expanded to include many countries in the production of a single product. In the early stages of development a network might consist simply of the production of one small part or component of a good in a low-cost country and then its re importation to the home country for assembly into the final good. This process has changed over the years so that it now involves many countries, and thus border crossings, in the production and assembly of a final product. [7] Thus, the development of cross-border production networks has led to the integration of the countries involved in the network.

As we mentioned earlier, a country's increased trade in parts and components is one indication of its increased participation in production sharing. Furthermore, as the trade (both imports and exports) in parts and components increases and more countries become involved in the production sharing system, their participation becomes more tightly woven into the network. This is true for East Asian countries on a global as well as intra-regional basis.

4.6.8 Trade in Parts and Components: Due to fairly recent (mid-1980s) revisions in the publication of trade data, it is now possible to separate the trade data for parts and components from that of final products in the machinery and transport sector (SITC 7) [8] and in the miscellaneous goods sector (SITC 8) of total manufacturing trade. This parts-and-components trade (also called "assembly trade" or "fragmentation trade") currently occurs largely in the machinery and transport equipment sector (SITC 7). Electronics and electrical equipment is a sub sector of SITC 7 and that sub sector is broken down further into 3-digit, 4-digit, and 5-digit groups that consist solely of components of manufactured equipment to be assembled. The assembly trade (exports and imports) of East Asia is heavily concentrated in electronics and electrical products. Over 80 percent of the region's total trade in 2000 was in parts and accessories of office machinery, telecommunications equipment, electrical circuit apparatus, and household electrical equipment.

Between 1992 and 2000, world trade in parts and components rose from US$ 336.8 billion to US$ 1,086.4 billion, or average growth of 18 percent per year. The share of these products in world manufacturing trade rose from 20.7 percent to 25.4 percent for exports and from 21.7 percent to 24.5 percent for imports between those two years.

East Asia's share of world imports of parts and components remained about the same in 2000 (33.1 percent) as it was in 1992 (33.5 percent). However, if Japan, whose share remained relatively unchanged during that period, is excluded from the calculation, then (developing) East Asia's share increases substantially, by nearly 14 percentage points. In addition, developing East Asia's share of world imports is nearly the same as its share of world exports in parts and components, particularly in 2000. Athukorala (2003, p. 12-14) argues that this finding reflects Japan's prominent role in assembly activities in East Asia and that Japan's large trade surplus can be attributed to the heavy involvement of Japanese companies in such activities. He also attributes the trade positions of Malaysia, the Philippines, and Singapore, all of which shifted from deficits to surpluses between 1992 and 2000, to growing intra-regional cross border trade in assembly products.

East Asia has a greater dependency on assembly trade than do NAFTA, the European Union, and the world. The share of parts and components in East Asia's total manufacturing exports was 32 percent in 2000 compared with 28.1 percent for NAFTA, 18.9 percent for the European Union, and 25.4 percent for the world. In 1992-2000, the contribution of parts and components to East Asia's export growth (43.5 percent) was also greater than the contribution to NAFTA's growth (30 percent), to the European Union's growth (22.2 percent), and to world growth (29.5 percent).

These regions' import shares of parts and components were in line with their export shares. Import shares in 2000 were 35.4 percent for East Asia, 22.8 percent for NAFTA, and 20.3 percent for the European Union. Although most countries within East Asia have fairly large assembly-trade shares, Malaysia, the Philippines, and Singapore are particularly notable for their shares that are 50 percent or higher for both exports and imports. In addition, assembly trade has contributed over 50 percent to export and import growth in these three countries, in Japan (exports only), and in Indonesia, Korea, and Thailand (imports only). The share of this type of trade in China's total manufacturing trade is also worthy of note because it has risen from 6.7 percent in 1992 to 14.5 percent in 2000 for exports and from 19.5 percent to 33.5 percent for imports. Parts and components contributed 42 percent to China's import growth between 1992 and 2000.

4.6.9 Intra-regional Trade in Parts and Components: Parts and components comprise a major proportion not only of East Asia's total trade (as previously discussed) but also of its intra-regional trade. This finding goes to the heart of the discussion in this chapter. In other words, significant intra-regional production sharing is taking place in East Asia and, in fact, has increased since the mid-1980s.

Between 1985 and 2001, the share of machinery and transport equipment (SITC 7) in developing East Asia's total intra-regional exports increased from 18.1 percent to 47.9 percent, indicating a significant rise in the relative importance of this sector in East Asia's intra-regional trade. Although this increase occurred for all developing East Asian countries, especially notable were the gains in share between 1985 and 2001 for China (32 percentage points), Malaysia (49 percentage points), the Philippines (44 percentage points), Singapore (34 percentage points), and Thailand (38 percentage points). Ng and Yeats (2003, p. 33) attribute these gains to the participation of these countries in international production networks and point out that China in particular specializes in the assembly of imported parts and components. The Asian Development Bank (ADB) reported recently that between 1995 and 2003, exports to China from all of Asia grew at an average annual rate of 16.9 percent (measured in US dollars), which was more than three times the 5.3 percent growth in world trade, due to China's "strong economic growth, stable yuan exchange rate, and the international segmentation of production processes."

The ADB also reported that during the same period, exports of precision instruments and electrical machinery to China from its nine major regional trading partners increased six fold, and exports of machinery, chemical products, and transportation equipment from the same countries increased threefold. In 2003, the main categories of exports from these nine economies to China were electrical machinery (34 percent share), machinery (17 percent share), chemical products (15 percent share), and textiles and apparel (6 percent share). In fact, over the past decade, nearly all major East Asian economies have experienced a change in the products they export to China from those in low value-added sectors to those in high value-added sectors. The ADB attributes this shift in product composition to an increase in production sharing as described below:

The PRC [China] has established a strong comparative advantage in downstream stages of production, especially for electronics products, largely a result of its massive foreign direct investment inflows and large supply of low cost labour. The final stages of production of some items have been moved to the PRC from other Asian economies. As a result, the PRC's demand for intermediate components from its nine major regional trading partners has grown sharply, while its exports of final goods to non-Asian industrial economies also increased significantly. The structural trade balances between the PRC and its major trading partners clearly show its role as an assembly centre for many exports from Asia to the United States and European Union.

Between 1995 and 2003, China's trade balances in machinery, electrical machinery, chemical products, and transportation equipment have become increasingly negative in the case of its nine Asian partners but increasingly positive in the case of the United States and the European Union. These findings indicate that China's participation in production sharing is both regional and global. Participation in production sharing on these two levels is also the case for East Asia as a whole.

East Asia's exports of machinery and transport equipment (SITC 7) increased as a share of its intra-regional exports between 1985 and 2001. However, they also increased as a share of its exports to Japan (from 3.5 percent to 35.4 percent) and to countries outside of East Asia (from 24.4 percent to 48.5 percent). Thus, this category of exports accounts for the largest share of both East Asia's intra-regional exports and its extra regional exports.

As we previously mentioned, the machinery and transport sector (SITC 7) includes trade in parts and components as well as in final goods, and it is the trade in parts and components that is relevant in assessing the degree of production sharing in the region. Ng and Yeats (2003, p. 53) found that "East Asian intra-trade in goods normally used in production sharing grew at an annual rate of 21 percent from the mid-1980s to mid-1990s. This was approximately 7 percentage points higher than East Asia's intra-trade in all goods." By 2001, East Asia's regional trade in parts and components had increased to 26.2 percent of its total regional manufacturing trade (excluding chemicals).

Furthermore, this regional trade in parts and components is fairly concentrated with nearly 85 percent of it accounted for by only four products: parts of office machinery (37.5 percent), parts of telecommunications equipment (27.7 percent), switchgear (12.9 percent), and electronic components (6.7 percent).The importance of parts and components in both the regional and non-regional trade of East Asia is further evident at the four-digit SITC level. For example, in 2001 several major products at the four-digit level, including "parts of office machinery" (SITC 759.9) and "parts of telecommunications equipment" (SITC 764.9), were among East Asia's top 30 four-digit SITC exports both on a regional and non-regional basis. The high degree of production sharing in East Asia is evident in the results of a survey of "high-performing" East Asian firms in seven East Asian countries presented in Yusuf (2003). These results indicate that internationally networked firms are prevalent in East Asia.

Of the non-Chinese firms surveyed, nearly one-quarter are internationally networked with 43.3 percent of those (or 10 percent of the total 326 firms) both importing parts and producing parts and final goods for foreign buyers. The results for Chinese firms in the survey are not quite as strong. Only 14.6 percent of these firms are internationally networked with just 32.2 percent both importing parts and producing parts and final goods for foreign buyers. Yusuf (2003) attributes the weaker result for the Chinese firms to China's "relatively recent and ongoing integration into the world trading system."

4.7 Japan and China in East Asian Production Networks

The roles of both Japan and China in production networks are worthy of special note. Japan's role has been pivotal historically in the establishment and expansion of production networks in East Asia, and China is already showing signs of becoming a key player in these networks.

In any discussion of Japan's role in the formation of production networks in East Asia, the flying-geese model always comes to mind. Japan established regional production networks in East Asia through its extensive foreign direct investment and the cross border activities of its MNCs. These activities included trade, investment, licensing, and sub-contracting. These original networks were extended as other countries in the region followed Japan's strategy of industrial development. Japanese MNCs have come under some criticism for allegedly continuing to utilize their own subsidiaries keiretsu-related firms for their large-scale sourcing throughout the region and thus limiting the opportunities for local firms to upgrade their capabilities. Yet, Japanese firms are recognized for their substantial impact on industrial upgrading through their substantial flows of technology, investment, and training resources to East Asian economies.

Today, Japan continues to play a major role in regional production networks as seen in Japan's heavy involvement in production sharing in East Asia. Local sales of Japanese overseas subsidiaries in the East Asian countries were between 18 percent and 58 percent of the subsidiaries' respective country sales, while local sales of Japanese subsidiaries in the United States and in the European countries were between 65 percent and 92 percent. Exports going directly to Japan from the United States and the European countries were only 1-2 percent, but exports to Japan from the East Asian countries were between 20 percent and 41 percent. Thus, the proportion of Japanese affiliates' exports that went to third countries (countries other than Japan or the country of operation) from the East Asian countries was around 30-50 percent, but the proportion from the European countries was smaller at 22-34 percent and that from the United States was only 6.4 percent. Although the composition of these exports is not known, these three sets of statistics indicate that Japanese overseas affiliates tend to export to Japan and to third countries from East Asia much more than they do from North America and Europe. This tendency is consistent with Japan's heavy involvement in the assembly trade of production networks in the region.

4.8 East Asia's Role in Assembly Trade

There are a number of reasons for East Asia's major role in assembly activities and the growth of production networks in the region. The reduction of trade barriers and the elimination of restrictions on FDI in East Asia have made the region attractive to MNCs, which were responsible for initiating and expanding production networks in the region. East Asia has lower wages in manufacturing than do countries in Europe and North America. Furthermore, significant differences in wages among the countries of East Asia have led to increased cross-border production sharing in parts and components, which has led to increased "intra-regional" production networks. MNCs tend to locate their assembly activities in countries where there are already other key participants so that countries such as Singapore, Korea, Taiwan (China), and Malaysia, which became part of international production networks early on, can attract even more assembly activities as networks grow. Over time, MNC affiliates in a particular country invest in the local production facilities and establish information links and become accustomed to the investment climate so that they are reluctant to withdraw even for cost reasons.

4.9 Concluding Remarks

The integration processes in Europe and East Asia developed along different paths. In Europe, the process was driven by governments and their policies, including the early creation of regional institutions, which strengthened over time to become a driving force for integration in their own right.

In Asia, where regional institutions are not well developed, integration has nevertheless progressed to a fairly high level, and the driving force behind it has been the market, or more specifically, multinational corporations and their production networks.

In recent years, parts and components have made up an increasingly large share of East Asia's total manufacturing trade, indicating the region's increasing involvement in production networks. As these production networks evolve and grow, they bind the countries involved in them into closer and closer cooperation.

And when the countries in the network are located within the same region, the process leads to deeper regional integration. Three points that have important implications for the future of regional integration in Asia can be drawn from this paper. First, China's role in regional production sharing has grown markedly in recent years.

China has been described as a specialist in assembly trade and the increase in its imports of parts and components from its major East Asian partners is an indication of its integration into regional production networks. Although China's role in these networks is not as prominent as Japan's role, there is little doubt that it will continue to expand and could approach that level during the next decade.

Second, although it has been emphasized on the market-driven nature of East Asia's regional integration and the weakness of its institutions, it should not be assumed that regional governments and their policies played no role at all in the integration process. In fact, as mentioned in our discussion, the increase in production sharing for some countries (for example, China and Singapore) was in part attributable to policy directives of their governments.

It could even be argued that the stage was set for market-driven integration in East Asia by the policy actions of East Asian governments and regional institutions. For example, the reduction of restrictions on trade and FDI was one of the reasons that production networks have developed so well in East Asia.

While much of this reduction has been on a unilateral basis, the effect of regional initiatives, such as AFTA, on trade barriers should not be overlooked. In addition, MNCs are attracted not only to countries with low labour and other costs but also to countries that are stable politically and economically, have good physical infrastructure and a skilled labour force, and that operate under the rule of law.

These characteristics are essential not only to attract FDI but also to ensure the continued growth of production networks. There is still much work to be done in these areas.

While tariffs have been significantly reduced, there are still non-tariff barriers in some Asian countries that can seriously inhibit trade flows. There is also considerable need for further reforms that could improve the commercial environment for both foreign and domestic enterprises. These reforms include "more effective R&D and other support schemes, better physical infrastructure, legal reform, improved education, and administrative reform."

Third, the participation of East Asian countries in production networks is growing not only on a regional basis but also on a global basis. While the ultimate and preferred goal for Asian countries might be full-fledged participation in international production networks, the current direction in the region is toward increased involvement in regional arrangements, such as free trade areas.

Although these arrangements tend to be bilateral or regional in scope and policy-driven in nature, they have the potential to lead to market-driven global production networks.

There is little doubt that market-driven regional, as well as global, integration will continue for Asia.

Notes

1. Leonard (2002) describes Hitler's role as one of unification "by the sword" in combination with the destruction of the self-confidence of Western European nations. He describes the roles of the United States and the Soviet Union as driven by self interest but benign in the case of the former and malign in the case of the latter.
2. The European Union called this process "pooling sovereignty" (European Communities 2003, p. 3).
3. Intra-European mobility remains very low (less than 0.2 percent of the European Union's total population) in spite of the Treaty of Rome's recognition of the principle of free movement for nationals of European Union countries and more recent measures taken to facilitate intra-European mobility. (World Bank, 2003c, p. 165).
4. For a detailed discussion of the contribution of Europe's regional institutions to integration see Gillingham (2003, Chapter 3, pp. 34-52).
5. While referred to as the "ASEAN Way," this particular type of human interaction is not unique to ASEAN but is generally characteristic of the interaction among persons and groups nearly everywhere in Asia in general.
6. These names include production sharing, production outsourcing, cross-border or international production fragmentation, distributed manufacturing, and dispersed manufacturing. The concept may include only production-related activities in the network or all stages of the value chain. (See Yusuf 2003, pp. 273-74 for a discussion of the differences in these terms).
7. The final stage of assembly is still generally located in other industrialized countries or in NIEs because it requires labour with a high level of technical and managerial skills, good domestic supply and service networks, and excellent infrastructure, among other things. However, China is emerging as a location for final assembly because of its large domestic market for the products concerned; the existence of this market reduces the risks associated with establishing facilities there.

(Athukorala 2003, p. 7).

8. SITC is the acronym for Standard International Trade Classification.

References

ASEAN. 2002. *Statistics of Foreign Direct Investment in ASEAN: Comprehensive Data Set.* 2002 edition. Jakarta: ASEAN Secretariat.

Asian Development Bank (ADB). 2004. *Asian Development Outlook 2004.* Oxford: Oxford University Press.

Athukorala, Prema-chandra. 2003. "Product Fragmentation and Trade Patterns in East Asia." Working Paper No. 2003/21. Division of Economics, Research School of Pacific and Asian Studies, Australian National University. Available online at http://rspas.anu.edu.au/economics/publish/papers/wp2003/wp-econ-2003-21.pdf.

Baldwin, Robert E. 2001. "The Implications of Increasing Fragmentation and Globalization for the World Trade Organization." In Leonard K. Cheng and Henryk Kierzkowski, eds., *Global Production and Trade in East Asia.* Boston: Kluwer Academic Publishers.

Barry, Frank and John Bradley. 1997. "FDI and Trade: The Irish Host-Country Experience." *Economic Journal.* 107(445):1798-811.

Borrus, Michael, Dieter Ernst, and Stephan Haggard, eds. 2000. *International Production Networks in Asia: Rivalry or Riches?* London and New York: Routledge.

Chia Siow Yue. 1997. *ASEAN: 30 Years of Existence and Challenges Ahead.* Seoul: Korea Institute for International Economic Policy.

Deardorff, Alan V. 2001a. "Financial Crisis, Trade, and Fragmentation." In Leonard K. Cheng and Henryk Kierzkowski, eds., *Global Production and Trade in East Asia.*Boston: Kluwer Academic Publishers.

Deardorff, Alan V. 2001b. "International Provision of Trade Services, Trade, and Fragmentation." *Review of International Economics* 9(2):233-48.

Ernst, Dieter. 2002. "Global Production Networks and the Changing Geography of Innovation Systems: Implications for Developing Countries." *Journal of the Economic sof Innovation and New Technologies* 11(6):497-523.

European Communities. 2000. "European Parliament Fact Sheets." Various issues. Luxembourg: Office for Official Publications of the European Communities. Available online at http://www.europarl.eu.int/factsheets/

European Communities. 2003. "How the European Union Works: A Citizen's Guide to the EU Institutions." Luxembourg: Office for Official Publications of the European Communities. Available online at http://europa.eu.int/comm/publications/booklets/eu_documentation/06/en.pdf.

European Communities. 2004. "Introducing the European Union." Luxembourg: Office for Official Publications of the European Communities. Available online at http://europa.eu.int/institutions/index_en.htm.

Feenstra, Robert C. 1998. "Integration of Trade and Disintegration of Production in the Global Economy." *Journal of Economic Perspectives* 12(4):31-50.

Gillingham, John. 2003. *European Integration, 1950-2003: Superstate or New Market Economy?* Cambridge, U.K.: Cambridge University Press.

Heaver, Trevor D. 2004. "Logistics in East Asia." In Shahid Yusuf, M. Anjum Altaf and Kaoru Nabeshima, eds., *Global Production Networking and Technological Change in East Asia.* New York: Oxford University Press.

Hummels, David, Jun Ishii, and Kei-Mu Yi. 2001. "The Nature and Growth of Vertical Specialization in World Trade." *Journal of International Economics* 54(1):75-96.

IMF (International Monetary Fund). 2002. *Direction of Trade Statistics Yearbook.* Washington, DC.

Japan, Ministry of Economy, Trade, and Industry (METI). 2002. "The Behaviour of Overseas Subsidiaries (Quarterly Survey of Japanese Business Activities): Results for January-March 2002." Tokyo, Japan. Available online at http://www.meti.go.jp/statistics/index.html.

Japan, Ministry of Economy, Trade, and Industry (METI). 2003. "Trends in Overseas Subsidiaries (Quarterly Survey of Overseas Subsidiaries): Results for April-June 2003." Tokyo, Japan. Available online at http://www.meti.go.jp/statistics/index.html.

JETRO (Japan External Trade Organization). 2003. *2003 JETRO White Paper on International Trade and Foreign Direct Investment (Summary).* Tokyo.

Jones, Ronald W. and Henryk Kierzkowski. 2001. "A Framework for Fragmentation." In Sven W. Arndt and Henryk Kierzkowski, eds., *Fragmentation: New ProductionPatterns in the World Economy.* New York: Oxford University Press.

Kartadjoemena, H. S. 2001. "ASEAN and the International Trading System: Regional Trade Arrangement vs. the WTO." In M. Than, ed., *ASEAN beyond the Regional Crisis:Challenges and Initiatives.* Singapore: ISAS.

Leonard, Dick. 2002. *Guide to the European Union.* London: The Economist Newspaper and Profile Books.

Navaretti, Giorgio B., Jan I. Haaland, and Anthony Venables. 2002. *Multinational Corporations and Global Production Networks: The Implications for Trade Policy.*

Brussels: European Commission, Directorate General for Trade, March. Market-driven regional integration in East Asia 73.

Ng, Francis and Alexander Yeats. 2003. "Major Trade Trends in East Asia: What Are Their Implications for Regional Cooperation and Growth?" World Bank Policy. Research Working Paper 3084. Washington, DC: World Bank.

Ozawa, Terutomo. 1999. "Pacific Economic Integration and the 'Flying Geese' Paradigm." In A. M. Rugman and G. Boyd, eds., *Deepening Integration in the Pacific Economies: Corporate Alliances, Contestable Markets and Free Trade.* Cheltenham, UK: Edward Elgar.

Ruane, Frances and Holger Görg. 2001. "Globalisation and Fragmentation: Evidence for the Electronics Industry in Ireland." In Sven W. Arndt and Henryk Kierzkowski, eds., *Fragmentation: New Production Patterns in the World Economy.* Oxford, U.K.: Oxford University Press.

Sakakibara, Eisuke and Sharon Yamakawa. 2003. "Regional Integration in East Asia: Challenges and Opportunities, Part I: History and Institutions." Policy Research Working Paper 3078. World Bank, Washington, D.C. Available online at http://econ.worldbank.org/files/27543_wp3078. pdf.

Sakakibara, Eisuke and Sharon Yamakawa. 2004. "Trade and Foreign Direct Investment: A Role for Regionalism." In Shahid Yusuf, M. Anjum Altaf and Kaoru Nabeshima, eds., *Global Change and East Asian Policy Initiatives.* New York: Oxford University Press.

Sturgeon, Timothy J. and Richard K. Lester. 2004. "The New Global

Supply Base: New Challenges for Local Suppliers in East Asia." In Shahid Yusuf, M. Anjum Altaf and Kaoru Nabeshima, eds., *Global Production Networking and Technological Change in East Asia*. New York: Oxford University Press.

Tan, Gerald. 2000. *ASEAN Economic Development and Cooperation*. Second edition. Singapore: Times Academic Press.

Tongzon, Jose L. 1998. *The Economies of Southeast Asia: The Growth and Development of ASEAN Economies*. Cheltenham, U.K.: Edward Elgar.

UNCTAD (United Nations Conference on Trade and Development). 1999. *Foreign Direct Investment and Development*. New York and Geneva: United Nations.

UNCTAD. 2002. *World Investment Report 2002: Transnational Corporations and Export Competitiveness*. New York and Geneva: United Nations.

UNCTAD. 2003. *World Investment Report 2003: FDI Policies for Development: National and International Perspectives*. New York and Geneva: United Nations.

Venables, Anthony J. 1999. "Fragmentation and Multinational Production." *European Economic Review* 43(3):935-45.

World Bank. 1994. "External Markets and China's Exports." In *China: Foreign Trade Reform (A World Bank Country Study)*. Washington, DC: World Bank.

World Bank. 2002. *World Development Indicators*. Washington, DC: World Bank.

World Bank. 2003a. *World Development Indicators*. Washington, DC: World Bank.

World Bank. 2003b. *Global Economic Prospects 2003: Investing to Unlock Global Opportunities*. Washington, DC: World Bank.

World Bank. 2003c. *Global Economic Prospects 2004: Realizing the Development Promise of the Doha Agenda*. Washington, DC: World Bank.

Yusuf, Shahid. 2003. *Innovative East Asia*. New York: Oxford University Press.

Yusuf, Shahid. 2004. "Competitiveness through Technological Advances under Global Production Networking." In Shahid Yusuf, M. Anjum Altaf, and Kaoru Nabeshima, eds. *Global Production Networking and Technological Change in East Asia*. New York: Oxford University Press.

Yusuf, Shahid, M. Anjum Altaf, and Kaoru Nabeshima, eds. 2004.

Global Production Networking and Technological Change in East Asia. New York: Oxford University Press.

5

Asian Economic Integration and Institution Building

5.1 Introduction

Since the 1990s, Preferential Trade Agreements of all kinds (from Free Trade to Custom Union, and Regional Community, from bilateral to regional) have been spreading all over the world. Almost every country is a member of at least one agreement. Many agreements -at least the most important ones- are organised on a continental basis such as Europe, America, Africa or, more recently, Asia. These regionalisation trends have revived the research on their economic rationale and on their compatibility with multilateral agreements.

The Asian movement toward regionalization known as ASEAN-10+3, +4 or +6 [1] is relatively new but it may become of major importance as it concerns Japan, China and India. These countries have contributed (Japan) or will contribute (China and India) to shape a completely new world. Their economic integration with ASEAN and their possible impact on the world economy using a CGE model are the subject of this article.

5.2 Open Regionalism versus AFTA

5.2.1 Open Regionalism: The traditional distinction introduced by Jacob Viner (1950) about the trade creation/trade diversion effect of preferential agreements is still valid. By definition preferential trade agreements (PTA) are discriminatory and therefore they may tend to reduce welfare. If a firm located within a PTA zone produces and exports a liberalised item, then it will benefit from the elimination (or reduction) of tariffs within the PTA, and the local consumer will benefit from reduced prices this will improve the producer's welfare as well as the consumer's welfare. On the contrary, if this producer is less efficient than outside producers and survives because of initial high tariffs it may nevertheless benefit from tariff elimination by the other PTA members if the difference in efficiency with external producers is lower than the remaining external tariff and/or if the resulting external tariff is higher than some of the previous ones. This will cause trade diversion and welfare losses for the consumer and global losses for producers.

With the new international trade theory several developments have questioned this issue.

Using a model of imperfect competition Krugman (1991) showed that, in a world with high trade costs, continental block formation could be welfare improving. Frankel and Wei (1993) estimated that 18 percent was the threshold value for transportation costs to allow for positive welfare gains in continental block formation. They found that the observed value for intercontinental transportation was around 15 percent, hence they concluded that regional discrimination was probably welfare reducing. But research made on specialisation show that in case of complementarily between the continental block members, a PTA could be welfare improving.

In order to reduce the discriminatory nature of preferential agreements, and also probably to differentiate it clearly from the European experience, the concept of Open regionalism was developed and supported by US and Australian (and the Eminent Persons Group Report to the 5th APEC Ministerial Meeting in 1993) economists in the APEC project to create an Asia Pacific Free trade Area by 2020. But no clear definition of Open regionalism was available at that time.

After the financial crisis of 1997-1998, there was renewed interest for regional build-up.

Wei and Frankel (1998) proposed a clear definition of open regionalism: a regional scheme, which does not reduce global welfare. The argument goes that regionalisation should not be regarded as an isolated regional affair but as a global trend on the three continental regions. Two proposals have been made to neutralise the negative impact of trade diversion:

The first one is the Macmillan proposal. It requires that there is no volume change in trade between the member and non-member countries after the formation of a block. This is achieved through a degree of external liberalisation by the members vis-à-vis the non-members. Given average parameters it would entail a reduction by 40 percent of former external tariffs in Asia, which might be politically unacceptable.

Wei and Frankel argue that this line of reasoning does not take into account the fact that the non member's countries are also engaged in other continental trade agreements. According to its promoters, AFTA remains inspired by the idea of open regionalism.

5.2.2 ASEAN Free Trade Area: Institutional integration in East Asia originated with the creation of the Association of South East Asian Nations (ASEAN) [2] in 1967. In 1992, ASEAN agreed to establish the ASEAN Free Trade Area (AFTA) through a Common Effective Preferential Tariff (CEPT) scheme, in order to attract foreign direct investment (FDI) from abroad. AFTA required that tariffs levied on a limited range of products (designed as "sensitive products") traded within the region be reduced to no more than 5 percent. Quantitative restrictions and other non-tariff barriers were also to be eliminated. Although originally scheduled to be achieved by 2008, the targets of AFTA were continuously brought forward. In fact, ASEAN suffers from two major problems: first, there is a lack of political will comparable to the Franco German engagement in Europe; second trade and investment within ASEAN-10 are second to their relations with the US, Japan or even EU-25.

In 1998, after the financial crisis, ASEAN leaders decided to accelerate the processes, involving that all tariffs on products in the inclusion list be reduced to a 0-5 percent range, and further to zero. They also decided to enlarge the inclusion list. New members agreed to the same objective with a delay. By the beginning of 2002, the ASEAN-6 had met AFTA's targets, and only 3.8 percent of products in the CEPT inclusion list, or 1,683 items out of 44,060, had tariff rates above five percent. The simple average tariff on goods traded under the AFTA scheme was about 2.7 percent in 2003, and 1.7 percent in 2004.

Vietnam is expected to achieve AFTA compliance in 2006, Laos and Myanmar in 2008, and Cambodia in 2010. ASEAN will eliminate all import duties by 2010 for the six original members and by 2015 for the new members.

5.2.3 From an ASEAN FTA to an ASEAN Community: Besides the liberalisation of trade in goods, ASEAN has endeavoured to take the next steps to create a Community. In October 2003, the ASEAN leaders agreed to achieve a dynamic, cohesive, resilient and integrated ASEAN Community by 2020, by creating the ASEAN Security Community, the ASEAN Economic Community, and the ASEAN Socio-cultural Community. The ASEAN Economic Community is to be a single market and production base. It aims to create a stable, prosperous and highly competitive ASEAN economic region by the year 2020, with free movement of goods and services, freer movements of capital, equitable economic development, and reduced poverty and socio-economic disparities. This ASEAN initiative was followed by projects concerning ASEAN-10 + 3, then +4 and lately +6. The additional four countries were Japan, Korea, China, and India, Australia and New Zealand. But the Kuala Lumpur summit in December 2005, due to strong political frictions within its participants, was not able to establish concrete steps in the direction of the creation of an Asian Community. Nevertheless the FTA fever continues to make progress.

5.2.4. Enlargement of the ASEAN FTA: ASEAN has extended its institutional integration instruments to other countries.

First, in November 2002, ASEAN and China signed the framework agreement on Comprehensive Economic Co-operation that plan to establish the ASEAN-China Free Trade Area (ACFTA) within ten years. In November 2004, ASEAN and China agreed to establish ACFTA by 2010 for the original six ASEAN member states and China, and by 2015 for the newer ASEAN member states.

Second, in October 2003, ASEAN and Japan signed the framework for Comprehensive Economic Partnership (CEP), and in November 2004, they agreed to start negotiations for an ASEAN-Japan CEP Agreement by April 2005.

Third, in November 2004, ASEAN and the Republic of Korea, as well as ASEAN and CER (Australia and New Zealand) agreed on a general framework to establish free trade areas.

Both negotiations started in early 2005 and are to be completed within two years. The ASEAN-Korea FTA will liberalise 80 percent of trade in products between the ASEAN-6 and the Republic of Korea, by 2009.

With India, the framework agreement was signed in October 2003, and negotiations started in January 2004. These different projects vary greatly depending on the partners' development level. A South-South agreement, such as ASEAN-China, can be negotiated within the 1979 GATT "enabling clause", which provides greater latitude to exclude products from the liberalisation scheme between developing countries forming FTAs. For example, ACFTA allows exemption of tariff reductions for a sensitive list of products, up to a ceiling of 400 tariff lines at the HS 6-digit level and 10 percent of the total import value, based on 2001 trade statistics for the ASEAN 6 and China; and 500 tariff lines at the HS 6-digit level for Cambodia, Laos, Myanmar and Vietnam.

By contrast, when one of the partners is a developed country, as in the case of a Japan-ASEAN FTA, the agreement must be notified under the GATT/WTO Article XXIV and must comply with the requirement of sectoral comprehensiveness (the agreement should substantially cover all bilateral trade). Therefore there are more obstacles to this second kind of arrangement and China may have advanced quicker than Japan in its negotiations with ASEAN.

The FTAs centred on ASEAN have different modalities and timeframes and will lead to free trade areas covering a large part of East Asia. (There are also arrangements between countries in Northeast Asia, such as between China and Japan, between China, Japan and the Republic of Korea, and so on.) These efforts by ASEAN members are expected at some point to establish a base for East Asian FTAs as well as economic and political communities, due to the political nature of these agreements. The leaders of ASEAN plus 3 are open to a possible enlargement of the East Asia trade region in which India, Australia and New Zealand could participate. This is probably an example of the "domino effect" (Baldwin 1993): exporters to regional blocks are strong pro membership forces, leading to enlargement of blocks. This in turn intensifies pro-membership lobbying. A good example of this tendency is given by Australia, which used to be rather opposed to Asian regionalisation (see Garnaut 2005).

Nevertheless there is also a risk that the spreading of bilateral agreements between Asian partners leads to some kind of "noodle bowl syndrome" as each agreement tends to be specific and include more or less stringent rules of origin. Even intra Asean FTA does not for the moment escape that limitation as lists of sensitive products are specific to each bilateral accord. The following simulations are made under the strong assumption that intra Asian agreements will converge towards a unique, truly plurilateral agreement, meaning that, for example trade between Indonesia and Thailand is in the end governed by the same rules as trade between Philippines and Malaysia, which has not been the case up to now.

To conclude this overview, it may be recalled that East Asia has durably maintained higher barriers to trade within

Asia than vis-à-vis other partners, as can be seen from the estimates made by ITC for the year 2002 (Table 5.1). In other words, East Asia, contrary to other regions like the EU or NAFTA, tends to discriminate against its members. This is well illustrated for the most sensitive sectors: agriculture, textile, clothing and food-beverage industries; by contrast, for industrial products there is no discrimination within East Asia and no preferential treatment.

Table 5.1: Applied Tariff in East Asia, the EU and NAFTA, by Sector, 2006 Ad valorem Tariff Equivalents (percent)

Importer	East Asia			EU-25			NAFTA		
Exporter	East Asia	NAFTA	EU-25	East Asia	EU-25	NAFTA	East Asia	EU-25	NAFTA
Agriculture	41.0	29.7	30.9	25.2	6.8	21.4	20.2	15.6	3.9
Light industry	26.8	8.3	12.8	4.9	0.0	2.2	8.7	9.6	0.1
Food and beverages	21.8	26.4	25.8	10.1	5.3	18.1	16.0	15.7	9.4
Textiles and clothing	7.3	7.6	7.8	6.2	0.0	4.9	10.9	9.7	0.1
Transportation machinery	4.6	2.8	8.6	3.4	0.0	6.8	3.3	2.9	0.0
Pottery products	2.9	3.6	4.4	1.4	0.1	2.9	5.7	5.6	0.5
Chemicals	2.4	3.0	2.7	0.8	0.0	4.9	4.1	4.2	0.2
Basic metals	1.8	2.6	2.3	1.5	0.5	4.0	3.0	2.7	0.3
Mining Products	1.7	2.6	1.7	0.4	0.0	0.3	1.4	1.8	0.1
General machinery	1.5	1.9	2.5	0.3	0.0	1.3	1.1	1.7	0.0
Electrical machinery	1.4	1.5	2.2	1.0	0.0	1.3	2.5	3.2	0.1
Others	1.4	1.7	2.6	0.6	0.1	0.8	3.2	1.3	0.0
Wood and paper	1.4	1.3	1.5	0.4	0.0	1.0	1.0	1.0	0.0
Precision apparatus	1.2	1.3	2.0	0.3	0.0	1.1	1.3	2.1	0.1
All products	7.4	5.5	7.2	7.6	1.9	7.7	5.7	5.3	0.7

Source: Market Access Map, calculations by ITC (2006).

A second conclusion might be that the APEC failure to bring significant results may first be due to its non continental content and second because of very divergent views of the real content of what was an open regional scheme: the US wanted clear and substantial commitments ("legal bindings") by country members, while ASEAN countries preferred to engage in limited and informal agenda corresponding to what is called the Musyawarch practice or "ASEAN way", based on consensus building. It turned out that these two views remained incompatible and the APEC project did not take off.

A third conclusion could be that East Asia needs strong partnership with the rest of the world but there is also a need for an Asian identity: financial crises, natural disasters, sanitary issues and even the rise of China have shown how necessary is enhanced cooperation within Asian countries.

5.3 Market Integration

In North America, trade among the three partners has grown quickly since the introduction of NAFTA more than a decade ago. Intra-regional trade, again, amounts to somewhat more than 40 percent of the total trade of the region. However, large asymmetries exist among the three member states (as in East Asia and the European Union). US trade with Canada and Mexico was roughly one-third of its total trade in 2003, whereas Mexico and Canada's trade within NAFTA was more than three-quarters of their total trade. Imports plus exports within the region represented 45.7 percent of Canadian GDP and 38.1 percent of Mexican GDP, but only 5.8 percent of US GDP.

The comparison across regions and over time suggests several observations. First, the overall association between institutionalization and the regional orientation of trade appears tenuous, as underscored by the fact that Asia ranks above North America despite lacking the regional equivalent of NAFTA. Second, while regional institutions can strongly facilitate regional trade and investment, which they appear to have done in Europe and North America, they are not strictly necessary for robust regional markets, as evidenced by East

Asia. Third, market integration is an ambiguous predictor of regional cooperation in related areas, such as monetary and financial matters. If the integration of goods markets were the leading factor, East Asia could be expected to seriously pursue exchange-rate stabilization and monetary cooperation, as did Europe in the 1970s. So, the relationship between market integration and institutionalization of regional cooperation is likely to hinge substantially on factors residing in the broader context.

5.4 Institutions: Concepts and Approaches

While the integration of markets is reasonably well defined—as the interpenetration of national markets, measured by flows of goods and capital and convergence of prices and interest rates—the concept of "institutions" is worth brief elaboration. After defining the term, we then review the explanations developed in the international political economy literature for the origins of institutions and the role that market integration plays in that process. Some analysts employ the term "institution" narrowly to refer exclusively to formal bureaucratic organizations with a legal charter. Other analysts refer to formal rules and procedures for collective governance, while still other writers include informal norms, expectations and patterns of behaviour under the definition of the term. Colloquial usage can be broader still and refer to things as varied as the currency, income tax, democracy and marriage as "institutions." This chapter examines the relationship between market integration, on the one hand, and institution-building and institutional design, on the other. We are interested in institutions that either eliminate or facilitate the elimination of barriers to trade and investment, including the harmonization of national regulations, regulatory frameworks and other legal, tax and policy changes that facilitate markets. We are also interested in the mechanisms through which common policies—such as the CAP, monetary union and "economic governance" in the EU context—are created and administered.

This paper thus requires a broader concept than that employed by economists' "new institutionalism" (Williamson 1985; North 1990).

The political economy of international regimes struck a broad and widely used definition of their focus of research that has sometimes been used synonymously with the term "institution". Regimes are "sets of implicit or explicit principles, norms, rules and decision making procedures around which actors' expectations converge in a given area of international relations" (Krasner 1983, 1). Goldstein, Kahler, Keohane, and Slaughter (2000, 387) define international institutions as "enduring sets of rules, norms, and decision-making procedures that shape the expectations, interests, and behaviour of actors".

The project on the Rational Design of International Institutions defines them somewhat more narrowly as "explicit arrangements, negotiated among international actors, that prescribe, proscribe, and /or authorize behaviour" (Koremenos, Lipson and Snidal 2001, 762). As such they have five key dimensions: membership rules, scope of issues covered, centralization of tasks, rules for controlling the institution, and flexibility of arrangements.

Another meaning, advanced by Milner (1998, 761), is "the means by which the diverse preferences of individuals are aggregated into choices or outcomes for the collective. Institutions here both shape and reflect the strategic interaction among agents". They are mechanisms to aggregate preferences (of individuals or states) and to exercise collective choice (See also Eichengreen 1998, 996).

This chapter thus employs the term "institution" to include both (a) explicit, formal commitments and organizations and (b) informal norms, rules, common understandings and expectations. The term encompasses formal bureaucracies, decision making procedures, informal consultative forums, patterns of cooperation, and informal agreements among states that facilitate, monitor and implement international agreements. With respect to East Asia, for example, the term "institution" can thus refer to ASEAN+3, the Chiang Mai Initiative, and Japan-Singapore Economic Partnership Agreement, SAARC, SAFTA as well as trilateral summit meetings, policy dialogue and the "ASEAN way" (principle of non-interference). The term does not include economic policies and regulations themselves (these are the focus of collective decision making within institutions); nor does it include private-sector networks, elite networks and transnational political and technocratic alliances.

Institutionalization is distinct from, but related to, "legalization". Legalization in its hard form refers to a particular variation of institutionalization. Hard legalization entails (a) binding rules of obligation, (b) precision in those rules, and (c) delegation to a third party of the interpretation, monitoring and implementation of those rules, dispute settlement, as well as perhaps the promulgation of further rules (Goldstein et al. 2000, 387; Abbott and Snidal 2000). The European Union is often cited as a case of relatively hard legalization (Alter 2000), NAFTA as a case of hardening legalization (F. Abbott 2000), while cooperation in the Asia-Pacific is described as non-legal (Kahler 2000).

Hard law holds a number of benefits over softer forms of institutionalization. As argued by F. Abbott (2000), it "(1) reduces intergovernmental transaction costs associated with trade and investment, (2) reduces private risk premiums associated with trade and investment, (3) promotes transparency and provides corollary participation benefits, (4) tends to restrain strategic political behaviours, and (5) may increase the range of integration effects by encouraging private actions to enforce intergovernmental obligations". But it also carries a number of disadvantages (discussed below).

The reciprocal relationship between market and institutional integration suggests, "institutions are simultaneously causes and effects; that is, institutions are both the object of state choice and consequential," as Simmons and

Martin (1998, 743) put it. "[S]tates choose and design institutions because of their intended effects. Once constructed, institutions will constrain and shape behaviour, even as they are constantly challenged and reformed by their member states".

5.4.1 Regional Economic Integration and Institutions: The implicit model of many analysts and policymakers through which economic integration leads to regional institution-building contains several channels. As trade and investment increase across borders, private actors demand elimination of costly barriers and provision of greater certainty in the security of contracts and investments. They petition governments to create regional agreements and institutions that underpin liberalization of tariffs and non-tariff barriers and harmonization of regulations. National politicians may accommodate those pressures as a matter of electoral necessity.

Governments can have their own motives for building regional institutions, such as managing the negative consequences of economic integration–policy externalities, regulatory arbitrage, races to the bottom, and dislocation of uncompetitive firms and their workers. States with autonomous policy preferences that are at odds with some private groups might also wish to move decision making to the regional level, where particularistic interests hold less influence over policy and legislation. The importance of economic integration for institutional integration is best appreciated by neo-functionalism, a school of integration politics championed by Ernst Haas in the early years of the European Community. Haas (1964) posited three specific mechanisms by which modest levels of integration produced an upward ratcheting of regional cooperation: functional spill over, political spill over, and cross-issue bargains mediated by autonomous institutions. Functional spill over captures the notion that cooperation in some areas (such as coal and steel) leads to cooperation in others (such as the Common Market) owing to interdependence among the sectors of advanced economies. Functional spill over is complemented by political spill over, through which societal groups interests' coalesce supra-nationally around expanding cooperation and institutions created to implement cooperative agreements become active (See, Kahler 1995, Moravcsik 1998 and Mattli 1999).

The dense network of regional institutions–the formal governing institutions of the EC as well as the more technical and less formal ones–facilitated bargaining and side payments to overcome deadlock on key issues. Some of the institutions of the European Union, the European Commission and European Parliament in particular, act in their own right to advance integration (For discussion of "supranationalism," see, for example, Sandholtz and Zysman 1989, Anderson 1995 and Moravcsik 1991). Martin (1993), for example, argues that these institutions were critical for smoothing the way to the Maastricht treaty agreement. Structural and cohesion funds served as side-payments to countries that were reticent to commit to the monetary union. Cohen (1993) argues that the presence of robust institutions distinguishes successful from unsuccessful monetary unions in the past.

A neo-functionalist thread can be woven through the history of European integration. The formation of the European Coal and Steel Community led to the Common Market and Common Agricultural Policy, which in turn led to the search for currency stability in the form of the "snake" and then the European Monetary System (McNamara 1993).

The Common Market and the expansion of the membership of the European Community led to the formation of the Single Market, an important feature of which was the elimination of capital controls and liberalization of trade in financial services. The free movement of capital within (and beyond) the European Union then forced member states to choose between accepting more flexible exchange rates, which would undermine the single market, or to press onward toward monetary union. (Padoa-Schioppa 1990 and 2004, Delors

Report 1989, European Commission 1990).

In theory and as interpretation of European integration history, neo-functionalism conceives of the relationship between economic and institutional integration as a virtuous circle. The simple forms of this approach bordered on the idealistic and naïve, however, as demonstrated by backsliding and long lapses in European integration. The approach also suffered from significant gaps in theory. Those gaps included insufficient attention to the role of national governments, precisely how institutions facilitate international cooperation, political backlash against regionalism on the part of private actors and coalitions, and, more generally, to the conditions that could generate the virtuous circle as opposed to backsliding. Simple neo functionalism would also have difficulty accounting for what might be called the "diseconomies" of dense institutionalization–inter-institutional conflict, policy incoherence, and gridlock in institutional reform—as well as for discontent over the "democratic deficit" and accountability in the European Union. These gaps have been addressed, though not necessarily filled, by subsequent approaches developed by political scientists.

5.4.2 Subsequent Approaches: Neo-liberal institutionalists argue that states create international institutions in order to overcome dilemmas of collective action. In the classic formulation, Keohane argued that under conditions of high transaction costs and uncertainty, institutions could help states overcome market failure in reaching international agreements, such as that modelled by the prisoners' dilemma game. "Chiefly by providing information to actors (not by enforcing rules in a centralized manner), institutions could enable states to achieve their own objectives more efficiently. Institutions would alter state strategies by changing the costs of alternatives; institutionalization could thus promote cooperation." Institutions affected outcomes by (a) providing information, (b) monitoring compliance, (c) increasing iterations, (d) facilitating issue linkages, (e) defining cheating, and (f) offering salient solutions (Katzenstein, Keohane and Krasner 1998, 662; Keohane 1984). When the coordination problem among states has multiple equilibria, institutions can provide mechanisms for solving distributional conflict (such as side payments in the form of EU cohesion funds for accession to the Maastricht treaty), signalling salient solutions and reducing bargaining costs. Once a particular equilibrium solution is chosen, institutions tend to lock it in (Katzenstein, Keohane and Krasner 1998). The logic applies equally to the regional and multilateral levels.

A key argument advanced by this approach is that international institutions should not be understood as coercive enforcers of hard rules against the will of member states. Instead, international and regional institutions are the instruments of states in their pursuit of mutually advantageous cooperation and integration. To conceive of institutions as hard constraints on national governments rather than their tools is to begin the analysis on the wrong foot.

Institutionalists juxtaposed their explanation to that of realism, dominated by the notion that powerful states create international institutions to serve their international interests. Hegemons create strong international institutions to support and defend a liberal international economic order from which they benefit, in the realist interpretation. The distribution of power in the international system is thus critical to creating and sustaining both international institutions and market liberalism. Again, the logic can be applied to both the global system and regions.

Domestic politics determine the preferences of states, whether operating within a realist or institutionalist framework, and complement both institutionalism and realism. National politicians respond to the demands of societal groups and their balance of influence in distributional conflicts when deciding to establish or change international institutions. Separately, international institutions may evolve depending on *knowledge and information.* As technical understanding becomes more broadly shared among expert communities, decision makers can converge on a specific set of institutional solutions to international problems (For reviews of explanations, see, for example, Kahler 1995, 6-11; Katzenstein, Keohane and Krasner 1998; among others).

Constructivism challenges the preceding causal arguments as far too rationalistic and adopts a sociological approach. For Katzenstein (1997), the key to understanding European integration lies not in the material interests of traded and non-traded goods sectors or their investors, but in the "Europeanization" of state identities, especially that of Germany, and shared norms. Norms about the conduct of regional relations shape regional institutions. In analyzing the Asian case, Katzenstein (1998) and Katzenstein and Shirashi (1998) argue that common norms arise from "the distinctive character of Asian state institutions," where the state is embedded in society and constituted by elaborate networks, to which reciprocity is critical to political consensus and legitimacy.

With such state systems, state sovereignty cannot be pooled in international organizations constituted by public international law–which presupposes European historical experience and concepts of sovereignty – and gives rise to the distinctively informal character of Asian institutions. Networks of public and private officials, corporations and organizations are thus critical to the formation of regionalism, though different network models (Japanese and Chinese) compete for dominance.

5.4.3 Comparison of Regions: The European Union clearly has the most highly elaborated set of regional institutions, based on treaties, with supranational organizations (the Commission, Parliament and Court of Justice), an intergovernmental body (Council), a capacity to establish secondary legislation, a body of law and regulations, as well as a broad set of common policies and instruments. Despite the pauses and lapses in the integration process, Europe is a paradigmatic case of the reciprocal interaction of economic and institutional integration.

NAFTA has a well-defined set of rules regarding trade and investment that, while incorporating agreement on labour and the environment, is considerably narrower in scope. A free trade agreement rather than a customs union, its penetration of national regulatory matters is relatively weak. Weakness of the few organizations created by NAFTA leaves the region without robust supranational or intergovernmental bodies or a regional capacity for secondary legislation. Some of the functional spill over from trade and financial integration has been handled on a bilateral or multilateral basis, such as the 1994-95 peso crisis. Despite proposals to develop NAFTA along the lines of the EU model (Pastor 2001), with regular summit meetings and institutions and a capacity for fiscal transfers similar to the EU structural funds, there is so far little political impetus in the United States for doing so. Rising economic integration of the region has not yet produced self-reinforcing iterations of liberalization and institution building, but could eventually do so.

East Asia now appears to be coalescing around the ASEAN+3 group, although other configurations remain relevant to regional cooperation. The Chiang Mai Initiative represents the most advanced cooperative agreement as a region thus defined. A number of sub-regional trade agreements have been struck, the most important of which could be the China-ASEAN agreement, or are under negotiation. A region-wide trade agreement, distinct from APEC, is discussed but does not appear imminent. Formal institutions within East Asia and the Asia Pacific are numerous but their degree of legalization, as defined above, has always been quite low. Policy dialogue among members of the region has recently intensified and is now quite robust, the ASEAN+3 meetings are institutionalized and broad in scope, and further initiatives are being considered. The considerable degree of economic integration could thus lead to further institution building, but this is not by any means clear.

5.4.4 Generalized Ability of the EU Model: The EU model is a demanding one in terms of institutional depth and political commitment and thus probably out of reach of other regions aspiring to integration. The EU experience nonetheless offers important lessons that can be applied in other regions.

Doing so, however, requires a clear understanding of (a) the nature of the EU model and (b) the lessons to be derived.

Kahler (1995, 85) urges careful interpretation of the role of European institutions. The importance of the supranational bodies of the EU stems not from their formal roles but from other, more subtle processes that revolve around them:

The nomenclature of the EU institutions (Parliament, Court) may obscure as much as it clarifies... The three institutional dimensions that set the EU apart from other regional groups lie instead in the degree of institutional delegation..., the scope of European bargains, and perhaps most important, the domestic political linkages constructed between European and national institutions. If there is a 'European model' for the future of other regional arrangements, it lies in these characteristics.

First, EU member states delegated more important and extensive functions to the EU institutions than have regions elsewhere. Second, bargains across functionally linked issues cumulated into an increasingly dense network of interdependent agreements.

Crucially, argues Kahler, Community enforcement of rules and law has been less important than "national reputational considerations that serve as a central binding device". Reneging in one issue area would have negative consequences for the government concerned in others.

The Stability and Growth Pact offers an object lesson in the role of hard rules in the European Union. These rules were designed to constrain governments' fiscal deficits and were given teeth in the form of painful sanctions. When they conflicted with the preferences of the large member states, however, the rules were effectively suspended and a broad discussion was launched on how to reform them. It is notable that reforms discussed as of this writing would place less emphasis on the hardness of the rule (and sanctions) and more emphasis on early sharing of information, analysis, consultation, debate and publicity—prior to, rather than subsequent to, governments' committing themselves to a fiscal path. Breaching the limits under the SGP has had substantial political consequences within the EU for relations between large and small states, providing the large with an incentive to conclude an agreement on SGP reform. The hard rule has been important not because it was enforced–to the contrary, it was violated–but because it altered the context in which member states bargained over economic policies and institutional reform.

Third, European institutions have developed deep connections to domestic political institutions and interest groups. "Those links, far more than the capabilities of European Institutions alone for monitoring and enforcement, provide a basis for ensuring that European bargains are implemented" (Kahler 1995, 86). Tacit collaboration between the Court of Justice, on the one hand, and lower national courts and private groups and firms, on the other, generated forward movement in cases such as Cassis de Dijon, which established the principle of mutual recognition underpinning the single market (See Burley and Mattli 1993, Alter and Meunier 1994, Slaughter and Mattli 1998). This general analysis is widely, though not universally shared, among analysts of European integration in political science.

The implications of this literature for proponents of regionalism elsewhere are not that they could bypass the creation of institutions, because they remain at the heart of each of the three processes, but that they must ultimately focus on delegation, institutions' roots in domestic politics, and the negotiation of pareto-improving cross-issue bargains.

Members of ASEAN+3 have been grappling with the issue of creating a secretariat but have reached no agreement, for example. If the context were somewhat broader, with more issues and institutional questions in play, a bargain could conceivably be negotiated across trade and finance, say, that parcelled out institutional prerogatives (See, de Brouwer 2004 on the design of a possible Asian Monetary Fund).

5.4.5 Political Integration: The argument that aspirations for political union underpin the evolution of the European Union is widely asserted in public commentary and some parts of the literature on the European economic integration. EMU, for example, is frequently cited as the product of widely shared political ambition for something akin to a United States of Europe (See, for example, Eichengreen 1992). The absence of such ambitions in East Asia and North America are cited as reasons for pessimism with respect to economic and institutional integration in those regions. While commitment to political integration plays a role, however, it has been substantially over-rated by some analysts.

Over the course of post-war history, first of all, economic projects for European integration have consistently received greater support than projects for political and security cooperation. Proposals for European Defence Community and European Political Community failed in the 1950s, for example, while the European Economic Community succeeded (See, for example, Dinan 2004). The Constitution for Europe would go some distance toward political integration, to choose a contemporary example, but its ratification will be decidedly difficult.

Second, while it is true that war in Western Europe has become "unthinkable", it has been "unthinkable" for quite some time, at least the 1960s and 1970s if not before. European integration has continued far beyond the point where interstate violence was a conceivable threat. Finally, ambitions for political union do not easily explain the successive enlargements of the membership. Britain, Ireland and

Denmark did not join the European Community because they wanted to participate in an ever closer political union. Many in successive enlargements are reticent, including the ten new members from Central and Eastern Europe. Indeed, the greater number and diversity of member states spawned by enlargements have created substantial barriers to political deepening.

For these reasons among others, many political scientists conclude that the political unity motive is a contributing but distinctly secondary motivation for European integration (See for example Moravcsik 1998). Analysis of political motivation should carefully distinguish between (a) ambitions for political union, (b) desire to avoid security conflict and war, and (c) political agreement on economic measures and the institutions necessary to implement them. Regional integration obviously cannot take place in the face of sharp security conflict, threats or interstate violence. Ambitions for political integration and a peace community can certainly reinforce regional integration, on the other hand, but they are not necessary.

Political agreements on the economic measures, common policies and regulations are indeed necessary, as is agreement on the institutions that would implement and monitor them. But the latter is a substantially lesser hurdle that the former. While the former is out of reach in East Asia, and probably in North America as well, the latter is achievable in both.

5.4.6 Diseconomies of Institutional Deepening: The European case illustrates not only the benefits but also the costs of institutional elaboration and complexity. Inter-institutional competition is rife within the European Union. The supranational institutions vie for prerogatives and influence among themselves as well as with national governments and institutions, such as national legislatures. While some of these inter-institutional conflicts can be ameliorated under the proposed Constitution for Europe, other inter-institutional conflicts will be created.

The proliferation of institutions thus weakens the

coherence of policy within the Union, a focus of the Sapir Group Report (Sapir et al 2003). Reform of these institutions, moreover, has become exceedingly difficult as member states are unwilling to surrender their prerogatives under one institutional framework for the sake of efficiency of decision making under another. Those institutional reforms that have been ratified (Amsterdam and Nice) have been modest, widely regarded as insufficient for a Union of twenty-five countries. The Constitution for Europe was negotiated to streamline the institutional structure and settle, hopefully once and for all, distributional conflict over voting schemes and limit institutional conflict. But the Constitution, which has fallen short of the hopes of many analysts (Devuyst 2004), might well not be ratified. This experience raises the question as to whether institutional deepening within the EU has reached a point of diminishing, or even negative, returns and suggests that other regions should institutionalize selectively.

5.4.7 Multilateral Context: The historical evolution of the three regions considered here illustrates the importance of the multilateral system in providing motives for regional cooperation and setting its agenda. In short, much of the impetus for regionalism springs from inadequacies of or discontent with multilateral institutions. If the multilateral regime fully satisfied the preferences of member countries for international cooperation, national governments would have little incentive to embark on regional projects. The Common Market was launched after the rejection of the International Trade Organization and after early rounds of GATT negotiations yielded only meagre results.

The multilateral trade regime would not soon provide much liberalization beyond border measures and would not provide for competition policy that could prevent gains from trade liberalization being captured by collusive agreements among firms. Because the international monetary regime was reasonably stable and expected to endure, by contrast, monetary integration was not prominent on the early agenda of

European integration. As the Bretton Woods regime broke down, however, Europeans experimented with the Snake and launched the EMS, the precursor to the monetary union (Henning 1998). Had the Bretton Woods regime survived, European monetary integration might have taken a very different course. Similarly, NAFTA was conceived and negotiated as a "GATT plus" agreement at a moment when the members of the GATT were having substantial difficulty concluding the Uruguay Round. Aspirations for regional cooperation in East Asia received powerful impetus from the 1997-98 financial crisis and resentment within the region of the International Monetary Fund and the United States for their handling of that episode (Henning 2002).

5.5 Conclusions and Implications

Our review of the interaction between economic and institutional integration in Europe, East Asia and North America generates a number of lessons and insights for regionalism. Desire for political integration is not a necessary precondition for regional institution building and integration. Political agreement on such institutions and the substance of cooperation is essential. But political support for economic cooperation is very different from aspirations for political integration or unification, and also very different from an elite consensus on using regional institutions to limit security conflict; it is also easier to achieve. This is good news for proponents of regionalism in South Asia and other parts of the world where there is little interest in pooling sovereignty in ways that Western European countries have done.

The state of the multilateral system and the role of key states have strong bearing on the substantive focus and timing of regional integration programs. When aspirations of a region are not satisfied by liberalization and cooperation provided at the multilateral level, they are more likely to explore or launch regional cooperative arrangements. When states are satisfied with multilateral regimes and content with the behaviour of systemically important countries, such as the United States, they are less likely to embark on regional programs or to strengthen existing regional institutions.

Regional arrangements should nonetheless be designed with due regard for the multilateral regime and its objectives. If constructed carefully, regionalism can complement rather than undermine aspects of the multilateral regime that function effectively. International financial cooperation, for example, would benefit from a set of principles that distinguish regional financial arrangements that are compatible with members' obligations in the IMF from those that are not (Henning 2002, 77-86). When appropriate, moreover, institutional arrangements should provide for external representation of the region as an entity in negotiations at the multilateral level.

Harder rules are not necessarily better rules. Rules are useful not because they are necessarily enforced–they are often violated–but rather because they alter the context in which bargaining takes place (The commonly made distinction between rules and discretion is a false dichotomy). Information, monitoring and bargaining among governments with stakes in cooperation across a number of issue areas, and therefore an interest in maintaining the confidence of their partners, is more important than enforcement of hard law to advancing integration. There is a danger that enforcement of hard legalization can produce domestic political backlash when rules conflict too strongly with domestic political imperatives (Goldstein and Martin 2000).

Regional economic integration and institution building Domestic political support is critical and substantially determines whether the relationship between economic and institutional integration becomes a virtuous circle. Regional institutions should nurture this support and find alliances in the domestic political arena. "Sink deep roots into domestic politics". Such roots are hard to construct or even identify ex ante: the tacit alliance between the ECJ and domestic courts was not anticipated at the outset of European integration and evolved only gradually. Regional institutions should not be designed, as they often are, in isolation from or without regard to domestic politics and the need to secure domestic constituencies.

The European case underscores the importance of making side-payments and concluding cross-issue bargains to assist governments in solving domestic political problems confronted in the process of integration. Political deadlock among member states was overcome on many occasions by exchanging concessions across policy areas and institutions. Such bargaining is facilitated by multi-sector economic integration and regional institutions (For an illustrative case within the G-7 context, see Putnam and Henning 1989).

Regional institution building can also reach a point of diminishing returns. Inter institutional competition, insufficient coherence of policy, and deadlock on institutional reform might suggest "diseconomies" of institutional scale within the European Union. For this reason, institution building in South Asia should be selective, designed with a view toward supplying the specific functions needed to negotiate, conclude and monitor agreements on trade, money, finance and regulations.

Notes

1. ASEAN+3: ASEAN+Japan, South Korea and China, ASEAN+6 includes three other countries India, Australia and New Zealand (invited to the Kuala Lumpur Summit in December 2005).
2. Established in 1967 by five founding members: Indonesia, Malaysia, the Philippines, Singapore, and Thailand were later joined by Brunei when it became independent from Great Britain. The initial objective at the time of the Vietnamese war was to foster regional stability and to promote political and economic cooperation.

References

Abbott, Kenneth W., Robert O. Keohane, Andrew Moravcsik, Anne-Marie Slaughter, and Duncan Snidal. 2000. The Concept of Legalization. *International Organization* 54, no. 3: 401-419.

Alter, Karen J. 2000. The European Union's Legal System and Domestic Policy: Spill over or Backlash? *International Organization* 54, no. 3: 489-518.

Anderson, Jeffrey J. 1995. The State of the (European) Union: From the Single Market to Maastricht, from Singular Events to General Theories. *World Politics* 47:441-65.

Baldwin, Richard E.1993, *A Domino Theory of regionalism,* NBER Working Paper Series No. 4465.

Burley, Anne-Marie, and Walter Mattli. 1993. "Europe before the Court: A Political Theory of Legal Integration." *International Organization* 47 (Winter): 41-76.

Calder, Kent, and Min Ye. 2003. Regionalism and Critical Junctures: Explaining the "Organization Gap" in Northeast Asia. Paper presented at the 2003 American Political Science Association Annual Convention, Philadelphia, PA (August).

Cohen, Benjamin J. 1993. Beyond EMU: the Problem of Sustainability. *Economics and Politics* 5 (July): 187-202.

De Brouwer, Gordon. 2004. Institutions to Promote Financial Stability: Reflections on East Asia and an Asian Monetary Fund. Australian Treasury Working Paper 2004-02 (September).

Delors Report [Committee for the Study of Economic and Monetary Union]. 1989.

Report on Economic and Monetary Union in the European Community. Luxembourg: Office of Official Publications of the European Community.

Dinan, Desmond. 2004. *Europe Recast: A History of European Union.* (Boulder/London: Lynne Rienner).

Devuyst, Youri. 2004. EU Decision-Making After the Treaty Establishing a Constitution for Europe. Policy Paper No. 9 (July). University Centre for International Studies, University of Pittsburgh.

Dinan, Desmond. 2004. Europe Recast: A History of European Union. London: Lynne Rienner Publishers.

Eichengreen, Barry. 1998. Dental Hygiene and Nuclear War: How International Relations Looks from Economics. *International Organization* 52, no. 4: 993-1012.

European Commission. 1990. One Market, One Money: An Evaluation of the Potential Benefits and Costs of Forming an Economic and Monetary Union. *European Economy* 44 (October).

European Commission. 2003. Quarterly Report on the Euro Area, No. III (30 September). Brussels: European Commission.

Feridhanusetyawan T. 2005, "Preferential Trade Agreements in the Asia-Pacific Region", IMF Working Paper, WP/05/149.

Goldstein, Judith, Miles Kahler, Robert O. Keohane, and Anne-Marie Slaughter. 2000.

Introduction: Legalization and World Politics. *International Organization* 54, no. 3: 385-399.

Goldstein, Judith, and Lisa L. Martin. 2000. Legalization, Trade Liberalization, and Domestic Politics: A Cautionary Note. *International Organization* 54, no. 3: 603-632.

Haas, Ernst. 1964. *Beyond the Nation State.* Stanford, CA: Stanford University Press.

Henning, C. Randall. 1998. Systemic Conflict and Regional Monetary Integration: The Case of Europe. *International Organization* 52: 537-573.

Henning, C. Randall. 2000. U.S.-EU Relations After the Inception of the Monetary Union: Cooperation or Rivalry? In C. Randall Henning and Pier Carlo Padoan, eds., *Transatlantic Perspectives on the Euro* (pp. 5-64). Washington, D.C.: The Brookings Institution and European Community Studies Association.

Henning, C. Randall. 2002. *East Asian Financial Cooperation.* Policy Analyses in International Economics No. 68. Washington, D.C.: Institute for International Economics.

Kahler, Miles. 1995. *International Institutions and the Political Economy of Integration.* Washington: Brookings Institution.

Kahler, Miles. 2000a. Legalization as Strategy: The Asia-Pacific Case. *International Organization* 54, no. 3: 549-571.

Kahler, Miles. 2000b. Conclusion: The Causes and Consequences of Legalization. *International Organization* 54, no. 3: 661-683.

Katzenstein, Peter J. 1997. *Tamed Power: Germany in Europe.* Ithaca, NY: Cornell University Press.

Katzenstein, Peter J., Natasha Hamilton-Hart, Kozo Kato, and Ming Yue. 2000. *Asian Regionalism.* Ithaca, NY: Cornell University Press.

Katzenstein, Peter J., Robert O. Keohane, and Stephen D. Krasner. 1998. *International Organization* and the Study of World Politics. *International Organization* 52, no. 4: 645-685.

Keohane, Robert O. 1984. *After Hegemony: Cooperation and Discord in the World Political Economy.* Trenton, NJ: Princeton

University Press.
Koremenos. Barbara, Charles Lipson, and Duncan Snidal. 2001. The Rational Design of International Institutions. *International Organization* 55, no. 4: 761-799.
Krasner, Stephen D. 1983. *International Regimes.* Ithaca, NY: Cornell University Press.
Krugman P. (1991), *The Move Towards Free Trade Zones,* in "Policy Implication of trade and Currency Zones", Symposium sponsored by the FRB of Kansas City.
Laurenceson, James. 2003. Economic Integration between China and the ASEAN-5. *ASEAN Economic Bulletin* 20, no. 2: 103-111.
Mansfield, Edward D., and Helen V. Milner, eds. 1997. *The Political Economy of Regionalism.* New York, NY: Columbia University Press.
Mansfield, Edward D., and Helen V. Milner. 1999. The New Wave of Regionalism. *International Organization* 53, no. 3: 589-627.
Martin, Lisa L. 1993. International and domestic Institutions in the EMU Process. *Economics and Politics* 5 (July):125-44.
Martin, Lisa L., and Beth Simmons. 1998. Theories and Empirical Studies of International Institutions. *International Organization* 52, no. 4: 729-757.
Mattli, Walter. 1999. *The Logic of Regional Integration: Europe and Beyond.* New York, NY: Cambridge University Press.
Mattli, Walter, and Anne-Marie Slaughter. 1998. Revisiting the European Court of Justice. *International Organization* 52 (Winter): 177-209.
Mayer, Frederick W. 1998. *Interpreting NAFTA: The Science and Art of Political Analysis.* New York, NY: Columbia University Press.
Milner, Helen V. 1998. Rationalizing Politics: The Emerging Synthesis of International, American, and Comparative Politics. *International Organization* 52, no. 4: 759-786.
McNamara, Kathleen R. 1993. Common Markets, Uncommon Currencies: System Effects and the European Community. In *Coping with Complexity in the International System,* edited by R. Jervis and J. Snyder. Boulder, CO: Westview Press.
Moravcsik, Andrew. 1991. Negotiating the Single European Act. In *The New European Community: Decision-making and Institutional Change,* edited by R. O.
Moravcsik, Andrew. 1998. *The Choice for Europe: Social Purpose*

and State Power from Messina to Maastricht. Ithaca, NY: Cornell University Press.

North, Douglass C. 1990. *Institutions, Institutional Change, and Economic Performance.* New York, NY: Cambridge University Press.

Padoa-Schioppa, Tommaso, ed. 1990. *Efficiency, Stability, and Equity: A Strategy for the Evolution of the Economic System of the EC.* Luxembourg: Office of Official Publications of the European Community.

Padoa-Schioppa, Tommaso. 2004a. *The Euro and Its Central Bank.* Cambridge, MA:MIT Press.

Padoa-Schioppa, Tommaso. 2004b. East Asian Monetary Arrangements: A European Perspective. Photocopy (July).

Pastor, Robert A. 2001. *Toward a North American Community: Lessons from the Old World for the New.* Washington, DC: Institute for International Economics.

Pedersen, Anders M. 2004. "Currency Unions and Foreign Trade," *National Bank of Denmark Monetary Review,* Second Quarter, at http://www.nationalbanken.dk/DNUK/Pulbications.nsf/side/Monetary_Review_2004_2_Quarter

Putnam, Robert D., and C. Randall Henning. 1989. The Bonn Summit of 1978: A Case Study in Coordination. In Richard N. Cooper, Robert D. Putnam, C. Randall Henning, and Gerald Holtham, eds., *Can Nations Agree? Issues in International Economic Cooperation* (pp. 12-140). Washington, D.C.: Brookings Institution.

Sandholtz, Wayne, and John Zysman. 1989. 1992: Recasting the European Bargain. World Politics 42 (October): 127.

Sapir, André, et al. 2003. An Agenda for a Growing Europe: Making the EU Economic System Deliver. Report of an independent study group established by the President of the European Commission. Brussels (July).

Viner Jacob. 1950, "The Customs Union Issue", New York, The Carnegie endowment for International Peace.

Wei, Shang-jin, Jeffrey A. Frankel 1998, *Open Regionalism in a World of Continental Trade Blocks*, IMF Staff papers Vol. 45, no. 3.

6

Role of India and China in Pan Economic Integration in Asia

6.1 Introduction

While rapid economic growth in East and South Asia and the emergence of China and India as major players in the global system are frequently cited and debated in the academic literature and popular press, much less attention is being placed on the rapid rise in intra-regional trade and investment, or "regionalization". Unlike the case of the European experience of economic integration, this process is being led by market forces without a strong role attributable to government-related cooperation policies. Moreover, recent studies show that the evolution of growth and development in the region is becoming increasingly self-sustained; Asia has not "de-coupled" completely from the OECD but it would appear that its self-sustainability has been rising. In addition, the region appears to be becoming more symmetric, from rising correlations of business cycles to increasingly-similar export structures and composition of the inflows of Foreign Direct Investment (FDI).

As the above process of integration intensifies, Asian economics have been negotiating various forms of formal economic integration arrangements, mainly as a way to support the market integration process. These arrangements are especially in the form of bilateral free-trade areas (FTAs) but also higher forms of cooperation, including monetary and financial cooperation. The ASEAN Economic Community, for example, aims to create a "single market and production base" by 2015. Asian economic integration raises myriad economic- and political-economy-related issues that are critical to the future of the region and Asia's most important trading partners in North America and Europe.

6.1.1 Regional Economic Integration in Asia: The rise of Asia is no longer an idea—it has become a sustaining reality. The Asian Development Outlook 2006, the flagship publication of the ADB, notes that developing Asia (excluding Japan) had expanded its export almost ten-fold from 1984 to 2004, while world exports grew just fivefold over the same period. Developing Asia's share of world exports doubled over the past two decades, reaching 21.3 percent by 2004. Asia not only expanded its share globally, but it also increased intraregional trade. As Table 6.1 shows, in 2004, intra-regional trade in developing Asia accounted for 44 percent of the region's total trade, jumped from just 21.6 percent in 1980. Needless to say, this magnitude of intra-regional trade has given rise to lofty aspirations for pushing further economic integration in Asia, ideally (or idealistically) toward an Asian free trade area or something more (such as an Asian Monetary Union).

Table 6.1: Intra-regional Trade Share (percent) of Selected Regions

Region	1980	1985	1990	1995	2000	2001	2002	2003
East Asian, including Japan	34.7	40.2	45.6	55.5	54.0	55.4	57.3	54.0
Developing East Asia	21.6	29.1	36.4	43.7	43.4	45.6	47.5	44.1
NIEs	7.7	10.7	14.3	18.1	16.4	17.5	17.1	16.1
ASEAN	18.0	20.3	18.9	24.1	25.7	24.1	24.4	24.0
NAFTA	33.8	38.7	37.9	43.2	48.7	49.0	48.3	46.0
European Union 15	52.4	52.5	58.6	56.8	62.2	62.1	62.4	64.4

ASEAN = Association of Southeast Asian Nations, NAFTA = North American Free Trade Agreement.

Notes: East Asia comprises Japan, ASEAN, PRC, newly industrialized economies (NIEs) of Hong Kong, China; Korea; Singapore; and Taipei, China. Developing East Asia excludes Japan.

Source: ADB 2006.

Although there is already a rather large amount of intraregional trade in Asia, a recent ADB study shows there is still room for Asia countries to gain from further regional economic integration in Asia. [1] Using the new Global Trade Analysis Project (Version 6) database with a dynamic global model, the study concludes, among others.

- Trade within the Asian region is far from reaching its potential, and policies that facilitate integration and more efficient regional trade accelerate growth and expand its basis, especially for lower-income Asia.
- Tariff barriers are only part of the challenge to further economic integration and trade expansion in the region.... A deeper and more inclusive Asian Free Trade Area can achieve for its members larger benefits than that would arise from global trade liberalization along WTO lines.
- The economies of the [ASEAN] have the most to gain (in domestic terms) from Asian economic integration, provided that this happens in a relatively uniform way.

In his speech the ADB President envisages a vision of Asia "free of poverty–diverse yet united, well integrated within itself and with the global economy, and contributing profoundly to the ongoing progress of humankind." He further remarks that, "Some sceptics may call this vision of deeply integrated Asia a pipe dream. Some say the disparities are too wide, the political divides too deep. But strong bridges for a united Asia, open to the world, are already being built".

Apparently, this study suggests that a RTA aiming at a deeply integrated Asia would bring substantial benefits to Asian countries regardless of whether the multilateral trading system ever delivers results. The fast growth of Asian trade and accelerated regional integration was, in substantial measure, due to the locomotive economic performance of East Asia. If Japan is included, intra-regional trade makes up for 54 percent of total trade in East Asia. The President of the ADB has remarked that this is higher than the 46 percent intraregional trade in the NAFTA region and is very much comparable to intraregional trade in the European Union before the 1992 Maastricht treaty There is a trade-foreign direct investment (FDI) nexus in Asia which, understood as the mutual reinforcement between trade and FDI, is a strong boost to regional economic integration in this area. FDI to the Asian developing countries from the more developed economies (Japan; Korea; Taiwan, China; Hong Kong, China) has helped shape totally new Asian production networks, in which cross-border production sharing is featured, with a high and increasing amount of intraregional trade in parts and components that are produced and assembled into final goods within Asia.

Apart from trade investment, Asian economic integration has also been seen in monetary and financial cooperation, and sub-regional cooperation in infrastructure. As noted by Kawai, in East Asia, "market-driven financial integration has also been underway as a result of the increased deregulation of the financial system, opening of financial services to foreign institutions, and liberalization of the capital account." [2] Regional financial cooperation, through the Chiang Mai Initiative (CMI), the ASEAN+3 economic surveillance process, and the Asian Bond Markets Initiative, has been taking root firmly in Asia. Although these efforts are being mainly undertaken in East Asia, South Asian countries have also started regional policy dialogue on financial cooperation. Sub-regional cooperation on infrastructure is a key part of the economic integration process in Asia.

Roland-Holst, Verbiest and Zhai observe that "if trade within the Asian region can be made more efficient, even by small by continuing improvements in reducing distribution costs, the gains would be much greater than those resulting from tariff or other trade policy reform". In this regard, connecting Asian countries through roads, ports, bridges, power and telecommunication networks is fundamentally important for another wave of income and growth and employment creation in Asia. One of the remarkable achievements in this regard is the Greater Mekong Sub-region Programme (GMS). Involving Cambodia, China, Laos, Myanmar, Thailand and Vietnam, the GMS has achieved international recognition with regard to the development of infrastructure to enable the development and sharing of the resource base, and promote the freer flow of goods and people in the sub-region.

6.1.2 Economic Role of China and India in Asian Economic Integration: China's rapid and massive rise as an economic power has an enormous impact on the global and regional economy. In terms of regional integration, China is playing the leading role in two aspects. First, China's import capacity has created the new basis for Asian regional growth: internal demand. With many Asian economies' exports to China rising by double-digit percentages over the recent years, that country has consolidated its position as the leading market for Asian traders. In 2003, China replaced Japan as the third largest importer in the world for merchandise trade and the biggest Asian market for both Asian and EU exporters. The result is that Asian countries are becoming less dependent on the North American and European markets, and more on the Chinese market, although the increasing Chinese demand for raw materials has been regarded as an important factor in reversing the long- term downward trend in the prices of non-oil commodities. [3]

A second profound impact of China's rise on Asian economic integration is that China plays a major role in shaping the new division of labour in Asia, largely as a result of the trade-FDI nexus mentioned previously. Deeper production-sharing practices within the [East Asia] region have contributed substantially to the rise of intraregional trade flows. In particular, China's emergence as a major production site for labour-intensive stages of production and assembly has exerted a huge impact on such flows, both within Asia and between Asian and the rest of the world. Goods that were previously processed and exported by other Asian countries are now finalised in China for export. This phenomenon explains, in large part, the increasing bilateral trade imbalances between China and its major trading partners; China has recorded growing trade surpluses with North America and Europe, while widening its trade deficit with the rest of Asia. Compared with China, India as a trader is much less significant. China's economy is 2.7 times larger than that of India's, and the annual FDI received by China is more than 10 times as large. China's share in world merchandise trade is roughly 6 times of India's. Needless to say, India, unlike China, is not yet a market important enough for Asian traders. However, there are two developments in India's foreign trade which deserve special attention.

First, India's merchandise trade has experienced a strong growth in recent years. Its merchandise exports grew 33 percent and 19 percent in 2004 and 2005 respectively, and import levels rose at even higher rates of 37 percent and 35 percent respectively (WTO 2005). India's merchandise trade with East Asian economies more than doubled from US$ 13 billion in 1997-98 to about US$ 27 billion in 2003-04. In fact, India expanded its trade with all East Asian countries except Japan over the same period. A UN report reveals that, although India is still far from having manufacturing-driven growth that has characterised the other rapidly growing Asia economies, the "structure of India's merchandise trade is likely to follow a sequence of changes similar to that of China, but with a lag of one or two decades," provided "the role of industrialization in India's further economic ascent is similar to that in the other fast growing Asian economies." [4]

Secondly, the recent growth of India's trade in services is almost unparalleled. The growth rate for the exports and imports of services were 66 percent and 53 percent in 2004, and 76 percent and 73 percent in 2005. In about five years since 2001, India moved from the 19th to the 10th position in the ranking of the largest traders of commercial services in the world. If such rapid growth rates are sustained, India is likely to overtake several countries, including China, in trade in services in a few years. No other major trading nation has enjoyed such remarkable growth in trade in services in the past few decades.

It has been observed that, given "the large size of the Chinese and Indian economies, and their specific patterns of demand, changes in the two countries' level and structure and demand will tend to have a much larger impact on the composition of world trade than those of Japan and the Republic of Korea during the economic ascent". China and India, with sustained rapid growth and rising living standards, will certainly play dominant roles in the process of economic integration in Asia.

6.2 RTAs Participated by China and India

RTAs are proliferating in Asia and worldwide. At the global level, almost every WTO Member is now a party to one or more RTAs. While Asia has jumped on the bandwagon of regionalism only recently, the current pace of development of RTA initiatives in this region is nothing but daunting. The ADB" observes in its most recent report on Asian economic development that, by 2005, a total of 36 RTAs involving Asian members have been formally notified to the WTO, with a much bigger number of agreements are under negotiation. The ADB has disclosed that in East Asia alone there are currently 16 FTAs under implementation, close to 22 under negotiation, and more than a dozen others proposed. Practically every East Asian economy has at least one bilateral agreement with its Asian neighbours in place and many have several overlapping accords. Although China and India jumped onto the bandwagon only recently, they can now be placed among the most active pursuers of RTAs. The regional initiatives of China and India will be examined in the following subsections.

6.2.1 China's Regional Trade Initiatives:

A. CEPAs with Hong Kong and Macau: Although China began embracing regionalism relatively recently, it appears to firmly believe that "a regional economic integration process consistent with WTO rules would not only promote regional but also worldwide liberalisation by achieving further tariff reduction and broader market access for services and investment". [5] China has been involved in over 15 RTAs. The Mainland and Hong Kong Closer Economic Partnership Arrangement (China-HK CEPA), signed in June 2003, marked the start of China's regional initiative, which was followed immediately by the signing of the Mainland and Macau Closer Economic Partnership Arrangement (China-Macau CEPA) three and half months later. The Closer Economic Partnership Arrangements (CEPAs) contains substantial unilateral concessions from China to the two formal Western colonies in merchandise and commercial services trade, and investment. Under the China-HK CEPA, China agreed to slash tariffs on imported goods of Hong Kong origin in stages, with full elimination of all tariffs no later than January 1, 2006. The CEPA rule of origin, which is relatively liberal, features a 30 percent value-added of Hong Kong's local content. In the area of trade in services, the mainland offers preferential treatment to Hong Kong and Macau service suppliers in 27 service areas, effectively granting business in these two economies the first-mover advantage.

B. China-ASEAN Free Trade Agreement: Considering that Hong Kong and Macau are two special administrative regions under Chinese sovereignty, ostensibly the two CEPAs are less regarded as RTAs. Among China's regional trade agreements, one of the most influential is the proposed China-ASEAN Free Trade Agreement (ACFTA). Coming almost as a surprise to his counterparts in the ASEAN countries, Chinese Premier Zhu Rongji proposed at the China-ASEAN Submit of November 2000 to form a "free trade agreement" between China and ASEAN. In November 2002, Chinese and ASEAN leaders signed the Framework Agreement on Comprehensive Economic Co-operation (hereinafter the Framework Agreement), which lays the groundwork for the eventual formation of a F.T.A. by 2010 for China and the six older members of ASEAN ("ASEAN 6", including Brunei Darussalam, Indonesia, Malaysia, the Philippines, Singapore and Thailand), and by 2015 for the newer ASEAN Members States (the "CLMV" countries including Cambodia, the Laos, Myanmar and Vietnam).

The Framework Agreement was amended by a Protocol on 6 October 2003 by the contracting parties at their annual submit in Bali (hereinafter the "Protocol"). On November 29, 2004, at the ASEAN+China summit in Vientiane, two agreements to implement the Framework Agreement were signed by ASEAN and Chinese leaders, the Agreement on Trade in Goods of the Framework Agreement on Comprehensive Economic Co-operation (the "Trade in Goods Agreement" or "TIG Agreement"), and the Agreement on Dispute Settlement Mechanism of the Framework Agreement on Comprehensive Economic Co-operation (the "Dispute Settlement Mechanism Agreement" or "DSM Agreement"). [6]

The Framework Agreement establishes only the preliminary measures for trade liberalisation between China and ASEAN countries as well as the agenda for further negotiations. The Framework Agreement commits the eleven countries have committed in the Framework Agreement to strengthen cooperation and to progressively liberalize and promote trade in goods and services and services as well as create a transparent, liberal and facilitative investment regime. This suggests that the proposed ACFTA will cover trade in goods and services, as well as, trade and investment facilitation.

The ACFTA Framework Agreement is known for its rather innovative Early Harvest Programme (EHP), under which the parties agreed to cut tariffs on certain products before the onset of the formal FTA. Briefly, eight categories of agricultural products and dozens of specific manufactured goods would be liberalised ahead of the planned establishment of free trade area. A key element of the EHP is that China has also given unilateral concessions to ASEAN members who feel they would not benefit as much from the EHP. This is because, for ASEAN's exports to China, all the products in Chapters 1-8 of the Harmonised System (HS) are covered for preferential tariff rates, while for exports to ASEAN countries, not all of the products in Chapters 1-8 are covered. ASEAN countries are allowed to come up with exclusion lists indicating the items for which they would not grant tariff concessions to Chinese goods. In essence, the EHP allows ASEAN products to be exported to China at significant concessionary rates so that ASEAN countries can actually benefit from the benefits of a free trade agreement even before the agreement itself is finalized.

The TIG Agreement represents the important second phase of the formation of the ACFTA.

From July 2005, China and the "ASEAN 6" have begun to reduce tariffs on commodities trade. On 20 July 2005, tariffs on more than 7,000 items, accounting for over 90 percent of all goods traded between China and ASEAN 6, were slashed to five percent or less.

The DSM Agreement represents another landmark achievement in China-ASEAN bilateral trade relations. It provides, first of all, a formal institutional design for solving trade and investment disputes between China and an ASEAN Member State. The significance of this agreement lies in its establishment of a rule-based setting for the resolution of economic disputes between the nations concerned, without which the governments are likely to resort to unilateral and retaliatory measures if they feel—sometimes rightly—that the multilateral trading system like the WTO does not provide for efficient and fair dispute settlement methods.

C. Other Signed RTAs: The Asia-Pacific Trade Agreement (APTA), known as the Bangkok Agreement between 1975 and 2005, is the first preferential trading arrangement among developing countries in the Asia-Pacific region, developed under the auspices of the United Nations

Economic and Social Commission for Asia and the Pacific (ESCAP). China joined the agreement in 2001, and started offering concessions from 2002. Presently, 749 tariff lines carry lower rates than the MFN rates committed under the WTO, mostly those involving textile products.

The significance of the APTA does not lie in the almost insignificant tariff concessions, given that the overall average applied tariff rate is 9.5 percent under the APTA compared with an MFN rate of 9.7 percent. The APTA is important symbolically for two reasons: (1) it provides a mechanism for giving special and differential treatment to the least developed countries; (2) it serves as a platform to link sub-regional RTAs In an area where the countries are at very varied stages of development, regional economic integration must involve compensation to the lesser developed members through special and preferential treatment. In this regard, the APTA mechanism provides a useful example. Further, APTA is the only agreement that currently link South Asia and East Asia, the two most dynamic sub-regions both of which are core parts of Asia. As such, it may serve an important role in consolidating the various sub-regional agreements in Asia. China signed an FTA with Chile on 18 November 2005, which has the effect of immediately eliminating 74 percent of Chile's tariffs, and 63 percent of China's tariffs within two years. By 2015, 97 percent of both countries' tariffs are to be eliminated. With Pakistan, China concluded an FTA Early Harvest Agreement on 5 April 2006, under which bilateral tariffs on certain products are to be gradually slashed and eventually eliminated between 1 January 2006 and 1 January 2008.

D. FTA Negotiations with New Zealand and Australia, and Potential Agreements with Other Nations: In China's pursuit of regionalism, the negotiations with New Zealand and Australia deserve special attention. For one reason, New Zealand and Australia are two developed OECD economies. More significantly, the contents of the negotiations are rather comprehensive, heralding the conclusion of final agreements which will bring about broader and deeper economic integration.

China and Australia signed the initial Trade and Economic Framework Agreement in October 2003. It sets out areas of strategic cooperation in areas including energy and mining, textile, agriculture, industrial products, IT, services, investment, intellectual property rights, and others. A joint feasibility study for a China-Australia FTA by the two governments was completed in March 2005, concluding that the FTA will bring tremendous benefits to both countries. Formal negotiations targeting for such an agreement were commenced on 18 April 2005. Negotiations for an FTA between China and New Zealand started even earlier, in December 2004, following the conclusion of the China-New Zealand Trade and Economic

Cooperation Framework on May 28, 2004, covering a broad range of economic areas, and a joint feasibility study completed in November 2004. It is highly likely that the China-New Zealand FTA will come into being before the China- Australia FTA.

In addition, China has initiated negotiations on bilateral FTAs with the Southern African Customs Union (SACU) and the Gulf Cooperation Council (GCC). It has started conducting feasibility studies on bilateral FTAs with India and Iceland.

6.2.2 India's Regional Trade Initiatives:

A. India's Involvement in Regional Integration in South Asia: SAARC/SAPTA/SAFTA/BIMSTEC: India is also a member of the APTA but this section will focus on India's trade agreements in South Asia. India is the founding member of the South Asian Association for Regional Cooperation (SAARC), which comprises all South Asian countries with the exception of Afghanistan. [7] SAARC members signed the South Asian Preferential Trade Arrangement (SAPTA) in April 1993, with the view to creating the South Asian Free Trade Area (SAFTA). As a framework merely for the exchange of tariff concessions through product-by-product or positive-listing approach, the progress of SAPTA in terms of tariff liberalisation has been rather slow. For instance, intra-SAARC trade rose slightly from 2.42 percent in 1990 to 4.7 percent in 2003, much of which was however attributed to unilateral, bilateral and multilateral (WTO) liberalisation, rather than to the SAPTA. [8]

The SAPTA was made into a regional trade agreement by all members of SAARC at the Twelfth SAARC Submit in January 2004, and came into force from January 1, 2006. Under Rule 7 of the phased tariff liberalisation programme, in two years, the tariffs of India, Pakistan and Sri Lanka will be slashed to 20 percent in two years, while Bangladesh, Bhutan, Maldives and Nepal (as Least Developed Countries) will reduce tariffs to 30 percent. In five to eight years, the contracting parties will bring tariffs down to 0-5 percent. The SAFTA includes also measures not covered by the SAPTA, such as the harmonisation of standards, mutual recognition of tests and accreditation of testing laboratories, trade facilitation measures such as simplification and harmonisation of customs clearance, important licensing, registration and banking procedures, and removal of intra-SAARC investment barriers.

The Bay of Bengal Initiative for Multi-sectoral Technical and Economic Cooperation (BIMSTEC) groups together Bangladesh, Bhutan, India, Myanmar, Nepal, Sri Lanka and Thailand. In the first BIMSTEC Submit in July 2004, the leaders adopted a Declaration calling for the establishment of a free trade area covering trade in goods, services, and investment, as well as mutual recognition of standards, customs cooperation, business migration, among others. For India, BIMSTEC is highly politically motivated, as it resolves the problem of slow movement in South Asian cooperation by eliminating Pakistan and including Myanmar and Thailand. The BIMSTEC is nevertheless instrumental for regional economic integration in Asia as it serves as a formal link between South Asia and Southeast Asia.

B. India-ASEAN FTA: Propelled by the ASEAN-China

FTA initiative, India and ASEAN signed a Framework Agreement on Comprehensive Economic Cooperation (CEPA) on October 8, 2003, which commits the parties to working towards the establishment of an ASEAN-India Regional Trade and Investment Area as a long-term objective. The CEPA includes a small list of exchanges of tariff concessions. Like the ASEAN-China FTA it also has an Early Harvest Programme (EHP) as a confidence building measure. However, due to disagreement on rules of origin as well as protectionist pressure from domestic industries in India, the EHP could not be implemented. [9]

A political aspect of the India-ASEAN CECP is India's ambition to compete with China for influence in Southeast Asia. As stated by Jayanta Roy, the Principle Advisor to the Confederation of Indian Industry, "like China, India is not competing with ASEAN economies in trade and FDI. An agreement with India will also give ASEAN countries a chance to reduce their excessive dependence on China as a trading partner".

C. India's Bilateral FTA Initiatives: India has signed a number of FTAs with its Asian neighbours. The India-Sri Lanka FTA, signed in December 1998, is one of India's earliest bilateral trade arrangements. India and Singapore signed a Comprehensive Economic Cooperation Agreement in July 2005, under which trade in goods, services, investment protection, standard and technical regulation, and other areas of economic and regulatory cooperation are addressed. A Framework Agreement for establishing Free Trade between India and Thailand was signed in October 2003. In addition, India is negotiating FTAs or joint exploring the possibilities of FTAs with China, Malaysia, Indonesia, Korea, Mauritius. Chile, the SACU, the GCC, and the MERCOSUR.

6.3 Asian Economic Integration: China and India

6.3.1 Different Types of Regionalism: In addition to unilateral and multilateral liberalisation, both China and India have intensified their regional initiatives. Countries have good reasons to embrace regionalism, as previously noted, including political and economic ones. This is however not to say that they should abuse their regional options. In a world economic interdependence is rapidly increasing, trading nations, while pursuing their national interests, must also consider their long-term interests by factoring regional, global, and even other countries' national interests into consideration. As the above analyses demonstrate, China and India are crucial players in the regional economic integration process in Asia. It also seems that both countries are actively pursuing regionalism, mainly in the form of bilateral FTAs. In promoting regional economic integration in Asia, China and India are faced with the following possible options:

- Bilateralism;
- Pan-Asian FTA; or
- Sub-regional integration in East Asia and South Asia respectively, with the two sub-regions linked through ASEAN-India FTA and China-India FTA.

This section discusses the various options, with a view to evaluating their different degrees of suitability for promoting regional economic integration in Asia.

6.3.2 Hub-and-Spokes Bilateralism: Both China and India are now obsessively negotiating and signing bilateral FTAs. The number of RTAs in which India is a party exceeds that of China. However, almost all of India's RTAs involve only "shallow" integration, in the sense that there has neither been substantial tariff reduction nor broad coverage of issues in those RTAs. They nevertheless deserve attention, not only because of India's recently demonstrated obsession with regional arrangements, but also because of the need to find an answer to the question of whether India can serve a leading role or as a hub in South Asia integration, which is obviously an important part of regional economic integration in Asia.

The bilateral initiatives of China and India are driven by both economic and political factors, including the so-called "domino effect" or "fear of exclusion". [10] The pursuit of bilateralism, if reaching its extreme, can lead to a hub-and-spoke situation. As the World Bank observes, in the hub-and-spoke pattern, "the largest markets sign individual agreements with a wide range of peripheral countries among which market access remains restricted". However, such system "can marginalize the spokes, where market access conditions are usually less advantageous than in the hub, which enjoys improved access to all of the spokes." In a region which accommodates several large economies, overlapping hub-and-spoke configurations tend to emerge. In the worst scenario, hubs have multiple FTAs with smaller spokes, but the spokes do not liberalise between themselves. This will not only create multiple layers of discrimination through exclusive trade preference and complex rules of origin, but also place the spokes at a disadvantage as foreign investment tends to move to the hubs in order to gain more market access.

Using a global "computable general equilibrium" model (GEMAT) to trace the numerical impact of trade globalism, regionalism, and bilateralism, ADB finds that, if two hub-and-spoke configurations in Asia are stimulated, namely the "China hub" and the "ASEAN hub", Compared to the Asian free trade scenario that extends MFN status to countries outside Asia, the Asian hub-and-spoke scenario generates somewhere between one fifth and one quarter of the global gains. Within developing Asia [excluding Japan], hub-and-spoke systems are inferior to regional free trade and to multilateral liberalisation initiatives. A [China] hub generates just over half the benefits of Asian free trade for Asian developing countries, and an ASEAN hub, which implicitly entails the removal of more trade distortions, about 70 percent of the benefits.

However, in pursuing trade bilateralism, the hub economies—which are China and ASEAN in the ADB model—gain larger benefits. For instance, China's welfare gains from having a regional hub position is almost four times that from pan-Asian free trade, and ASEAN is also better off by becoming a hub than under the Asian free trade scenario. India is not treated as a hub in the ADB report, presumably because its foreign trade and investment is not comparable to that of China or ASEAN. According to the conventional hub-and-spoke theory, India, as the largest economy in South Asia, will benefit from a sub-regional hub position in that area. India however will lose 0.24 percent of its GDP in the "China hub" system, and its GDP will negligibly increase by 0.08 percent in the "ASEAN hub" system. Put simply, India has none or little to gain if other big economies such as China and ASEAN are placed in the position of hubs.

6.3.3 Asian Free Trade or Asian Economic Community: The ADB report, consistent with the findings of Roland-Holst, Verbiest and Zhai, offers the conclusion that the "estimated benefits from free trade in Asia (with the extension of MFN to the rest of the world) are nearly as large as those from global free trade". Further, there will be no trade diversion as "no country or global region loses under the assumption of Asian free trade". This finding is reaffirmed by the IMF 2006 report, as discussed above. This is because, for most Asian developing countries, the bulk of gains from global free trade will still originate from trade liberalisation in Asia. However, given China's foreign trade structure (i.e. its strong trading links with non-Asian markets), its gains from Asian free trade are less than half those from global trade liberalisation. India's gain from pan-Asian free trade is a 1.15 percent expansion in its GDP, slightly higher than the projected benefits from global trade liberalisation. Furthermore, in spite of overall gains, "Asian free trade could lead to a significant deterioration in the terms of trade for Asia's two mammoth economies, the PRC and India". This is because these two nations now mainly trade with non-Asian countries, while their increased demand for goods produced in other parts of the world would not be compensated by increase in the demand for their exports outside Asia, thus creating lifted import prices relative to export prices.

India has been advocating an Asian Economic Community for years. As the Indian Prime Minister has enthusiastically indicated, "we envision an Asian Economic Community, which encompasses ASEAN, China, Japan, Korea and India. This community of nations would constitute an 'arc of advantage', across which there would be large-scale movement of people, capital, ideals and creativity." The basic idea is to bring the major blocs in East and South Asia, including Japan, ASEAN, China, India and Korea, which are collectively called the JACIK economies, to create an FTA or Asian Economic Community. This community, with a combined population of 3 billion, Gross National Income (G.N.I.) of US$ 16 trillion, total exports of US$ 1.66 trillion, and foreign exchange reserves of US$ 1.6 trillion (in 2003), will be the largest trade bloc in the world. This FTA based community will eventually force other Asian economies to join, thus eliminating the "noodle-bowl" problems.

6.3.4 An East Asia Bloc and a South Asian Bloc Linked with Bilateral FTAs: A More Viable Route for Asian Economic Integration: East Asian economies have developed strong economic interdependence and integration with the global economy through external liberalisation and internal, market-driven, reforms. In recent decades, the independence is further strengthened by the newly developed Asian division of labour system cantered on China which is on the top of vertical trade in East Asia. In addition to trade and FDI, East Asia economic integration is also linked by financial and macroeconomic interdependence.

Economically, East Asian economic integration, via the creation of an East Asian trade bloc, is a viable option confirmed by numerous studies. Gilbert, Scollay and Bora, using the methods of both the CGE and gravity models, credibly demonstrated that East Asian economies are natural trading partners and hence integration agreements tend to be building blocks in moves to achieve free trade in the Asia-Pacific region. Specifically, it is argued that East Asian integration would be based on arrangements in which Northeast Asian economies would necessarily form the core. As such, the proposed Japan-Korea and China-Japan-Korea FTAs, plus the proposed ASEAN+3 FTA which serves as the link between Northeast Asia and Southeast Asia, are therefore essential elements in the construction of an East Asia FTA. With regard to the welfare-enhancing effects of the relevant FTAs, the findings of Gilbert, Scollay and Bora are as follows:

- Japan-Korea FTA produces relatively weak benefits for the two participating economies (0.3 percent of GDP for Korea and close to zero effect for Japan). The widespread negative effects on non participants are negligible when expressed as a percentage of initial GDP, reaching 0.1 percent of GDP only in the case of Vietnam.
- Including China in the proposed arrangement significantly improves the welfare outcome for Korea and Japan, to 0.7 percent and 0.1 percent of GDP, respectively. In China's case, however, the welfare gain is negligible. With the inclusion of China in the FTA, the negative effects on non-members start to appear significant, particularly for Taiwan, China, and for the ASEAN economies, which compete directly with China in many markets.

The negative welfare effects on the ASEAN economies are converted into positive effects, if the proposal is expanded into an ASEAN+3 FTA, comprising the 10 ASEAN economies plus China, Japan, and Korea. Proportionately to GDP, the ASEAN economies and Korea are the biggest gainers from this arrangement, although for Korea there is only a marginal improvement in the welfare outcome relative to the outcome from the China-Japan-Korea FTA. In comparison with the latter arrangement, Japan enjoys a slightly larger welfare gain, although as a percentage of GDP, the gain is still small. The welfare effect on China is negligible, although very slightly inferior to that from the China-Japan-Korea FTA.

In the case of South Asia, it has been pointed out that enhanced regional cooperation, including regional integration, is an imperative if the countries in the region are to strengthen their competitive position, both individually and as a group, so as to attract foreign private capital from outside and even within the region to widen and diversity their production base. Because the trade barriers between South Asia countries are traditionally high, trade liberalisation through a FTA or custom union would substantially increase intra-regional trade and foreign investment.

According to one study, the FTA approach (i.e. SAFTA), if removing all intra-regional tariff barriers, would lead to GDP growth, trade expansion, and welfare gains for all South Asian countries, although the extent of benefits would vary among the members. For instance, Sri Lanka would benefit the most from free trade in the region, with real GDP expanding by two percent. India and Bangladesh have lesser gains (0.8 percent and 0.3 percent GDP expansion respectively), while the rest of South Asian countries is projected to gain 0.9 percent in real GDP. India's lesser gains in GDP growth can be compensated by benefits obtained in other aspects, as, for instance, "India appears to enjoy a positive contribution from terms of trade movements towards increase welfare gains in comparison to the other FTA members". If South Asia opts to achieve regional integration via a custom union, the benefits are strikingly much more significant. Needless to say, given the political economy in this region, a custom union is nearly impossible in the near future, although a preliminary FTA (SAFTA) has already been instituted. A possible route for Asian economic integration is that East Asia and South Asia progress to achieve sub-regional integration respectively, while developing bilateral FTAs between countries in these two sub-regions simultaneously.

6.3.5 Concluding Analysis: Which Asian Regionalism is Acceptable to China, India, and Other Asian Economies? As discussed above, the benefits from regionalism cannot be taken for granted. Countries have no incentives—not to mention obligations—to pursue regional economic integration unless immediate or long-term gains outweigh the costs. As the preceding section shows, neither China nor India is among the largest economic beneficiaries of regional economic integration in Asia. Economically, China gains the most from a system of bilateral FTAs in which it is a hub. According to the ADB, China's welfare gains are projected to be 0.41 percent of its 2025 baseline G.D.P. from a PRC-hub regime, 0.22 percent of the same GDP from global trade liberalisation, and only 0.11 percent of it from Asian free trade. Even in the scenario of China-Japan-Korea FTA or ASEAN+3, China's welfare gains are at best "negligible".

That is to say, for China, the gains from pan-Asian free trade (Asian regionalism) are less than half those from global free trade (multilateralism), and only a quarter of those from bilateral FTAs (China regionalism). China also does not gain much from East Asian regionalism according to Gilbert, Scollay and Bora. Presumably, if India is put in a regional hub position, its income would rise much faster than that from other channels. Hence, the question: Why a country such as China or India would pursue a region wide RTA such as an Asian FTA or an East Asian FTA or an Asian Economic Community India might have a stronger incentive for an Asian Economic Community, as India will relatively gain more welfare from a pan-Asian free trade arrangement. However, it is not easy to convince China to sincerely endorse such an idea. It seems that the Chinese practice of RTAs parallels both Chinese regionalism (cantered on China as the hub) and multilateralism. This can be seen from China's active pursuit of WTO accession as well as the sheer number of bilateral RTAs it has concluded and is negotiating.

In Asia only, it is exploring bilateral arrangements with important economies such as ASEAN, Korea, Japan, India, and Pakistan. It has not demonstrated strong interest in regional economic integration in Asia, be it Asian Economic Community or Asian FTA. Where East Asian economic cooperation is concerned, China's Prime Minister Wen Jiabao has warned that the cooperation should not be "close, exclusive and directed against any particular country," indicating that "China takes the position that in pursuing regional cooperation, it is imperative to be open minded and promote open regionalism so as to achieve progress for all countries and development in all regions." This type of open regionalism, as almost all other countries, including non-Asian countries such as U.S., EU, Russia, and arguably Australia and New Zealand, are equally welcomed and treated, will cause Asian regionalism to lose its distinctive identify and eventually the momentum to develop into full regional economic integration. This practice, featuring the parallels of multilateralism and Chinese bilateralism, is generally in line with China's economic interests, and is presumably not against its interests in other aspects.

Obviously the gains and costs have both economic and political dimensions. Trading nations have a wide range of considerations when they seek to negotiate RTAs. Apart from the traditional trade gains, countries might want to strengthen domestic policy reform, as is the case of the Mexican negotiating position on NAFTA. The underlying philosophy is that "a regional trade treaty can underpin domestic policy reforms and make it more secure; that is, by binding the country to the masthead of an international trade treaty, any future reversal of domestic policy reform becomes more difficult to implement." [11] They might also pursue RTAs to increase multilateral bargaining power with third countries by negotiating a preferential agreement, as the case of the European Community or MERCOSUR.

RTAs might also be used to make access to the larger economy's market more secure for the smaller economy. This was Canada's obvious purpose in forming the Canada-U.S. free trade agreement. A further objective is the formation of strategic linkages with trading partners in a RTA, which can help underpin security arrangements among the participating countries. The strategic objective was the central theme in early European integration which was aimed at preventing a fresh outbreak of European war by bringing Germany and France together through a trade agreement. Finally, regional agreements could be used tactically to achieve multilateral negotiating objectives. For example, in the Uruguay Round of GATT negotiations, it was widely thought that it was to the U.S. advantage to have regional trade negotiations underway, so that in dealing with recalcitrant multilateral negotiating partners, the United States could threaten to actually play the bilateral card, and engage in active discussions with prospective regional partners.

Needless to say, not all the above objectives will apply to a country negotiating a RTA. One or two objectives might be dominant in some cases, while in others multiple objectives exist Either way, it is often the case that non-economic, strategic, objectives quite rightly occupy the central place in RTA negotiations. Further more, although countries are not required to practice altruism in the international trade arena, big trading powers, as their policy would have tremendous impact on other countries, are expected to take into account not only their national interests, but also regional and global interests, in their policy-making. China and India, as the two most dynamic trading nations, shoulder such a responsibility.

But does this responsibility translate into an obligation not to pursue (self-interest oriented) bilateralism. Isn't it right that China or India can maximise its national interest by mainly focusing on bilateralism and, while possible, multilateralism. Obviously, China could achieve its economic and strategic goals through signing bilateral FTAs with its Asian neighbours. For the following reasons, it is submitted that China and India should pursue regionalism on a broader basis—namely involving more Asian countries with fewer agreements—instead of focusing on hub-and-spoke regionalism.

First, both China and India, and undoubtedly all Asian economies, have a long-term interest in broader liberalisation on a multilateral basis which will lead to greater net benefits for all trading nations. In fact, China's projected gains from bilateralism and India's projected gains from pan-Asian free trade are also based on the assumption that multilateral trade liberalisation, which might move at unsatisfactorily slow pace, does not stop. As China and India—and especially China at this stage—are heavily dependent on non-Asian markets such as North America and Europe (both of which are unlikely to sign FTAs with China and India in the foreseeable future), global trade liberalisation is actually crucial to their trade and economic growth. Therefore, countries like China and India should make sure that their regionalism supplements multilateralism despite the slow progress of the latter, but it should not stand in the way of global free trade. In this sense, bilateralism, featuring a hub-and-spoke system of FTAs, is more likely to harm the multilateral trading system in the long run as they are more likely to become stumbling blocks for the global free trade. In contrast, as the above sections show, an Asian FTA, East Asian FTA, and South Asian FTA are more likely to be building blocs with more trade-creating effects.

Second, the many bilateral FTAs signed by the hubs, be it China, India, or ASEAN, contribute greatly to the complexity of trading rules and to the potential costs of trade. In essence, systemic problems such as the "spaghetti bowl phenomenon" should not be overlooked. By creating a large number of (overlapping) bilateral FTAs, the hubs also create problems for the multilateral trading system. When the problems arise, they might hurt the hubs' long-term interests in global free trade. As such, it is in the interest of the hubs, in this case China and India, to minimise the number of RTAs by consolidating then into a regional one encompassing more countries.

Third, China's and India's fast growing trade frictions with non-Asian countries have generated the need for the two Asian giants to explore other markets. This is especially urgent for China, as its astronomical trade surpluses with the United States and EU have led to enormous protectionist pressure in the latter two trading powers. Building an alternative, integrated, market in Asia through Asian regional economic integration can strengthen the negotiating position of all Asian countries, most significantly China and India, with respect to their trade relations with the U.S. and EU.

Additionally, both China and India have political and security interests in a more integrated, economically interdependent Asia. Take the ASEAN-China FTA as an example: although it is believed that the long-term benefit of the ACFTA will be enormous to both sides, commentators have observed that "China's [RTA] approach, as a strategic movement, must be viewed in a larger context that embraces both economic and geopolitical considerations, with the latter playing a relatively more important role at this stage." Specifically, "China's worldwide RTA movement, which has primarily engaged its Asian neighbours at this stage, is aimed at expanding its political influence through peaceful economic exchange and cooperation." On the part of ASEAN, China's proactive pursuit of a regional trade pact offers a "win-win" opportunity which ASEAN cannot afford to reject, as remarked by ASEAN's spokesman: "there is no other way [for ASEAN] to deal with China but to engage it in regional process. China is important as a neighbour politically, in terms of security and is also important as an emerging economic power."

Especially in recent years, China has made gestures, accompanied by many concrete measures, to allay the fears of its neighbours about the growing Chinese economic and military power. China has emphasised that its major objective at this stage is to seek a friendly international and regional environment to facilitate its endeavours at economic development. But for China's small neighbours, they would like the added reassurance that the bilateral relations with China are contained in a multilateral and, if possible, regional framework.

Consequentially, if China is to succeed in its "good

neighbour" policy, it has to help create a regional economic architecture to support it. The same logic can also be applied to China's bilateral relations with other Asian countries, even including Japan. India is also located in a region (South Asia) where political relations are tense and there is significant distrust between countries. India and Pakistan have long-standing hostilities towards each other. Serious political differences also exist between India and other smaller South Asian countries, which are reinforced by the rigid positions of political and military leaders toward each other in this area. There is, in addition, a fear of Indian dominance in bilateral relations. Like China, India also has the crucial task of introducing a regional framework which is open to other regions as well as to the multilateral system in order to create a harmonious regional setting for its economic development.

In brief, although the economic gains from regionalism (based on a China and India playing the role of hubs in their respective regions) are not necessarily larger than bilateralism, leading Asian giants like China and India do have a long-term interest in regional economic integration in Asia if non-economic objectives are taken into consideration. As to the type of regionalism to be adopted, it is submitted that the best route for the realisation of Asian integration is sub-regional integration in East Asia and South Asia, while linking the two by bilateral FTAs. The next section presents an analysis of this approach and puts forward policy recommendations for China and India on Asian economic integration.

6.4. Policy Recommendations

China and India are among the most important economies in Asia. Since the 1997 Asian financial crisis, regional trade in Asia has become increasingly integrated, particularly with China, since China's rise as both a production centre and a final export market for the region has been a key factor in boosting intra-Asian trade and investment. China and India are also active participants in the growing number of regional economic cooperation initiatives, including bilateral and regional trade agreements as well as Asian cooperative measures in the areas of finance and investment.

China and India, together with other Asian countries, share the imperative to promote regional economic integration in this continent. Given the size of their economies and the central location of their development in international politics and economy, China and India should take the lead in this endeavour. The scope of gains from Asian regionalism can be formidable if it is realised through well-designed RTAs which complement the unilateral and multilateral liberalisation approach and anchor domestic reform programmes to increase economic efficiency and improve competitiveness. In light of the above, the following policy recommendations regarding Asian economic integration are made, with a special focus on the role of China and India.

6.4.1 Routes for Asian Economic Integration: East Asian FTA + South Asian FTA + others = Asian Free Trade. While it is unlikely that the trend of bilateral initiatives in Asia will stop, it is wise for the region as a whole to have a coordinated regionalisation policy. As suggested by Wang (2006) [12] and noted above, the hubs and spokes systems, while inducing larger benefits for the hubs, may damage the spokes because of discrimination in other spoke markets. Hubs and spokes regimes not only add layers of discrimination in the region, but also lead to greater resistance to multilateral liberalisation. This is not in the long-run interest of the economies which have the potential to be—or already are—hubs, including China, India, Japan, and ASEAN, as all of them are still heavily dependent on markets outside Asia.

A pan-Asian free trade area or an Asian economic community is unlikely to be achieved or even seriously discussed. Asia is no more than a geographic concept, with the sub-regions sharing no common heritage. Countries in each sub-region, including East Asia, South Asia, Central Asia, however share not only geographic contiguity but also common cultural, social and economic characteristics. Furthermore, the numerous sub-regional initiatives have demonstrated that the countries involved are preparing for economic and financial integration at the sub-regional level. It is hence submitted that East Asia and South Asia should strive to realise their sub-regional integration respectively, while linking the two sub-regions with bilateral integration agreements between individual countries.

Economic integration in East Asia should aim at creating an East-Asia wide FTA (EAFTA) comprising ASEAN, China, Japan and Korea. East Asia is now in a better position to achieve integration ahead of other sub-regions, because its intra-regional trade had reached 55 percent in 2004. There has also been a rapid rise in intra-regional investment flows, shaping a visible trade-investment nexus. As discussed in the previous section, various studies conclude that an EAFTA offers visible and meaningful benefits to all participating countries while generating little trade diversion. Although China may not gain as much as other East Asian countries do, it however has a long-term strategic interest in such an arrangement. For one, China would profit from the costs advantages of input imports from the regional partners in the EAFTA community, which will make the Chinese products more competitive in third markets. Being part of an integrated regional market can also strengthen China's negotiating position vis-à-vis other global trading powers.

Despite possessing enormous physical resources and comprising 22 percent of the global population, South Asia is the least integrated economic region of the world. The largest economy accounting for 70 percent of the total sub-regional GDP, India should take the lead in South Asia integration under the auspices of the SAFTA. Although the businesses in this area believe that intra-regional trade will triple in five years if South Asia regional integration is facilitated, especially in the areas of trade, traffic and transport, integration in this sub-region has been hampered by long-standing political hostility and the existence of a protectionist mentality. However, as a business leader of Pakistan has remarked, "if USA could allow MFN status to China whom it considered archenemy for five decades and Russia and USA having long standing conflicts in social, political and economic fields could become allies, what is restraining the countries of South Asia from economic integration."

Furthermore, South Asia countries, most importantly India, should conduct significant reduction in tariff and non-tariff barriers. India is one of the most protected major markets in the world, with high level of tariff and non-tariff protection for its domestic industry. India's vibrate economic growth in the recent decades, mainly as a result of trade and investment liberalisation, is however a strong proof that liberalisation, not protection, is the engine for economic growth.

The two sub-regions should not pursue integration separated and isolated from each other. Rather, the two, before the time is right to consolidate them into one, should be connected by bilateral arrangements between countries in the two regions. Most notably, India is negotiating an FTA with ASEAN and has concluded a FTA with Singapore. China and Pakistan has signed an early harvest agreement and have started negotiating a comprehensive FTA. More link-ups between the two sides should be encouraged provided that the bilateral arrangements follow the guidelines discussed below and serve as building blocks for global trade. If an Asian Economic Community is formed by consolidating the East Asian FTA and the SAFTA, other Asian countries will be compelled to join it. Eventually, a pan-Asian economic community will be accomplished through these routes.

6.4.2 Establishing a China-India FTA: In terms of using bilateral FTAs to link East Asia and South Asia, a China-India FTA will be most helpful in this regard. China-India trade is one of the most rapidly growing bilateral trade relationships in the world. During 1995-2003, the average annul growth of merchandise trade between the two countries was 26.4 percent, a figure higher than each country's growth rate with other trading partners. In 2003, the growth rate of bilateral trade in services was 125.5 percent. Still, the small share of the two countries in each other's foreign trade suggests enormous potential for trade expansion. [13] Arvind Panagaria, a distinguished economist who has generally been "critical the discriminatory trade blocs not just because such arrangements fragment the global trading system but also because they often hurt economic efficiency within the countries forging the arrangements", nevertheless favours an India-China FTA. [14]

Panagaria has beautifully stated the following reasons in support of a Sino-India deal in the interest of both Asian economic integration and global free trade, as well as China's and India's national competitiveness: The case for an India-China FTA is based principally on its strategic value. During the last decade, with the creation of the NAFTA, several expansions of the EU and a host of smaller FTAs in Latin America, Asia has suffered from a diversion of these regions' trade away from it. One response to this trade diversion for Asia would be to move towards a bloc of its own. Such a bloc may give Asia the necessary leverage to pry open the NAFTA and EU blocs to outsiders through multilateral liberalisation. If one accepts this argument, an India-China FTA is probably the best starting point for such an Asian bloc. For example, as an alternative, even if India and China both make good on their respective framework agreements with the members of the Association of

Southeast Asian Nations (ASEAN) to forge FTAs with them, an effective Asian bloc will not form without these two countries signing an FTA agreement with each other. On the other hand, if India and China signed an agreement, chances are much higher that the remaining countries in Asia will rush to sign agreements with them. Presently, the ASEAN is driving the integration process in Asia but with the emergence of India and China as major economic powerhouses and the relative stagnation faced by the most populous ASEAN country,

Indonesia, its ability to serve as the engine of the Asian integration has substantially diminished.

An India-China FTA also has the advantage that it will help promote an alternative FTA template that focuses on trade integration rather than non-trade subjects including labour standards, intellectual property rights and even restrictions on the use of capital controls. These subjects are integral parts of the US FTA template that the US may eventually want to turn into the WTO template. An Asian bloc that relies on a "trade only" template will be an effective instrument of countering the US template in the future WTO negotiations. Internally, India can surely benefit from cooperation with China in shaping its labour-intensive industry. In particular, direct competition with China may help push some of the key reforms necessary to stimulate the expansion of the labour-intensive industry. With the wages in China now rising, the time for India could not be more opportune for moving in a big way into such labour-intensive sectors as apparel, footwear and toys. Likewise, China could gain from increased interaction with India in the information technology sector.

6.4.3 China and India Should Lead Asia: China and India, as well as some of their Asian neighbours, all have crucial interests in global trade liberalisation, partly because their exports mainly go to markets outside Asia. In this sense, Asian regionalism is merely adopted as the “second-best” strategy due to the stalemate in the multilateral trade negotiations. The best framework for harvesting sustainable benefits from liberalisation is still the global one, while regional arrangements represent the middle ground on the spectrum of frameworks. Nevertheless, in the current situation of world trade, there seems to be no viable alternative to regionalism for trading nations.

It is widely recognised that Asian regionalism must be, first of all, “open regionalism”. There is however no fixed definition on what constitutes open regionalism. Difficult questions will be raised if open regionalism must mean, as some commentators suggest, open membership, which means that every country, be it geographically located in the region or not, can join on the same terms. This renders it possible that a R.T.A. can eventually encompass the entire world and hence—at least theoretically—lead to multilateral liberalisation. This will render the concept of Asian economic integration senseless (or make it become global economic integration) as it is, by definition, economic integration in Asia, which is pursued because of the very reason that global integration is halted by slow negotiations at the multilateral level. As such, it is inconceivable that membership of a regional arrangement is "open" for all countries of the world.

More often, the membership of a regional integration group is strictly confined to a given geographic area. The openness of regional groupings, in a more practical way, should lie in its willingness to extend intra-regional concessions and preferential treatment to non-members. As such, Wei and Frankel define open regionalism concisely as "external liberalisation by trade blocs, that is, the reduction in barriers on imports from non-member countries that is undertaken when member countries liberalize the trade among themselves." This is not to say that all the concessions and privileges must be offered to non-members on an MFN basis–this would probably cause the regional integration arrangement to lose its regional nature. As Wei and Frankel points out, the degree of liberalization on imports from non-members need not be as high as that from member countries".

Therefore, developing countries are encouraged to adopt a three-pronged strategy that integrates unilateral, regional, and multilateral liberalisation initiatives. The success of Asian emerging economies, including East Asia economies and India, is to a large extent attributed to the unilateral government reform programs. In the practice of open regionalism, Asian countries are encouraged to reduce their trade and investment barriers unilaterally to the maximum extent possible in order to improve their competitiveness and reduce poverty, as well as to avoid trade diversion effects. Although it is not an obligation embodied in the regional integration agreement, members are free to extend its regional liberalisation to non-members on a mutually reciprocal or even unconditional basis. Further, Asian countries participating in the integration process should take this as an opportunity to consolidate their diverse views and form consensus to push the multilateral trade negotiations ahead.

6.4.4 China and India Should Conduct Deeper Integration: It has been advocated that the new wave of regionalism should practice "deep integration" as opposed to "shallow integration". In the scenario of shallow integration, mainly trade in goods is liberalised among members. "Deep integration" goes beyond trade, involving investment, services, product standards and technical regulations, competition policy, and even environmental and labour standards, among others. In short, deep integration may induce welfare gains for participating countries by lowering the costs of production and improving efficiency in general, and for non-participating countries by avoiding trade diversion through stimulating trade.

Regional agreements in Asia are increasingly comprehensive in scope, going beyond reduction/elimination of tariffs and tariff barriers. In the Asian context, deep integration should be achieved through investment liberalisation, financial cooperation, and trade facilitation. Asian countries either heavily rely on foreign investment for economic development or aspire to attract foreign investment. Hence Lee and Park observe that "the movement of East Asian countries toward RTAs has been motivated by facilitating investment and providing a more flexible environment for the operation of multinational firms". In most Asian FTAs, investment commitments are cantered on national treatment and/or MFN treatment for foreign investors alongside rules on expropriation, compensation and repatriation of earnings. Countries have also committed to the creation of liberal and competitive environments for investment, as well as improve transparency in their legal systems. [15] Frankly, in China's and India's regional initiatives, the investment commitments are rather general, with little details to guide the practice.

If Asian countries wish to continue to draw investment from each other and from outside the region, they should take efforts to liberalise their investment regime, relax restrictions on foreign ownership, remove discriminative performance requirements, and provide impartial dispute settlement procedures. It is important to stress that these countries should however seek to strike a balance between investment liberalisation and promotion of competitiveness of domestic industries.

Trade in services is another important area in which deep integration should be sought. Unfortunately, Asian integration in the trade in services is very shallow. SAFTA does not even have a service dimension. In East Asia, although ASEAN's F.T.A. initiatives, including ASEAN-China, ASEAN-India, ASEAN-Japan, and ASEAN-Korea, commit the parties to conduct GATS-plus liberalisation, it is questionable that the voluntary nature of the commitment will lead to significant progress. [16] Again, China and India, with growing comparative advantage in certain services sectors, should take the lead in liberalising regional services. Initial liberalisation at the regional level may help create economies of scale, nurturing efficient and competitive domestic and regional firms which can stand up to competition from outside the region, and provide opportunities for learning-by-doing. Further, as some commentator correctly noted, "regulatory co-operation, such as harmonisation and mutual recognition of domestic regulations in financial, professional and a range of other services, may be more feasible in a regional context". [17] Needless to say, the building of a strong and flexible regulatory framework, which ensures fair competition, and regulates and remedies market failures, should accompany the whole liberalisation process.

A danger of regional agreements is that countries will tend to avoid making tough liberalisation decisions by excluding whole sectors from preferential arrangements. This can happen to trade in both merchandise (especially the agricultural sector) and services. For instance, the Japan-Singapore FTA totally excludes the agricultural sector. Although it is widely recognised that reduction of trade barriers in agriculture is particularly important for poverty reduction, whereby tremendous gains can be conferred on the poor households of the less developed countries in this region, for most of the major Asian economies, including ASEAN, Japan, Korea and India, agriculture is still viewed as a sensitive sector placed outside the liberalisation agenda.

In this regard, China's commitment to a regime of low protection in agriculture demonstrates that the country is taking the lead on some issues relating to regional liberalisation. China's WTO commitments in agriculture are already impressive, and its stance toward agricultural trade at the regional level warrants further attention. Under the EHP of the ASEAN-China FTA framework agreement, China undertakes to grant unilateral concessions to agricultural products of ASEAN countries provided that the latter also commit to some degree of agricultural liberalisation. It is remarked that "China's binding to low tariff levels as part of its agricultural policy therefore offers scope for the liberalization of agriculture in a regional setting, which could set in place a favourable political dynamic for more open agricultural sectors through East Asia". [18] One would question the effectiveness of this approach as the Chinese method is to "induce"–with the imposition of no compulsory obligations–trading partners to liberalise by offering unilateral concessions. The fact that this approach cannot readily deliver reciprocal commitments implies that it may have a limited potential as a vehicle for trade liberalisation. Without a more formal and institutionalised approach, the liberalisation process in sensitive sectors such as agriculture and financial sector can be unsatisfactorily slow.

6.4.5 Asian Countries Should Develop Common Guidelines for Bilateral FTAs: As analysed above, regional integration in Asia will have to be achieved through a web of regional and bilateral FTAs. Every agreement adds to the layers of discrimination and worsens the systemic problems of regionalism. For example, on rules of origin alone, a survey of several RTAs in Asia demonstrates that the "spaghetti bowl" effect is apparent. For instance, under the Singapore-Australia FTA, the general rule of a specified threshold of local value content is either 30 percent or 50 percent. In the Japan-Singapore FTA, each product has one corresponding specific rule of origin, although a significant portion of the rules require 60 percent of local content. Such a world of complex clauses governing rules of origin, criticised the President of the Asian Development Bank, "could create a bureaucratic tangle that might put individual companies off trading together." [19]

It is suggested that, to cure the systemic problems and facilitate deeper integration, East Asian and South Asian countries should establish an institution to develop common standards and best practices to guide the regional FTAs. This body, with the participation of all interested Asian countries and under the auspices of a regional forum such as the East Asia Summit or ASEAN+3 cooperation, should produce a set of guidelines and principles for Asian FTAs, with a view to ensuring that the regional FTAs lead to integration rather than fragmentation of trading relations in Asia. It is highly possible that bilateral and sub-regional arrangements, if designed with measure incorporated to mitigate distortions and inefficiencies, can deepen regional economic integration and even "present additional opportunities to those currently accommodated within the multilateral framework".

The suggested guidelines for sub-regional and bilateral trade agreements in Asia should include the following which is nevertheless not an exhaustive list:

First, Asian FTAs should at least be WTO-consistent. This

not only refers to compliance with GATT Article XXIV and GATS Article V. The bottom line is that every FTA should be WTO-plus. Further, they must follow, to the widest extent, the principles, terminologies, concepts and rules embodied in the WTO, although they are encouraged to develop liberalisation-oriented rules for areas not covered by the WTO.

Second, deeper integration and comprehensiveness in Asian FTAs should be sought. Numerous studies show that agreements with deeper and broader integration can lead to larger trade and income effects. WTO disciplines also require regional FTAs to eliminate barriers to trade and investment between the parties, including tariffs and non-tariff restrictions in goods, services, and investment. Furthermore, given Asia's relatively backwardness in infrastructure, comprehensive cooperation in trade facilitation should be the focus of any FTA in this region.

Third, Asian FTAs should adopt liberal, or at least non-restrictive, rules of origin. The best solution is to have an Asia-wide set of rules of origin. If this is not possible, the rules of origin in Asian FTAs should at least be transparent, clear, and consistent, and have "transparent and consistent implementing regulations (e.g. accounting practices, paperwork for certification of origin) that are chosen at the minimum level needed to prevent trade deflection". As the bottom line, they should not serve as trade policy mechanism for protecting "sensitive sectors" or special interest. In brief, a set of Asian "best practice guidelines" for rules of origin can be an invaluable contribution to Asian economic integration.

Fourth, there should be clear rules on how technical barriers to trade can be employed for legitimate purposes such as the protection of public health and safety. There should be "clear and simple codes that guide technical barriers to trade, such as product standards and phytosanitary standards to protect public health and safety (based on the WTO agreements on standards). Likewise, agreements that cover environmental and labour standards should embrace the rights of partners to establish and implement their own laws and regulations in conformity with existing international obligations in the areas of environmental protection and labour rights and conditions".

Fifth, harmonisation of regulatory standards may or may not be required in Asian FTAs, depending on the readiness of the participating economies. Countries are encouraged to adopt international standards provided that all parties have the capacity to implement it. Mutual recognition is also encouraged. However, it is important to realise that, given the diverse backgrounds of the Asian countries, regional cooperation in standards can be very difficult. The best starting point is that all members of the FTA should maintain an open and transparent system, with standards published and easily accessible to businesses and the public.

Finally, dispute settlement procedures should be established in Asian FTAs to promote legalism in trade relations. Disputes should be resolved, first, through amicable consultations. If bilateral consultations do not offer solutions, then an independent third party should be established to resolve the disputes in an impartial, expeditious manner, and its decisions should be fully implemented. Mediation should be allowed in the whole process of dispute resolution. Further, the parties should avoid duplication with the WTO dispute settlement mechanism where appropriate.

6.5 Conclusion

Asian economic integration is caused and pushed forward by the painful experience from the Asian financial crisis, the delay in global trade negotiations of the Doha Round, concern at the rise of the giant Chinese and India economies, as well as some strategic and political considerations. It is a "second-best" approach which Asian countries unfortunately have to follow. In the process of regional economic integration, China and India, given the size of their populations, as well as their central strategic positions in international and regional relations, will inevitably play fundamentally important, if not entirely dominating, roles. This chapter has suggested that regional economic integration in Asia should first of all realise sub-regional integration in East Asia and Southeast Asia, while linking up these two sub-regions with bilateral FTAs, among which the most important one should be a China-India FTA. Eventually, all the FTAs will be consolidated into one pan-Asian FTA. China and India must take the lead in promoting Asian economic integration. They are advised to lead the region to practice open regionalism (with whatever Asian identity) and conduct deeper integration. Lastly, it is suggested that Asian countries should, at this stage, establish an institution to develop common principles and guidelines for the sub-regional and bilateral FTAs.

Notes

1. David Roland-Holst, Jean-Pierre Verbieft & Fan Zhai, "Growth and Trade Horizon for Asia: Long-term Forecasts for Regional Integration" (2005) 25(2) Asian Development Review, pp 76.
2. Masahiro Kawai, "East Asian Economic Regionalism: Progress and Challenges" (2005) 16 Journal of Asia Economics 29, pp 34.
3. UNDPPO (United Nations Development Policy and Planning Office), World Economic Situation and Prospects 2005 (Geneva: The United Nations, 2005) at 28-29.
4. UNCTAD (United Nations Conference on Trade and Development), Trade and Development Report, 2005 (Geneva: The United Nations, 2005), pp 43, 69.
5. World Trade Organisation, Trade Policy Review: People's Republic of China – Report by the Secretariat (WTO Document No.: WT/TPR/S/161) (Geneva: WTO, 2006) at 45.
6. The text of the DSM, TIG Agreements are available at the ASEAN Secretariat's official website at <http://www.aseansec.org/16635.htm>.
7. SAARC members hence include Afganistan, Bangladesh, Bhutan, India, Maldives, Nepal, Pakistan, and Sri Lanka.
8. Jayanta Roy, "South Asian Regional Trade Agreements: Perspectives, Issues and Options" (Paper presented at the International Trade Roundtable "The WTO at 10 Years – The Regional Challenge to Multilateralism", Brussels, Belgium, 27

June 2005), online:
<http://mba.tuck.dartmouth.edu/cib/news/itr_2005_pdf/Roy.pdf

9. See Ministry of Commerce and Industry, Government of India, "India's Current Engagements in R.T.As.", (New Delhi, India: Ministry of Commerce and Industry, 2006), online<http://commerce.nic.in/india_rta_main.htm> and Amita Batra, "Micro pains, macro gains" Financial Express (20 May 2006), online:
<http://www.financialexpress.com/fe_full_story.php.content_id=127689>.
10. Richard Baldwin, A Domino Theory of Regionalism (Working Paper No. 4465) (Cambridge, Massachusetts National Bureau of Economic Research, 1993).
11. John Whalley, "Why Do Countries Seek Regional Trade Agreements." In Jeffrey A. Frankel, ed., The Regionalization of the World Economy (Chicago: The University of Chicago Press, 1998) at 63-72.
12. Wang Jiangyu (2006), 'China, India, and Regional Economic Integration in Asia: The Policy and Legal Dimensions' in Singapore Year Book of International Law .
13. 127 Report of the India-China Joint Study Group on Comprehensive Trade and Economic Cooperation (New Delhi, India: India-China Joint Study Group, 2005) at 20, online: Ministry of External Affairs (India)
<http://meaindia.nic.in/treatiesagreement/2005/11ta1104200504.pdf>
14. Arvind Panagaria, "An India-China Free Trade Area." (The Economic Times, 20 April 2005), online <http://www.columbia.edu/~ap2231/ET/et77_April20_05.htm>.
15. O.G. Dayaratna Banda & John Whalley, "Beyond Goods and Services: Competition Policy, Investment, Mutual Recognition, Movement of Person, and Broader Operation Provisions of Recent FTAs Involving ASEAN Countries" NBER Working Paper 11232 (Cambridge, Massachusetts: National Bureau of Economic Research, 2005) at 15-17.
16. Tubagus Feridhanusetyawan, "Preferential Trade Agreements in the Asia-Pacific" IMF Working Paper WP/05/149 (Washington D.C.: IMF, 2005) , pp 24.
17. Kathie Krumm & Homi Kharas, eds., East Asia Integrates: A Trade Policy Agenda for Shared Growth (Singapore: the World

Bank and Oxford University Press, 2003) at xxxii, online: <http://web.worldbank.org>.

18. Homi Kharas, "Trade and Economic Integration in the Asia Pacific Region" in Organisation for Economic Co-operation and Development (OECD), ed., Regional Integration in the Asia Pacific: Issues and Prospects (Paris: OECD, 2005) , pp 107.
19. David Pilling, "ADB chief hits out at 'noodle bowl' trade" Financial Times (Asia) (2 February 2006), pp 1.

References

Akamatsu, K. 1962."A Historical Pattern of Economic Growth in Developing Countries." Developing Economies (preliminary issue): 3-25.

Eichengreen, B, and R, Hausmann 1999. *"Echang Rates and Financial Fragility."* Working Paper 7418, Cambridge, Mass.: National Bureau of Economic Research.

Eichengreen, B. 2002. "What To Do with Chiang Mai Initiative?" Berkley University Website.

Kenen, R. 1969. "The Theory of Optimum Currency Areas: An Eclectic View." In R. Mundell and A. Swoboda (eds). 1969, Monetary Problems of The International Economy. Chicago: University of Chicago Press.

Kwan, C.H. 2001, Yen Bloc, Brookings Institution Press, Washington, D.C. Fukao, Ishido, and Ito, 2003, Vertical Intra-Industrial Trade and Direct Investment in East Asia, RIETI discussion paper 03-E-001.

Mckinnon, R.I. 1963. *"Optimum currency areas"*, American Economic Review, Vol. 53, September 717-725.

Mckinnon, R.I. 1998. "Exchange Rate Coordination for Surmounting the East Asian Currency Crisis". Asian Economic Journal. Vol. 12, Number 4, December 1998.

Mckinnon, R.I. and Ohno.K.1997. *Dollar and Yen.* Cambridge. Massachusetts: The MIT Press.

Mckinnon, R.I. 2000. After the Crisis, the East Asian Dollar Standard Resurrected: An Interpretation of High-Frequency Exchange Rate Pegging. Economic Department, Stanford University, mckinnon@leland.stanford.edu.

Mundell, R. 1961. "A Theory of Optimum Currency Areas." *American Economic Review* 51:657-64.

Mundell, R. 1997. "Adapting the Agenda for Monetary Union?" in

M.I. Blejer et al. (eds), Optimum Currency Areas: New Analytical and Policy Developments, International Monetary Fund, Washington.

Radelet, S. and J.D. Sachs. 1998. "The East Asian Financial Crisis: Diagnoses, Remedies, Prospects," *Brookings Papers on Economic Activity*.

Sakakibara, Eisuke and Yamakawa, Sharon. 2004. Market-Driven Regional Integration in East Asia, Paper for the Workshop on "Regional Economic Integration in a Global Framework", 22-23 September 2004, Beijing.

Trivisvavet, Tanawat: Do East Asian Countries Constitute An Optimum Currency Area? Durham University. April. 2001.

UNCTAD, 2001. *Trade and Development Report.*

7

NAFTA: Economic Integration in North America

7.1 Introduction

Some analysts consider the North American Free Trade Agreement (NAFTA) part of a larger economic integration process that goes beyond narrowly defined trade policy (Pastor 1992, Weintraub 1993b). Because of US initiatives, issues with only tenuous direct connections to trade have come under negotiation. A harmonization of national policies that appears tantamount to a broad movement toward integration seems to be under way. But is it? NAFTA clearly makes trade freer on a broad front among the signatories and will result in the efficiency enhancements typical of trade openings. However, in many cases, what may at first look like integration appears on further scrutiny simply to be a continuation of a Hegelian dialectic over trade policy. [1] To show why a Hegelian dialectic appropriately characterizes what took place with NAFTA and the parallel agreements and why economic integration seems a less appropriate characterization, we begin by considering the antecedents of the NAFTA negotiations. The events that precipitated NAFTA began, at the very latest, in the 1970s. From the end of World War II until the late 1970s, US trade policy involved an unconditional interpretation of the most favoured nation (MFN) clause of the General Agreement on Tariffs and Trade (GATT). [2]

The United States was the world's principal proponent of a multilateral approach to international trade liberalization. But by the late 1970s, the United States had become frustrated with GATT. The sources of frustration were the caravan effect (GATT negotiations emulate a caravan that moves only as fast as its slowest camel); the free-rider problem (some countries, chiefly the less developed ones, have benefited from the multilateral system without much lowering their own barriers); and the rise of trade-related issues not covered by GATT, such as direct foreign investment, trade in services, and intellectual property rights (Primo Braga 1989, 245).

Over time, these three problems became more frustrating for the United States. While the caravan effect is self-explanatory, both the free rider problem and trade-related issues not covered by GATT deserve more detailed attention. Although many countries had entered GATT because they wanted open foreign markets, they were often less interested in opening their own. For the less developed countries (LDCs), whose competitive positions against the developed nations were unfavourable in many industries, these predilections were considered understandable. GATT allowed the LDCs to surrender less protectionism than the industrialized nations and offered LDCs special openings to the developed countries under the generalized system of preferences (GSP). [3] But to some countries, these special opportunities were not enough. A historical peculiarity of GATT offered countries a freeway to still more protectionism.

Because pre-World War II protectionists had focused their energies on tariffs, tariffs are what GATT had been designed to lower. Over time, many GATT signatories simply replaced their tariff barriers, which are discouraged by GATT, with other, GATT-legal barriers. Quantity restrictions, expressed through quotas and permits, became commonplace, as did regulations and standards concerning "product quality." Export subsidies became popular. Detailed regulations against direct foreign investment surfaced. Some countries became harbours for intellectual piracy, maintaining weak patent and copyright protection in order to become centres for unlicensed production.

7.2 Innovations in US Trade

During the 1980s, particularly in LDCs, these innovations

in protectionism proliferated in response to terms-of-trade shocks and foreign debt problems. Surmising that the raw materials price booms of the 1970s would continue in the 1980s, many LDCs had devised debt-led growth strategies and found foreign bankers to support them. But at the end of the 1970s, a shift in U.S. monetary policy triggered a sudden rise in interest rates, making debt a tortuous route to any goal. At the beginning of the 1980s, the prices of the LDCs' traditional raw materials exports entered a protracted slump. To address their new balance-of-payments and debt problems, [4] many LDCs adopted philosophies more reminiscent of eighteenth-century mercantilism than of GATT, and they expressed them through GATT-legal non-tariff innovations. Meanwhile, certain technological developments caused the United States to find foreign protectionist innovations increasingly baneful. Since the 1960s, innovations in transportation and communications had inspired a rise in "production sharing," in which firms located one portion of a total manufacturing operation in Taiwan, another stage in Singapore, and perhaps another in Mexico. By the 1980s, further revolutions in communications and in production technology had allowed a surge in opportunities for US trade in services.

This surge prompted the United States to push its trading partners to permit more such trade. Trade in services, however, involves complications that are less common in the goods trade. Much services trade operates most efficiently in locations where producer and consumer physically meet. For trade in services, someone must travel, typically the seller. The service producer prefers to locate itself and its capital-goods inputs at the market, so the buyer will not have to travel to use them.

But in international trade, locating at the market means that the host country's investment rules have an overriding effect on sales opportunities. Rules that restrict foreign investment hinder US services trade. Moreover, because many U.S. services exports involve specialized technological knowledge—embodied in machinery, in software, or in employees—the development and profitability of such trade often depends on the protection of intellectual property rights. The risk of technology theft has a chilling effect. By the 1980s, the accelerating pace of technological development, together with the increasing ease of pirating new technology, made such risk steadily greater. Since these factors made opening trade more attractive to the United States at the same time that LDC innovations in protectionism were raising trade barriers, the United States launched a program of what came to be called "aggressive reciprocity." [5]

Section 301 of the Trade Act of 1974 and its revision, "Super 301," under the Omnibus Trade and Competitive Act of 1988 allowed the United States new manoeuvrability in threatening unilateral trade retaliations. The United States used these threats to extract trade openings from other countries and to induce trading partners to tighten their intellectual property protection. (Such was the case, for example, with Brazil and computer software.)

Innovative protectionists soon contrived to apply measures expressly designed to open trade to quite different purposes. For example, the United States used Section 301 and Super 301 to negotiate "voluntary" export restraints, a US innovation in protectionism in which exporting countries "volunteer" to restrict their exports to the United States. Foreigners slow in volunteering were not long in receiving US threats of 301-based trade sanctions. The United States also stepped up countervailing actions, such as raising duties, against countries it charged with dumping or other "unfair" trade practices. [6] In many cases, the merits of these charges have been questionable (Bovard 1992). In sum, in the context of US trade policy, two types of dialectics were operative.

First, a dialectic operated between forces in the United States that wanted free trade abroad but not so much at home, and foreign countries that also wanted free trade abroad but not so much at home. That is, as one side developed innovations in both liberalization and protectionism, they were countered by those of the other side.

Second, the realignment in trade patterns that inspired the United States' initiatives at the GATT negotiations also changed who wanted protectionism and who did not. Some US firms that had favoured protectionism discovered that changes in production technology and in markets had made freer trade agreeable. Other traditional protectionists found that these same changes favoured increased protectionist efforts.

To illuminate this redistribution of protectionist pressures, some details of the dynamics of production-sharing deserve attention. Production sharing simply meant that it became more common for US firms to export partially manufactured products for further processing abroad, and then to import, perhaps for further processing in the United States before final sale. As such trade developed, firms and industries carrying out production sharing inclined increasingly toward trade liberalization at home (Gonzalez and Velez 1992). After all, producers who import their inputs often benefit from low trade barriers. Manufacturing firms' lobbying efforts on behalf of protectionism began to diminish (Magee 1990). Moreover, US production-sharing manufacturers became more interested in negotiating liberalized foreign investment laws in foreign countries that made attractive platforms for production-sharing operations. These interests were consistent with those of US service-exporting firms, even though the latter intended to sell abroad the products of their foreign operations. On the other side of the dialectical process, U.S. labour groups viewed increased US manufacturing operations abroad as signifying fewer union jobs in the United States. Accordingly, unions increased both direct and indirect pressure toward restricting trade.

In an innovative example of indirect pressure, US labour organizations began to ally with groups that were concerned about environmental problems abroad. These allied organizations accused US firms of moving operations abroad to take advantage of looser environmental laws or enforcement. They petitioned Congress for measures that might impede firms from re exporting to the United States. Such measures could not only discourage some firms from continuing to operate abroad, even if environmental considerations had not been the motive underlying their locations, but could discourage others from establishing foreign operations in the future.

7.3 NAFTA as the Next Step

These redistributions of pressures for and against trade liberalization manifested themselves further in the establishment of the negotiating frameworks that would lead to NAFTA. The opportunities for a free trade agreement had increased with the decline of protectionist pressures from US manufacturers. US labour organizations, however, urged negotiation for parallel agreements without which, unions argued, NAFTA itself would promote a type of competition that was destructive. The progress of the parallel negotiations offered much evidence to suggest that protectionists saw the discussions of side agreements as a second chance to sink NAFTA. As one after another agreement was reached on environmental and other issues, none was adequate. Disparities between US and Mexican labour and environmental laws— or their enforcement—increasingly attracted charges of "social dumping" (AFL–CIO 1992).

One major sticking point in the parallel negotiations implies a great deal about whether the US agenda involved integration or whether it reflected the protectionist side of a dialectical process. Although all three parties concurred that violation of the parallel covenants ought to incur penalties, the United States was unique in arguing that the penalties ought to include selected revivals of protectionism. Canadian and Mexican negotiators, perceiving a contradiction in the use of protectionism to achieve free trade, favoured fines. Moreover, some of NAFTA's moves toward what has been referred to as integration can also be seen as attempts by US protectionists to broaden their efforts against freer trade by pushing issues that Canadians and Mexicans may perceive to involve their national sovereignty. In any case, the efforts of pro- and anti-protectionist forces have jointly determined NAFTA and will likely determine how the agreement will evolve over time. [7] To more fully elucidate these competing forces—and the likely outcomes of their conflict over the life of the agreement—we selectively discuss NAFTA itself, its expected effects, and the political forces that will influence its implementation. It has also been considered in more detail the emergence of the parallel agreements.

7.3.1 Negotiated NAFTA: Liberalization and Protectionism: In arguing that NAFTA may signify something besides economic integration, we have focused on the parallel agreements because they reflect both protectionist and liberalizing pressures. But NAFTA itself reflects the same opposing forces. NAFTA does not free trade, but it certainly liberalizes it. Over a fifteen-year period, NAFTA initially reduces and ultimately eliminates all tariffs and most non-tariff barriers between Canada, Mexico, and the United States. Moreover, NAFTA is a GATT-forward agreement; no signatories can increase their tariffs on imports from countries within or outside the free trade area. Although full elimination of tariffs will take fifteen years, about 68 percent of goods imported from Mexico could enter the United States without tariffs as soon as the agreement goes Sierra Club, Friends of the Earth, the Humane Society of the United States, and other environmental groups declares:

Take the Marine Mammal Protection Act. It specifies that yellow fin tuna cannot be imported from countries that violate a US law that limits the number of dolphins killed while catching the tuna. Mexico currently violates this law. But under NAFTA, the manner in which a product is produced (in other words, the way fish are caught) cannot alone prevent their import. Good-bye dolphin protection.

The United States in 1990 outlawed Mexican tuna to protest fishing practices that had resulted in thousands of dolphin deaths. Nearly four years later the US embargo continues—despite the fact that Mexican dolphin kills today are negligible. That Mexico, the world's fourth largest tuna producer, could respond so dramatically to US environmental concerns and still fail to break down an environmentally inspired trade barrier has prompted many policymakers to question whether the tuna—dolphin issue has shifted from a US policy of protecting global resources to one aimed at protecting a domestic tuna industry' into effect. At the same time, 50 percent of US exports to Mexico are now tariff-free. Other, less obvious merchandise trade barriers also were removed. In the traditional in-bond, or *maquiladora*, industries' performance (export) requirements [8] and restrictions on domestic sales evaporated when the agreement went into effect. Moreover, NAFTA addresses much more than merchandise trade. In a tri-national context, the agreement realizes the United States' long-held goals of liberalizing trade in services and foreign investment rules abroad, and it tightens the protection of intellectual property. It is important to note that, in this context, NAFTA represents an achievement the United States has had more difficulty realizing in a broader multilateral context. [9]

Although NAFTA opens Canada and the United States, it accomplishes its most significant liberalizations in Mexico. NAFTA expands Canadian and US companies' ability to establish or purchase a business in Mexico and facilitates their ability to sell out if they want to leave. NAFTA also loosens previous restrictions on expanding operations for such companies, and it removes restrictions on profit remittances to foreign countries. Local content requirements are eliminated, although NAFTA wide content rules will exist. Through NAFTA, Mexico extends temporary work permits to service providers from Canada and the United States and removes licensing and performance criteria.

Despite much liberalization, however, NAFTA initially retains protectionist elements, some of which persist indefinitely. NAFTA protects sensitive sectors-such as agriculture, minerals, banking, textiles, and apparel-by stretching out the phase-in time. This protection is temporary. But as the synthesis of liberal and protectionist pressures, NAFTA contains other types of protection that are not only permanent but also raise trade barriers above pre-NAFTA levels. [10] In a number of sectors-notably automobiles, textiles, and apparel-NAFTA imposes North American content rules, some of which appear to increase protectionism. Under the Canada-United States Free Trade Agreement, for example, automobiles could be imported duty-free if they contain at least 50 percent Canadian-US inputs. For auto imports to receive NAFTA benefits, the North American rule is 62.5 percent. For textiles or apparel to qualify for "free" trade under NAFTA, all components-starting with the yarn or fibre-must be made in North America. This NAFTA covenant extends and strengthens the protectionism inherent in the broader, multinational Multi -fibre Agreement. Nevertheless, NAFTA unequivocally liberalizes trade in North America. It is also noteworthy that the agreement offers only minimal opportunities for trade diversion, in which efficient non-NAFTA producers would be squeezed out of trade with NAFTA countries simply because the treaty reduces trade barriers among North American countries only (Primo Braga 1992). However, the increase and permanence of domestic content requirements signals that protectionism has found a place even in the North American Free Trade Agreement.

7.4 Trade-related Effects on the United States

Although the most famous description of NAFTA's ultimate effect is the "sucking sound" of jobs going to Mexico, more serious attempts to gauge the effects of NAFTA exist. [11] These studies do not all take the same approach, and their results vary considerably. Some studies involve static models.

A few are dynamic. Some accommodate capital flows, but most do not. Others are historically based. However, the majority involve computable general equilibrium (CGE) models, are highly disaggregated, and find positive but small welfare and output effects for the United States. [12] After all, Mexico begins NAFTA as a small market relative to Canada, and the United States has already signed a free trade agreement with Canada.

Most CGE models assume either rigid wages and flexible employment, or flexible wages and full employment. The rigid wage models typically find small percentage gains in employment, while the flexible wage models find gains in wages. Both types, of course, show similar income gains. In a model that a little more fully accommodated characteristics of the real world-with somewhat flexible wages and less than full employment-the effect of NAFTA will probably include less employment growth than the rigid wage models, less wage growth than the full employment models, and about the same income growth as either. Static CGE models without capital flows typically show the smallest effects, regardless of NAFTA country. [13] Some static CGE models incorporate increasing returns to scale. As output grows, income grows even more. Even these show only small percentage gains in real income, real wages, and employment. The empirical importance of scale effects, as opposed to pure improvements in efficiency from greater competition, remains small (Tybout and Westbrook 1993 and Backus, Kehoe, and Kehoe 1991). Dynamic models portend larger effects on growth, especially for Mexico (Young and Romero 1991).

Two other branches of the literature are less consistently sanguine about the effects of NAFTA for the United States. The first branch, whose foremost representative is Leamer (1991), offers arguments based upon factor price equalization through trade and migration. These arguments are consistent 14 Exceptions include silk and flax (Barry and Siwicki 1993, 138) with the Stolper–Samuelson theorem that opening trade will decrease low-skilled wages in the United States because Mexican exports are intensive in low-skilled labour. However, Hinojosa-Ojeda and Robinson (1992) argue that the relative sizes of the U.S. and Mexican economies and NAFTA's long phase-in period mean the Stolper–Samuelson effect will be small; it would be swamped by the other, growth-enhancing effects of the agreement. A second branch of the literature regards NAFTA from an historical point of view. Although some of this literature (Hufbauer and Schott 1992; Weintraub 1991) offers conclusions consistent with those of the CGE models, a series of briefing papers from the Economic Policy Institute (EPI) does not. These papers derive historical parallels, abstracting from individual industry experiences, to hypothesize about the US macro-economy. Their narratives typically assume, for example, that what has happened in the automobile industry is an accurate guide to what will happen in the US macro-economy. For the Economic Policy Institute, the results of NAFTA for the United States are negative.

An interesting artefact of the EPI papers is their argument that "free trade" over the last fifteen years has, despite US employment growth during that time, been a principal cause of the movement of jobs to other countries. In fact, there is evidence to suggest that US policy has been increasingly protectionist over this period, although the Economic Policy Institute authors may view the increase as too small to budge the United States from free trade. However, the authors do not discuss the empirical evidence presented by Gruben (1990a and 1990b) and Truett and Truett (1993) that jobs that went to Mexico during this period would otherwise have gone to Asia. The Economic Policy Institute authors not only dismiss the United States' increases in employment and declining unemployment rates during this period, but they do not deal with the claim that jobs move to other sectors in an economy rather than to other countries.

Nevertheless, arguments that picture massive movement of jobs to Mexico seemed to carry weight even after NAFTA passed. Moreover, the idea that foreign countries are taking jobs to which Americans are entitled continues to be a focal point of the larger US protectionist movement.

7.4.1 Sectoral Effects: If most studies of the impacts of NAFTA suggest overall expansion for the United States, why did protectionists turn so much of their energy against the agreement? In a broad sense, the answer is that the opening of trade shifts resources and production from less competitive to more competitive sectors, inspiring renewed political efforts from the less competitive. According to traditional Hecksher–Ohlin–Samuelson analysis, the sectors that will prove most competitive (and therefore gain most from trade) will use the nation's relatively more abundant factors of production relatively intensely. Compared with most other countries, and certainly with Mexico, the United States has a relative abundance of physical capital (plants and equipment) and human capital (an educated work force). Industries that require relatively low-skilled labour or low levels of physical capital to make tradable products will find much to dislike about NAFTA unless they can establish operations abroad.

Nevertheless, displacement of workers across sectors of the U.S. economy will likely be small in both absolute and relative terms, because the sizes of the economies and work forces of Mexico and Canada are small compared with those of the United States. Most studies suggest that US sectors that lose include sugar refining, fruits and vegetables, apparel, and household appliances. Sectors that gain include chemicals, instruments, machinery and equipment, motor vehicles, instruments, and rubber and plastic. Neither the output and employment gains of the winners nor the losses of the losers appear to be large, according to most models, but losers appear to find cold comfort in such estimates. Finally, an important reason reactive anti-liberalization lobbying is typically strong-regardless of the nature and benefits of the particular trade initiative-is that it is easier for those who are likely to lose their jobs to know they are likely to lose them than for those who may gain jobs to know they would be the ones to gain them. After all, even if new jobs are created, someone else might get them.

7.4.2 Services: As technological advances have increased opportunities for US trade in services, the United States has intensified efforts to negotiate openings for it. Services trade negotiations demand a different focus from goods trade negotiations because service trade protectionism differs from goods trade protectionism. Domestic services providers cannot be protected by tariffs and quotas. Imports of services are not easily detected by customs officers at international borders.

Instead, services trade protectionism emphasizes laws that focus not on the product, but on the producer. Some countries outlaw foreign owned service companies of various types and prohibit foreigners from acquiring controlling ownership in existing domestic companies. Some bestow monopolies on particular domestically owned producers. Some regulate foreign-owned companies differently than domestically owned firms of the same type. As a final complicating factor, one country's regulations for its service firms will typically differ substantially from another country's regulations for its service firms. The ideal solution is to harmonize regulations. In many cases, NAFTA's services openings reflect less protectionism than the clauses for goods trade. NAFTA does not create full harmonization, but it moves in that direction and it particularly opens Mexico. NAFTA provides for national treatment, which means that a US firm in Mexico is supposed to be treated regulatorily as if it were a Mexican firm. National treatment under NAFTA is not de jure, but de facto. That is, foreign firms may still face different regulatory treatment than domestic firms, as long as the effect of the regulations is equivalent and does not place foreign firms at a competitive disadvantage.

The services that received the most attention in the NAFTA negotiations were finance, insurance, transportation, and telecommunications. NAFTA does not change requirements for foreign banks' entry into the United States and Canada, but the opening of the Mexican financial system is among the agreement's most significant achievements. Because the standards for entry are tied to the size of the Mexican banking system, they will change over time. But in the context of the size of the Mexican banking system at the end of 1992, entry into Mexican banking by Canadian or US firms would require the commitment of reserves and paid-up capital of between US$ 20 million and US$ 60 million. Requirements will likely go up, not down, in the future. Although this means US banks may be slow to move into Mexico, their presence there will grow over time. Requirements for entry into brokerage, bonding, insurance, leasing, and warehousing are more liberal. One would expect more initial entry by US specialists in these areas.

Transportation services on both sides of the border stand to gain under NAFTA, especially in trucking. Eighty-two percent of freight in Mexico is moved by road (USITC 1991, 4–48). Mexican exports of trucking services to the United States will likely increase if border and inland infrastructure improvements continue to take place in Mexico. The longer term implications of NAFTA include increases in US trucking services as well, but NAFTA will have only a marginal effect on other transport services. Other transport services will be affected only marginally by NAFTA (USITC 1991, 4–48). Clearly, trade in goods is transport service intensive and infrastructure development on both sides of the border will be needed.

Trade in telecommunications and related goods trade received a large boost from the privatization of Telefonos Mexicanos (TELMEX) in 1991. Basic telephone services are the main service traded between the United States and Mexico, with the United States being a net importer of these services. NAFTA should shift the balance of trade in favour of the United States in the basic services especially in related equipment, as the investment in this sector increases over the coming years.

7.4.3 Intellectual Property Rights Protection: Because of the importance of intellectual property protection in facilitating services trade and foreign investment, NAFTA's coverage of this topic has received much notice. Moreover, it has been argued that the provisions on patent and trade secrets offer the highest standards of protection achieved in any trade negotiations (USITC 1993, 3-7).

One of the most significant provisions of this section, and in NAFTA in general, is the codification of national treatment. This codification ensures that the intellectual property of firms from any two NAFTA countries will be legally treated in the third as if it had been developed in that country. A second important general provision is the strict limitation on the use of compulsory patent licenses, which has affected Canada's process for patenting pharmaceutical patents. A third important detail obligates the signatory countries to enforce intellectual property rights against infringement not only internally but also at the border. That is, NAFTA includes sanctions not only against the production of pirated products, but against their importation.

Despite these and other provisions, including those for judicial procedures to ensure enforcement, Canada, Mexico and the United States all offered strong intellectual property protection before NAFTA was signed. Indeed, NAFTA implies few significant changes in US intellectual property laws and will not much change Mexican patent law, which was upgraded in 1991 to a level consistent with those of major industrial countries. One of the most important aspects of intellectual property protection in NAFTA is that it helps ensure the durability of Mexico's new intellectual property law. Still, differences between the Mexican, Canadian, and US legal systems offer opportunities for complications.

Under Mexican law, precedent does not automatically control the implementation of law. Protection in most cases is extended to a firm or individual only if that party successfully litigates the issue. The costs of gaining effective protection are accordingly high. Under NAFTA, the effects of such divergences in legal systems may be reduced, but there is clearly much to suggest that NAFTA's service-related clauses do not constitute harmonization.

7.4.4 Migration: From the United States' point of view, a raison d'être of NAFTA is the hope that it will ease pressures on migration from Mexico to the United States. Because trade openings tend to equalize real wages across countries (factor price equalization), the argument goes, incentives for cross border migration would decline. Results reported by the United States International Trade Commission (1991) from partial equilibrium models show such convergence, most of it from an increase in Mexican wages. Hinojosa-Ojeda and McCleery (1990) model migration, trade, and capital flows with dual labour markets (high wage and low wage) in both the United States and Mexico, and add a maquiladora sector. According to their results, NAFTA would decrease migration because wages would rise more in Mexico than in the United States. The picture clouds when one incorporates Mexico's large and inefficient *ejido* (or collective farm) system, as do Levy and Van Wijnbergen (1992) and Hinojosa-Ojeda and Robinson (1991).

Under NAFTA, US exports of maize and soybeans could not only offer competition to the ejidos but could accordingly induce worker dislocation in this system. The result could involve increases in migration to the United States.

The Mexican government's recent restructuring of the ejido system, to facilitate infrastructure and capital goods investment through partnership or leasing agreements with business organizations, may allow more competitive operations. However, these same steps may induce some ejido farmers . Mexico, however, must amend its law to reverse the burden of proving infringement of process patents, placing the burden on the accused infringer to take their money and leave, even if the extra income might also motivate them to remain in

Mexico instead of migrating to the United States. The long phase-in period of NAFTA for agricultural products typical of the ejidos, however, gives the farmers more time to make their deals and their decisions before competition intensifies, which will smooth and slow the transition.

7.5 Beyond NAFTA

In the parallel agreements and even in NAFTA itself, the United States has pushed its agenda in directions that blur the demarcation between trade issues and public policy actions that only indirectly affect trade. In some contexts, it is easy to see why this blurring could occur. For example, if a country's zealous health standards on food imports could be seen as impediments to trade, why not differences in environmental protection and workplace standards?

Workplace conditions and environmental protection have been pushed to the forefront of the NAFTA debate. During the vote on fast-track status, President Bush committed to trilateral side or parallel negotiations on the harmonization of environmental policies, labour laws, and worker retraining or other adjustment assistance. Upon assuming office, President Clinton voiced his support for NAFTA with the caveat that the side agreements be completed before the treaty would be submitted to Congress for ratification.

7.5.1 Environmental Concerns: All three NAFTA countries consider environmental problems to be important policy issues. Mexico's pollution problems, especially those in Mexico City and along the border, have become acute. In the NAFTA negotiations, a principal environmental concern has been that loose regulations constitute an unfair trade advantage. The question, then, is what are the likely environmental effects of NAFTA?

Two common fears about NAFTA are that the consequent economic growth in all three countries, but especially Mexico, will cause more pollution and that Mexico will be a haven for polluting US manufacturers. Plausible as conjectures, these issues seem less compelling in light of recent research and current Mexican policy efforts. Grossman and Krueger (1991) statistically model the interaction of trade, growth, and pollution in a cross-section of countries. They show that, when per capita income in a country is very low, higher output (and therefore income) generates higher pollution. But beyond a per capita income of US$ 5,000, pollution control becomes a normal good. Further increases in income cause pollution to fall. Since Mexico's per capita income in 1988 was almost exactly US$ 5,000, Grossman and Krueger's results suggest that the increased growth in Mexico due to NAFTA will improve Mexico's environment.

The evidence likewise suggests that laxer environmental regulation was not significant in motivating U.S. firms to relocate in Mexico. Environmental abatement costs in the United States are low, averaging between 1 percent to 2.5 percent of total production costs (Grossman and Krueger 1991, and Cropper and Oates 1992).

Moreover, firms that relocated typically had lower abatement costs in the United States before moving than those that did not relocate (Grossman and Krueger 1991, 27). This correlation may be spurious. But if one considers that heavy industry typically both pollutes more and requires higher job skills than light industry, and that firms that move to Mexico go there for lower-skilled workers, this result seems less implausible.

Nevertheless, some US firms have indeed moved to Mexico because of stepped-up environmental regulation in the United States. Some California furniture companies, for example, moved operations to Mexico after California tightened regulations on paint coatings and solvents (Grossman and Krueger 1991, 22). However, the number was small relative to the total number of furniture producers in the state of California, let alone in the rest of the United States.

Some of the environmental concern stems from two inaccurate assumptions. The first is that Mexico continues to be lax in environmental regulation; the second is that NAFTA does not address environmental issues. The first assumption ignores improvements in Mexican policy over the last decade. Under the Salinas administration, the budget for the Mexican environmental authority (SEDESOL) grew from US$ 4 million in 1989 to about US$ 68 million in 1992 (Hufbauer and Schott 1993, 92). In 1993, Mexican government expenditures on environmental protection approached 1 percent of gross domestic product. The powers of Mexico's environmental authority have been expanded significantly since its creation, and the government is preparing market-based environmental reforms such as auctioning pollution rights. Moreover, the Mexican government has lately closed a number of polluting factories, most notably PEMEX's Azcapotzalco refinery in Mexico City.

But not all environmental concerns are mistaken. Geographically, an important environmental issue is the U.S-Mexico border, and with good reason. Environmental damage there is significant. Raw sewage and water problems date at least to the 1950s. With the development of the border's maquiladora plants, beginning in the 1960s, dumping of toxic chemicals has aggravated the dangers.

However, the United States and Mexico have already entered into side agreements for the border. The most comprehensive is the so-called Mexican-U.S. Integrated Border Protection Plan, for which the United States has pledged US$ 379 million and Mexico has pledged US$ 466 million (Globerman 1993, 296–97). Some find the effort lacking, but the program is an important step. NAFTA does address the environment directly.

Signatories must commit to a half-dozen additional international environmental agreements, and each country agrees not to lower existing environmental protection, or health and safety standards, to attract investment. Individual countries may maintain stricter standards than NAFTA requires.

However, some of NAFTA's significant environmental components are not in NAFTA proper but in the parallel agreements. Under the dispute settlement mechanism outlined in the parallel agreement on the environment, individuals or groups in one country can file complaints about environmental abuses in another, and representatives from each of the disputing countries will be chosen and will attempt to negotiate a settlement. If this fails, the complaint goes to a panel of experts for adjudication. A country that receives an unfavourable ruling has sixty days to enforce it. If the country fails to enforce, it may incur up to a $20 million fine. If the government of the country fails to pay, the complaining country may level tariffs against the products of the offending industry.

It should be noted that NAFTA-related agreements differ from most trade pacts in that disputes in the latter are almost always required to involve directly trade-related issues. By contrast, according to the office of the US Trade Representative, [14] "any environmental or natural resource issue may be addressed" by NAFTA's environmental commission. The parallel agreement offers more than the usual scope of international adjudication opportunities to those concerned about environmental abuses.

7.5.2 Workplace Conditions: US labour organizations typically express concerns that Mexico's workplace regulations—including those related to safety and health, child labour, benefits, and hours of work—will send US firms over the border. However, Mexico's workplace regulations are strong and, in some cases, tighter than those in the United States. Mexican law establishes 14 as the minimum working age. Persons ages 14 through 16 may not work more than six hours per day and are prohibited from working in occupations designated as hazardous. Minors may not work more than a forty-eight-hour week (Weintraub 1993a, 28–29). Mexican regulations on maternity leave, sick leave, and profit sharing are more generous to workers than those of the United States.

Nevertheless, legitimate concerns about enforcement remain. It is these concerns that inspired the parallel negotiations and agreement on labour. The labour commission, which serves as the review body for the parallel agreement, has a broad mandate that covers worker benefits, industrial relations, and occupational health and safety. In NAFTA's labour-related dispute settlement framework, the form of litigation itself offers particularly strong opportunities for protectionist pressures. For example, the dispute settlement process will operate under the influence of a joint advisory committee, along with evaluation committees of experts made up of representatives from labour-supported organizations. This commission is supposed to provide expert advice on regulatory matters and will have a high degree of access to commission proceedings.

7.5.3 Adjustment Assistance and Retraining: Programs that assist and smooth relocation of displaced workers are fully consistent with the application of the theory of economic welfare to trade policy. But the creation of such programs does not depend on a trade agreement between the United States and other nations. However, not only will fiscal budgetary problems make such programs difficult to pass in the future, but similar promises of adjustment assistance were made during the 1980s but not honoured. Conroy and Glasmeier (1992-93) argue that current policies are inadequately designed and constructed to account for the dislocations that NAFTA will bring. They suggest that the European Economic Community's approaches to funding special adjustment programs be followed. It has been concurred that worker dislocations deserve attention.

However, Sala-i-Martin and Sachs (1991) observe that the United States, at least, ensures regions against income shocks. They show that a US$ 1 reduction in a US region's per capita personal income triggers a 34 cent decrease in federal taxes and a 6 cent increase in federal transfers. In the EEC, they note, the comparable tax reduction is only about half a cent.

They argue that "the current European tax system has a long way to go before it reaches the 34 cents of the US federal government."

7.6 Whither NAFTA?

NAFTA and the parallel negotiations have been described as a move toward greater economic integration, and many of their traits are consistent with it. They offer a framework for harmonizing much more than just directly trade related rules and regulation. But in the context of recent US trade history, they may also be seen as part of a dialectical progression in which shifting protectionist and free trade interests compete to synthesize a new trade policy. US manufacturers' protectionist lobbying diminishes, as labour union pressures increase. Seeking new allies to replace some once-protectionist industrialists, labour organizations associate themselves with environmentalists. Meanwhile, some US manufacturers profess to find new forms of unfairness among their competitors abroad and so do some agriculturalists. In Mexico, policy innovations and new inter industry and inter-group conflicts materialize.

As a result of these conflicting and changing pressures, NAFTA liberalizes trade on some fronts, particularly in services, and increases protectionism on others, as in the rules for increased domestic content in autos and textiles.

Despite NAFTA's soft spots, the agreement offers an important opportunity not only to increase trade in North America, but to signal US commitment to free trade in general-and to free trade in particular with respect to intellectual property rights protection, trade in services, and trade-related aspects of foreign investment.

However, in NAFTA such increased integration as occurs is largely a side effect of a dialectic that continues. At the same time the Clinton administration pushed to open the United States to freer trade with Mexico and Canada, it entered into new agreements with Mexico to restrict the effects of openings in some types of agriculturally related trade, including sugar and fruit juice. Meanwhile, while NAFTA opens trade, NAFTA related agreements open broader opportunities for protectionists to reduce trade through appeals against environmental and workplace enforcement in areas with little direct effect on the international exchange of goods and services. NAFTA opens trade, but the dialectic goes on.

Notes

1. We use the term Hegelian dialectic, in the context of trade policy, to signify the process by which innovations in trade liberalization are countered by innovations in protectionism and are succeeded by some synthesis that is temporarily acceptable to each of the two competing sides, followed by yet another innovation in liberalization, countered by yet another innovation in protectionism, followed by yet another synthesis, and so on. It should be noted that Kane (1988) poses the evolution of financial regulation in the same way, while Gruben (1992) describes NAFTA as a game that leads to a dialectical progression.
2. The MFN clause requires a member nation that lowers tariffs on specific products from a given country to lower them to all nations. However, less developed countries receive "special and differential treatment" that exempts them from certain aspects of the MFN in the interests of economic development. In supporting the unconditional interpretation of the MFN, the United States persistently has contested the policy of special and differential treatment.
3. The GSP allows virtually duty-free entry of designated products from designated developing countries (the LDCs) into the United States and other developed nations.
4. Latin America's debt-led commercial policies, which mixed export incentives with import restrictions, did help Latin America begin to generate balance-of-trade surpluses from 1983 on. Even so, the region's external debt continued to mount. That is, the regional surplus in the balance of goods and non-factor services remained too small to offset the deficit in the factor services balance (interest, profits, and dividends) (Primo Braga 1990).

5. It is important to note that the United States continued its program of aggressive reciprocity even after Latin American countries began to lower their trade barriers in the broad-based liberalization efforts of the late 1980s and early 1990s. This pattern is one of many that raise questions as to how many of the United States' announced efforts on behalf of free trade are really acts of disguised protectionism.
6. Between 1970–75 and 1980–85, U.S. countervailing actions went up by more than 1,000 percent (Nam 1987).
7. As an example, in an attempt to secure votes sufficient to ratify NAFTA, the Clinton administration entered into NAFTA related agreements that were not part of NAFTA in order to re-erect barriers in orange juice trade that NAFTA would have lowered.
8. For example, before NAFTA, U.S. automobile manufacturing subsidiaries in Mexico had to export at least two units of value added for every unit imported. NAFTA eliminates such requirements.
9. At the 1982 GATT ministerial meetings, the United States attempted to launch a new round of negotiations focused on these issues but was defeated. These same issues have been addressed at the subsequent Uruguay Round but, from the perspective of U.S. goals, with limited success.
10. See Morici (1993), Johnson (1993), Barry and Siwicki (1993), and USITC (1993).
11. Space precludes a systematic treatment of these studies, but more comprehensive overviews than what we offer can be found in Lustig et al. (1992) and Globerman and Walker (1993).
12. These include Hinojosa-Ojeda and Robinson (1991), Hinojosa-Ojeda and McCleery (1990), KMPG Peat Marwick (1991), Brown, Deardorff, and Stern (1991a and 1991b), and USITC (1991). See Brown (1992) for a survey.
13. See Brown (1992, 35–37), Hinojosa-Ojeda and Robinson (1991 and 1992), Hinojosa-Ojeda and McLeery (1990), and Roland-Holst, Reinert, and Shiells (1992).
14. This quotation appears in Sheehan (1993).

References

Backus, David K., Patrick J. Kehoe, and Timothy J. Kehoe (1991), "In Search of Scale Effects in Trade and Growth," Federal Reserve Bank of Minneapolis Research Department Working

Paper no. 451, February.

Ballew, Paul, and Robert Schnorbus (1992), "NAFTA and the Auto Industry: Boon or Bane?" Federal Reserve Bank of Chicago, *Chicago Fed Letter*, no. 64, December.

Barry, Eric, and Elizabeth Siwicki (1993), "NAFTA: The Textile and Apparel Sector," in *Assessing NAFTA: A Trinational Analysis,* ed. Steven Globerman and Michael Walker (Vancouver: The Fraser Institute).

Bayoumi, Tamar, and Barry Eichengreen (1992), "Monetary and Exchange Rate Arrangements for NAFTA," mimeo, University of California at Berkeley.

Berry, Steven, Vittorio Grilli, and Florencio Lópezde- Silanes (1992), "The Automobile Industry and the Mexico–U.S. Free Trade Agreement," NBER Working Paper Series, no. 4152 (Cambridge, Mass., National Bureau of Economic Research, August).

Bhagwati, Jagdish (1991), *The World Trading System at Risk* (Princeton, N.J.: University of Princeton Press).

——— (1989), "Is Free Trade Passé After All?" *Weltwirtschaftliches Archiv*, vol. 125, no. 1.

Blecker, Robert A., and William E. Spriggs (1992), "Manufacturing Employment in North America: Where the Jobs Have Gone," Briefing Paper, Economic Policy Institute.

Bovard, James (1992), "The United States' Protectionist Antidumping and Countervailing Subsidy Laws," paper presented at "Liberty in the Americas: Free Trade and Beyond," a conference sponsored by the Cato Institute and the Centro de Investigaciones Sobre la Libre Empresa, Mexico City.

Brown, Drusilla K. (1992), "The Impart of a North American Free Trade Area: Applied General Equilibrium Models," in *North American Free Trade: Assessing the Impact*, ed. Nora Lustig,

Barry P. Bosworth, and Robert Z. Lawrence (Washington, D.C.: The Brookings Institution).

———, Alan V. Deardorff, and Robert M. Stern (1991a), "A North American Free Trade Agreement: Analytical Issues and A Computational Assessment," mimeo, University of Michigan, October.

——— (1991b), "Some Estimates of a North American Free Trade Agreement," mimeo, University of Michigan, October.

Chant , John F. (1993): "The Financial Sector in NAFTA: Two Plus

One Equals Restructuring," in *Assessing NAFTA: A Trinational Analysis,* ed. Steven Globerman and Michael Walker (Vancouver: The Fraser Institute).

Conroy, Michael E., and Amy K. Glasmeier (1992– 93), "Unprecedented Disparities, Unparalleled Adjustment Needs: Winners and Losers on the NAFTA 'Fast Track,'" *Journal of Interamerican Studies and World Affairs* Winter, 1–37.

Cropper, Maureen L., and Wallace Oates (1992), "Environmental Economics: A Survey," *Journal of Economic Literature* 30 (June): 675–740.

Faux, Jeff, and Thea Lee (1992), "The Effect of George Bush's NAFTA on American Workers: Ladder Up or Ladder Down?" Briefing Paper, Economic Policy Institute.

Federal Reserve Bank of Dallas (1991), *North American Free Trade: Proceedings from a Conference*, Dallas, June 14.

Gilbreath, Jan (1993), "Fish or Foul?" *Hemisfile*, November/December, 10–11.

Globerman, Steven (1993), "Trade Liberalization and the Environment," in *Assessing NAFTA: A Trinational Analysis,* ed. Steven Globerman and Michael Walker (Vancouver: The Fraser Institute).

Grossman, Gene M., and Alan B. Krueger (1991), "Environmental Impacts of a North American Free Trade Agreement," NBER Working Paper Series, no. 3914 (Cambridge, Mass., National Bureau of Economic Research, November).

Gruben, William C. (1993), "Free Trade, Globalization, and U.S. Labour: What Are the Long Run Dynamics?" in *The North American Free Trade Agreement: Labour, Industry and Government Perspectives*, ed. Mario F. Bognanno and Kathryn J. Ready (Westport, Conn.: Greenwood).

——(1992), "North American Free Trade: Opportunities and Pitfalls," *Contemporary Policy Issues* 10 (October): 1–10.

——(1990a), "Mexican Maquiladora Growth: Does It Cost U.S. Jobs?" Federal Reserve Bank of Dallas *Economic Review*, January, 15–29.

——(1990b), "Do Maquiladoras Take American Jobs? Some Tentative Econometric Results" *Journal of Borderland Studies*, Spring, 31–46.

——, John H. Welch, and Jeffrey W. Gunther (1993), "U.S. Banks, Competition, and the Mexican Banking System: How Much

Will NAFTA Matter?" Federal Reserve Bank of Dallas *Financial Industry Studies*, October.

Grunwald, Joseph (1991), "Opportunity Missed: Mexico and Maquiladoras," *The Brookings Review*, Winter.

Hanson, Gordon (1992a), "External Economies, Vertical Integration, and Trade: Theory and Evidence from Mexico," mimeo, University of Texas at Austin.

——(1992b), "Agglomeration, Dispersion, and the Pioneer Firm: Theory and Evidence from Mexico," mimeo, University of Texas at Austin. Heston, Alan, and Robert Summers (1991), "The Penn World Table (Mark 5): An Expanded Set of International Comparisons," *Quarterly Journal of Economics*, vol. 106, 327–68.

Hinojosa-Ojeda, Raul, and Robert K. McCleery (1990), "U.S.–Mexico Interdependence, Social Pacts, and Policy Alternatives: A Computable General Equilibrium Approach," mimeo, University of California at Berkeley, October.

——, and Sherman Robinson (1992), "Labour Issues in a North American Free Trade Area," in *North American Free Trade: Assessing the Impact,* ed. Nora Lustig, Barry P. Bosworth, and Robert Z. Lawrence (Washington, D.C.: The Brookings Institution).

——, and Sherman Robinson (1991), "Alternative Scenarios of U.S. Mexico Integration: A Computable General Equilibrium Approach," mimeo, University of California at Berkeley, October.

Hirsch, Seev (1989), "Services and Service Intensity in International Trade," *Weltwirtschaftliches, Archiv*, vol. 125, no. 1.

Hufbauer, Gary C., and Jeffrey J. Schott (1992), *North American Free Trade: Issues and Recommendations* (Washington D.C.: Institute for International Economics).

——(1993), *NAFTA: An Assessment* (Washington D.C.: Institute for International Economics).

Johnson, Jon R. (1993), "NAFTA and the Trade in Automotive Goods," in *Assessing NAFTA: A Trinational Analysis,* ed. Steven Globerman and Michael Walker (Vancouver: The Fraser Institute).

Josling, Tim (1993), "NAFTA and Agriculture: A Review of the Economic Impacts," in *North American Free Trade: Assessing the Impact,* ed. Nora Lustig, Barry P. Bosworth, and Robert Z.

Lawrence (Washington, D.C.: The Brookings Institution).

Junco, Alejandro (1991), "The Case for an Internal Mexican Free Trade Agreement," *Wall Street Journal*, March 22.

Kane, Edward (1988), "Interaction of Financial and Regulatory Innovation," *American Economic Review*, May, 328–34.

Kehoe, Timothy (1992),"Assessing the Economic Impact of North American Free Trade," Centre for Economic Research, Department of Economics, University of Minnesota, Discussion Paper no. 265, October.

KMPG Peat Marwick (1991), *The Effects of a Free Trade Agreement Between the U.S. and Mexico: Executive Summary* (Washington, D.C.: The Brookings Institution).

Krugman, Paul (1989),"Is Bilateralism Bad?" NBER Working Paper Series, no. 2972 (Cambridge, Mass.: National Bureau of Economic Research).

Leamer, Edward E. (1992), "Wage Effects of a U.S.–Mexican Free Trade Agreement," NBER Working Paper Series, no. 3991 (Cambridge, Mass.: National Bureau of Economic Research, February).

Levy, Santiago, and Sweder Van Wijnbergen (1992), "Maize and the Free Trade Agreement Between Mexico and the United States," *The World Bank Economic Review* no. 3, 481–502.

López-de-Silanes, Florencio, James R. Markusen, and Thomas F. Rutherford (1992), "The Auto Industry and the North American Free Trade Agreement: Employment, Production, and Welfare Effects," mimeo, Harvard University.

Lustig, Nora (1991), "Bordering on Agreement," discussion paper, The Brookings Institution, February 25.

——, Barry P. Bosworth, and Robert Z. Lawrence (1992), *North American Free Trade: Assessing the Impact* (Washington, D.C.: The Brookings Institution).

Magee, Stephen P. (1990), "The Decline of Lobbying in the U.S. Over Trade Policy, 1950–1986,"mimeo, University of Texas at Austin.

McLeod, Darryl, and John H. Welch (1991), "Free Trade and the Peso," mimeo, Federal Reserve Bank of Dallas.

Mody, Ashoka (1990), "New International Environment for Intellectual Property Rights," in *Intellectual Property Rights in Science, Technology, and Economic Performance: International Comparisons*, ed. Francis W. Rushing and Carole Ganz Brown,

(Boulder, Colo.: Westview Press). 203-39.

Morici, Peter (1993), "NAFTA Rules of Origin and Automotive Content Requirements," in *Assessing NAFTA: A Trinational Analysis,* ed. Steven Globerman and Michael Walker (Vancouver: The Fraser Institute).

Nam, Chong-Hyun (1987), "Export Promoting Subsidies, Countervailing Threats, and the General Agreement on Tariffs and Trade," *The World Bank Economic Review*, September.

Pastor, Robert A. (1992), "NAFTA as the Centre of an Integration Process: The Non-trade Issues," in *North American Free Trade: Assessing the Impact*, ed. Nora

Lustig, Barry P. Bosworth, and Robert Z. Lawrence (Washington, D.C.: The Brookings Institution), 176–98.

Primo Braga, Carlos A. (1992), "NAFTA and the Rest of the World," in *North American Free Trade: Assessing the Impact,* ed. Nora Lustig, Barry P. Bosworth, and Robert Z. Lawrence (Washington, D.C.: The Brookings Institution), 210–34.

——(1991), "The North–South Debate on Intellectual Property Rights," in *Global Rivalry and Intellectual Property: Developing Canadian Strategies* (Ottawa: The Institute for Research on Public Policy).

——(1990), U.S. Policies and Prospects for Latin American Economic Integration," in *United States Policies and the Latin American Economies,* ed. Werner Baer and Donald V. Coes (New York: Praeger).

——(1989), "U.S.–Latin American Trade: Challenges for the 1990s," *Economic Impact*, no. 2.

Primo Braga, Carlos A., Raed Safadi, and Alexander Yeats (1993), "Regional Integration in the Western Hemisphere: 'Deja Vu All Over Again,' " mimeo, The World Bank.

Roland-Holst, David, Kenneth A. Reinert, and Clinton R. Shiells (1992), "North American Free Trade, Liberalization, and the Role of Non-tariff Barriers," mimeo, Mills College, April.

Sali-i-Martin, Xavier, and Jeffrey Sachs (1991), "Fiscal Federalism and Optimum Currency Areas: Evidence for Europe from the United States," NBER Working Paper Series, no. 3855 (Cambridge, Mass.: National Bureau of Economic Research, October).

Sheehan, James M. (1993), "NAFTA—Free Trade in Name Only," *Wall Street Journal*, September 9.

Smith, Russell E. (1990), "United States Policies and the Labour Sector in Latin America," in *United States Policies and the Latin American Economies*, ed. Werner Baer and Donald V. Coes (New York: Praeger).

Smith, Wesley R. (1992), "Protecting the Environment in North America with Free Trade," *The Backgrounder*, no. 889, The Heritage Foundation.

Truett, Lila J., and Dale B. Truett (1993), "Maquiladora Response to U.S. and Asian Relative Wage Rate Changes," *Contemporary Policy Issues* 11 (January): 18–28.

Tybout, James, and M. Daniel Westbrook (1993), "Trade Liberalization and the Dimensions of Efficiency Change in Mexican Manufacturing Industries," Working Paper no. 92–03, Georgetown University.

U.S. International Trade Commission (1993), *Potential Impact on the U.S. Economy and Selected Industries of the North American Free - Trade Agreement*, USITC, January.

——(1991), *Review of Trade and Investment Liberalization by Mexico and Prospects for Future United States Mexican Relations: Phase III*, USITC, February.

——(1990a), *Review of Trade and Investment Liberalization by Mexico and Prospects for Future United States Mexican Relations: Phase I*, USITC, April.

——(1990b), *Review of Trade and Investment Liberalization by Mexico and Prospects for Future United States Mexican Relations: Phase II*, USITC, October.

Weintraub, Sidney (1993a), "The North American Free Trade Agreement as Negotiated: A U.S. Perspective," in *Assessing NAFTA: A Trinational Analysis*, ed. Steven Globerman and Michael Walker (Vancouver: The Fraser Institute).

Welch, John H. (1991), "A Preliminary Survey of Issues Surrounding a U.S.–Mexico Free Trade Agreement," mimeo, Federal Reserve Bank of Dallas, March.

——(1993), "The New Face of Latin America: Financial Flows, Markets, and Institutions in the 1990s," *Journal of Latin American Studies*, vol. 25, 1–24.

Young, Leslie, and José Romero (1991), "A Dynamic Dual Model of the Free Trade Agreement," in Federal Reserve Bank of Dallas.

8

African Economic and Monetary Integration

8.1 Introduction

Monetary and economic integration may evolve from trade links, as well as, historical and cultural ties. The process entails the harmonization of macroeconomic policies, legal frameworks and institutional architectures, towards nominal and real convergence. Other objectives of monetary union include the enlargement and diversification of market size, the promotion of intra-regional trade and the strengthening of member countries' bargaining power in the global economy.

Regional economic cooperation in Africa dates as far back as the beginning of the last century. The cooperation primarily focussed on the facilitation of international trade and payments, as well as infrastructure. In the process of deepening cooperation, African countries have formed a number of regional economic communities with overlapping memberships. However, the presence of these groupings is yet to translate into a substantial increase in trade within the continent. While the share of African countries' exports to other African countries grew from about 4 percent in the 1980s to 12 percent in the first half of the 2000s, this growth is very low compared to other regional groupings outside the continent. More efforts are needed to promote trade within the various regional economic communities.

In addition, there has been very little manufacturing or intra-industry trade, with petroleum, cotton, livestock, maize and cocoa accounting for most of the trade within the continent. Among the prescriptions that policymakers could choose to promote and address the challenges impeding the flow of goods and services within the continent is the creation of a stable macroeconomic environment. This could be achieved if member countries of the RECs commit to follow economic programmes that include the effective management of inflation and public finance stability, so that the actions of investors and entrepreneurs can translate into sustainable economic growth and development. This is why most of the RECs are pursing macroeconomic convergence programmes to support regional integration initiatives, particularly in the area of trade and monetary cooperation.

Africa has had a chequered experience of monetary and financial cooperation, dating back to the pre- and post-colonial eras. This chapter will focus on the current monetary cooperation arrangements being pursued by the African regional economic communities, preceded by a brief historical background of Africa's experience with monetary and financial integration.

8.2 Africa's Experience with Monetary Cooperation

Although the promotion of regional economic integration among African countries dates back to the colonial days, a conscious effort at the continental level was made only in 1991, when a single monetary zone for Africa was for the first time mainstreamed in the Organization of African Unity's Treaty. The *Abuja Treaty* established the African Economic Community and adumbrated stages for the attainment of a single monetary zone for Africa by 2028, monetary cooperation between different countries in Africa has been going on for a long time. During the colonial period, French and British colonies had in place common monetary arrangements. At the time, these arrangements were established to facilitate the administration of the colonies and the collection of seignior age, rather than to promote exchange rate management and fiscal policy.

In the British colonies, the monetary arrangement involved a currency board with the colonial currency pegged to and backed by the pound sterling. However, the British colonial administration received its seignior age revenues through interest earned on investment of the reserves in British Government securities. In the case of the French colonies, the colonial franc was pegged to the French franc and backed by a convertibility guarantee of the French Treasury.

The British and the French monetary cooperation arrangements were not the same. The British currency boards were rooted in English central banking and therefore performed functions similar to those of the Bank of England. The French currency boards in the colonies followed the guidelines and principles of French central banking. Hence, like the Banque de France, the French currency boards lent significantly to the local banking system as the currencies were backed by the French Treasury. During the colonial period, a number of monetary arrangements existed in the Eastern and Southern Africa regions. In East Africa, a common currency area was established in 1919 for Kenya, Uganda and Tanganyika (now Tanzania) with the creation of the East African Currency Board (EACB). Tanganyika joined in 1920 after it became a British territory and the same year EACB was given the responsibility of issuing the legal currency for Kenya, Uganda and Tanganyika. In 1936, Zanzibar joined the common currency area. During the Second World War, the East African shilling was used as legal tender in Somaliland as well as in parts of Ethiopia and Eritrea, and in 1951 Aden was included in the currency area.

As part of its functions, EACB issued the East African shilling as a local currency in exchange for the pound sterling at a fixed rate of 20 shillings per pound sterling. EACB also issued limited loans to participating governments, even though Tanganyika and Uganda did not benefit much from this credit facility. Between 1960 and 1965, important changes took place at EACB. In 1960, the Board's operational centre was moved from London to Nairobi and appointees of the participating countries replaced the members of the Board who had been nominated by the British Government. In the following years, activities of the Board were expanded and modernized. The

Board strengthened its role as a central bank by introducing new policies and methods for credit, banking and other currency operations.

Following the independence of participating countries, the East African monetary arrangement became a subject for consideration. Studies were commissioned to salvage the East African Monetary Union. [1] But the political decision by member countries led to the disintegration of the East African currency system. The Finance Ministers of Kenya, Tanzania and Uganda announced in 1965 that separate currencies and national central banks would be created for each country. Consequently, in 1966/67, the functions of EABC were terminated in all three countries following the issuance of national currencies by Tanzania (in June 1966), Uganda (in August 1966) and Kenya (in September 1966). In 1969, the East African shilling ceased to be legal tender.

A monetary system similar to that of East Africa was established for the Federation of Southern Rhodesia (now Zimbabwe), Northern Rhodesia (now Zambia) and Nyasaland (now Malawi). A Southern Rhodesia Currency Board (SRCB) was established in 1938 by a colonial Act. The functions of SRCB included the following:

- The issuance of local currency in exchange for pound sterling at a fixed rate of one-to-one
- The management of the pound sterling reserves that were placed in a "currency fund" which was invested either in British government securities or held in liquid form in England
- Limited investment in bonds and stocks issued by the three participating governments. A currency board replaced SRCB in 1954. Two years later in 1956, the Bank of Rhodesia and Nyasaland was created by the federal parliament. It played the role of a central bank by:
- Regulating the monetary system of the federation
- Exercising the sole right to issue notes and coins
- Exchanging local currency to pound sterling at a fixed rate

of one to one

- Maintaining 25 percent in gold as a means of safeguarding the external value of the local currency
- Fixing the minimum cash reserve, liquidity ratios and rate of discount/rediscount as a means of controlling bank credit expansion.

The Federation of Rhodesia and Nyasaland dissolved in 1963 and was followed by the closure of the Bank of Rhodesia in 1964. The assets and liabilities of the Bank were distributed among the central banks of the three countries. As in the case of the EAC, the Federation failed for political and economic reasons. Member countries felt that there was unequal distribution of benefits from the federal arrangement. Southern Rhodesia was considered to be deriving more fiscal, industrial and commercial gains to the detriment of Northern Rhodesia and Nyasaland, which were relatively underdeveloped and did not make as much use of the monetary system and its facility. This led to the decision by the three governments to create their own central banks that would enable them to exercise their autonomy on monetary and fiscal matters.

South Africa, Basutoland (Lesotho), Bechuanaland (Botswana) and Swaziland had their own currencies during colonial time. But after 1881, the pound sterling became the standard currency in these countries and remained in use until 1961. The Reserve Bank of South Africa was established in 1921. It started issuing its own currency (the South African pound) in 1923, which was accepted as legal tender in the other countries. There was no exchange control in these countries. In 1961, the rand was introduced as the currency of South Africa and was used in Lesotho and Swaziland under a customs union agreement.

In 1974, the Rand Monetary Agreement (RMA) was signed and the rand became the only legal tender in the RMA zone, which included Botswana, Lesotho, South Africa and Swaziland. However, Botswana pulled out from RMA in 1975. Lesotho and Swaziland – which became independent in 1966 and 1968, respectively, felt that the RMA deprived them of instruments of monetary control. This feeling became more compelling in 1985 when the rand was faced with severe depreciation vis-à-vis major currencies. Consequently, the RMA was amended in 1986, giving Lesotho and Swaziland more autonomy.

8.2.1 Monetary Cooperation after Independence: Most of the British colonies abandoned monetary cooperation when they gained their independence. Some of the French colonies continued to maintain the colonial system of monetary cooperation after independence. These are the monetary unions in West and Central Africa. The franc-based currencies in these unions have only been devalued once against the French franc (by 50 percent in January 1994). Post-independence saw most of the African countries setting up their own central banks which issued national currencies in large part to assert the sovereignty of the countries after independence. This meant that the currency board arrangements that were put in place during the colonial era were abolished and replaced with national central banks. It must be noted that in West Africa, Sierra Leone and the Gambia continued to operate their own currency board-type arrangements for a few more years after independence until 1971 when Gambia left the sterling peg. The East African Currency Board, which covered Tanzania, Uganda and Kenya, also retained its common currency until 1966 when it was replaced with sovereign currencies because of fiscal imbalance and dissatisfaction with the distribution of benefits within the East African Community.

It must be noted that the franc-based currency unions or the currency boards that operated in Africa appear to be very different from the arrangements of the European Monetary Union system. Both the currency boards and monetary unions operated on a fixed peg, which is different from the floating exchange rate of the euro. A notable exception is the South African rand zone, where Lesotho, Namibia, Swaziland and, for a time, Botswana have their currencies pegged at par with the South African rand. Under this arrangement, the member countries of the zone allow the rand to circulate alongside their currencies and receive a payment in lieu of seignior age. The sharing of seignior age and the flexibility of the peg vis-à-vis the outside world makes the rand zone very similar to the euro zone.

8.2.2 Challenges of Monetary Policies in Post-Independence Africa: With the abandonment of currency boards and the creation of sovereign central banks, the conduct of monetary policy varied from one independent African country to another. Most of the policies followed in post-independent Africa were weak, with a few exceptions. Honohan and O'Connell (1997) indicate that post-independence monetary policy in Africa took sharply different routes in different countries. Some countries pursued policies that rationed and controlled goods and services, while others embarked on massive government expenditure at the expense of uncontrollable inflation. Chamley and Honohan (1993) show that, by and large, the increased government expenditure was financed either through financial repression or through inflation quasi-tax. The negative consequence of financial repression and high inflation was felt in the 1980s, and to rectify the appalling situation, African governments, on the advice of the Bretton Woods institutions, removed the controls and reduced central bank financed government expenditures. These moves were meant to institute a market oriented monetary policy.

Hanohan and Lane (2000) point out that market-oriented central banking did not last for long as African governments relied on the monetary system for resources. These governments borrowed heavily from the banking system, resulting in high nominal interest rates and persistent and substantial excess returns.

8.2.3 Challenges of the CFA Zone: Although the franc-based monetary unions were established in West and Central Africa for political expediency, they are built on a solid institutional foundation. Hanohan and Lane argue that the underlying economic philosophy of the franc zone was based on open and competitive market principles. The multinational central banks governing the zone are independent of the member countries and have stringent rules for monetary financing of fiscal deficits. Consequently, the inflation rates in the zone are the lowest in Africa. In addition, the zone has open and liberalized capital accounts and encourages the operations of foreign-owned banks.

Despite the sound framework of single currency, freedom of capital movements and multinational central banks, the CFA zone suffered severe crises in the 1980s. Before the mid-1980s, the franc zone countries enjoyed solid economic performance. The fixed exchange rate with France reduced any macroeconomic uncertainty and encouraged external investment. The growth rates of the economies in the zone were high and CFA franc notes were used by trans-boundary traders in preference to unstable and inconvertible local currencies in neighbouring countries such as Ghana and Nigeria. The banking system of the zone functioned better than those of neighbouring countries and consequently attracted significant deposits of flight capital from those countries.

However, economic prosperity of the zone did not last forever. In the mid-1980s, the banking system in the zone collapsed due in part to the rigidities of its institutional mechanisms. Political pressures from governments forced the banks to lend to state-owned enterprises, regional and political groupings, governments' own suppliers. Consequently, in the early 1990s, almost all of the economies in the zone went into deep recession. At the same time, parallel markets in the zone opened up as capital movements were blocked and international payments had become extremely difficult. Furthermore, a majority of the banks failed and depositors of the remaining banks had difficulty accessing their funds for years. Banks that continued to exist started to discriminate against their deposit and lending customers.

The environment also provided limited operations of inter-bank markets. The central banks also faced difficulties in covering their operating expenses, because of the loans they had made to the failed banks. Hence, the CFA came under heavy pressure, leading market participants to anticipate a devaluation of the currency. The part played by the banks in the crises cannot be overlooked. Most of the banks operating at the time were jointly owned by the national governments and one of four major French-based banks, with key senior management being French nationals seconded from the parent banks in France. Hanohan and Lane (2000) argue that the objective of the French shareholders of the banks was nothing more than profit maximization. They were more concerned about protecting the commercial interests of their French customers in Africa.

Although the banks were supposed to be autonomous, the structure of the ownership and control by government functionaries made it easier for commercially doubtful lending to take place. Furthermore, the banks were not constrained by loanable resources. Despite the difficulties in mobilizing deposits, they were able to lend through the funds secured from the two regional central banks. Although the central banks were restricted from lending to governments, they were free to refinance loans through the banking system, effectively providing the banks with loanable resources. The interest of the central banks to preserve the quality of their own balance sheets (in order to ensure adequate revenue to meet their substantial operational expenses) was not sufficient to limit their lending to the banks. The statutory arrangements were understood by parties to provide the central bank with a government guarantee for lending to banks. Although independent, the central banks acted as the agents of the fiscal authorities, refinancing politically directed or government-inspired bank loans that could never be repaid.

The challenges of monetary policy in the CFA zone clearly demonstrate that rule based monetary and banking arrangements do not guarantee sound monetary policy. The rules in the franc zone at the time appeared very rigid and perhaps induced banking practices that violated sound banking principles. However, Hanohan and Lane (2000) suggest that three rules were in place to guarantee favourable outcomes and appeared to immunize the zone against the consequences of mistaken policies in other areas.

First, the exchange rate rule was used as a tool for macroeconomic stability. However, the rule could not cope with the pro-cyclical public sector wage policy and the policy of raising official purchasing prices of cash crops, particularly coffee and cocoa. This made labour in the formal sector uncompetitive, and the crop credits provided by the banks for the purchasing of crops at unrealistic prices were not being repaid. The inability of the banking system to find a satisfactory mechanism to fund merchants' working capital also contributed to the failure of the system.

Second, the rule that the banking sector could not lend to the government more than a fraction of its annual revenue needs acted as a safeguard against inflationary pressures. However, the rule was circumvented by indirect borrowing through public enterprises and other associated bodies and through the payment of government arrears to its suppliers. The consequence was an increasing degree of illiquidity in the system as payments discipline collapsed.

Third, the rule that each national government was responsible for the debts of any insolvent bank to the central bank delegated bank regulation to national authorities. While this rule was aimed at preventing central banks from lending to unsound banks, it failed to inspire national responsibility. This led to massive bank insolvency, amounting to at least 10 percent of zone-wide GDP. External shocks and the recession only exacerbated the poor lending decisions and consequent insolvency of the banks.

It should be noted that the franc zone worked very well for two decades and offered protection against macroeconomic instability before the crisis. It was just a few months before the crisis that it was discovered that institutional structures and mechanical rules could not withstand political interference and pressures and the volatility of the external environment. The lessons learned here suggest that there is a strong need to have consistent macroeconomic and financial fundamentals to support a fixed exchange rate system, irrespective of other institutional rules. In other words, mechanical application of automatic rules is no guarantee for a well functioning banking system.

Although the rules governing the franc-zone were put in place to guard against monetary instability, they have not been robust enough to alleviate the impact of fiscal mismanagement. In fact, the exchange rate peg has exacerbated the real economic effects of imprudent fiscal and financial policy. That is why Collier (1991) suggests that institutional arrangements governing regional central banks have to be adequate to guarantee their role as quasi-external "agencies of restraint" on the national governments. Furthermore, it has to be recognized that monetary unions or rules based monetary systems such as currency boards have their limitations and must be applied with caution.

8.2.4 Recovery of the CFA Zone: To deal with the challenges of the French franc crisis, the CFA franc was devalued in 1994. Since then the region has witnessed several years of recovery and comparatively rapid economic growth, as well as lower-than-expected pass-through of imported inflation into domestic consumer price indexes (CPIs). The banking crisis in the CFA franc zone was also addressed by introducing new institutional arrangements in the early 1990s, including the centralization of responsibility for bank supervision in the two regional banking control commissions. This centralization provides a new multinational "agency of restraint" to political pressures and interference.

The pegging of the currencies in the zone to the euro instead of the French franc also provides confidence in the monetary arrangements in the zone as it ensures greater nominal and real exchange rate stability on average vis-à-vis trading partners. Since the peg to the euro, the CFA zone has not faced any significant new challenges. Following the success of EMU and the desire to strengthen the continental integration agenda, most African regional economic communities are pursuing monetary cooperation programmes, in the hope that a common currency would protect African countries from contagious or correlated capital movements and financial crises.

8.3 Monetary Cooperation Arrangements of the Regional Economic Communities

This section begins with a review of the current monetary framework of the regional economic communities, followed by an assessment of their monetary cooperation arrangements, focussing on established macroeconomic convergence criteria. It concludes with an assessment of the challenges and constraints in implementing the convergence criteria.

8.3.1 Monetary Arrangements of Southern African: Development Community (SADC): SADC has designed a framework of macroeconomic convergence targets for its members. However, monetary cooperation amongst them began in 1980 when the Southern African Development Coordinating Conference (SADCC) of nine member countries was formed to pursue common regional development projects, particularly infrastructure projects, so as to minimize the dependence of member States on the apartheid-based South Africa. After the independence of Namibia and South Africa in the early 1990s, SADCC was transformed in 1992 into the Southern Africa Development Community (SADC), with a focus on regional economic integration and development. Membership also grew from nine to fourteen, until Seychelles pulled out more recently. [2]

The strategic goals of SADC, as contained in its *Regional Indicative Strategic Development Plan* (RISDP), are as follows: promoting equitable, self-sustaining economic growth and socio-economic development in the sub region with the view of alleviating poverty; strengthening common cultural, social and political values, as well as maintaining democracy, peace, security and stability; and achieving complementarily and sustainable environmental and resource utilization. Despite the lack of a framework for SADC on macroeconomic convergence, Maruping (2005) indicates that a Memorandum of Understanding (MOU) has been drawn up on the subject. The MOU, which requires the signature of at least two thirds of the membership to become effective, lays down the institutional framework for the monitoring and surveillance mechanisms, macroeconomic indicators and targets, data requirements, and monetary and fiscal policy cooperation parameters for the member countries. The MOU was designed to ensure that member States achieve financial and economic stability, strengthened institutional structures and sound macroeconomic policies.

The drafters of the MOU believe that, without guidance on the targets of macroeconomic variables in the SADC zone, member States would not achieve optimal fiscal balances and would therefore experience high deficits, unsustainably high or rising ratios of public debt to gross domestic product, wide external current account and financial imbalances, and market distortions resulting in high rates of inflation and stifling of growth amongst SADC member countries. Although there is no legal framework on macroeconomic convergence criteria, a Committee of Central Bank Governors of the member States provides guidance on macroeconomic convergence in the SADC region. The committee asks member States to use the following macroeconomic convergence criteria and benchmarks: inflation rate to reach single digit by 2008, 5 percent by 2012 and 3 percent by 2018; ratio of budget deficit to GDP should not exceed 5 percent by 2008, with 3 percent as an anchor, and within a 1 percent band by 2012 through to 2018; and nominal public debt-to-GDP ratio should be less than 60 percent by 2008 and beyond to 2018 (Table 8.1).

Table 8.1: Macroeconomic Convergence Criteria

Criteria	2008	2012	2018
Inflation rate (percent)	Single digit	5 percent	3 percent
Fiscal deficit as percent of GDP	< 5 percent	Between the range of 2 percent and 4 percent anchored at 3 percent	
Government debt as percent of GDP	< 60 percent of GDP	< 60 percent of GDP	

Source: SADC Secretariat

There are several reasons why the SADC Committee of Central Bank Governors is concerned about macroeconomic convergence in the zone. First, SADC is focused on pursuing developmental programmes aimed at promoting sustainable economic growth in the region. In order for the economies in the region to achieve their full potential, an enabling environment that includes sound monetary policy needs to be established. Hence, the central banks have an important role to play in facilitating growth and development in the zone.

Second, SADC is a regional integration area (RIA) made up of countries with unequal economies. The theory of regional integration as an instrument of development, and the experience of RIAs like the European Union, suggest that small economies would eventually converge to the bigger economies when these economies are fully integrated. In other words, regional integration allows lesser-developed member States to "catch up" to the more developed ones.

Third, macroeconomic convergence could be instrumental in driving the process of regional integration. In the EU, macroeconomic convergence is considered important for economic integration and criteria (conditions) have been determined for joining the economic and monetary union. Although monetary integration in SADC is a long-term goal, macroeconomic convergence is an important ingredient for market integration in a RIA.

In addition to various protocols that provide the legal framework for monetary and financial cooperation, SADC tracks progress in harmonization and convergence processes among its member States through the following roadmap and milestones: elimination of exchange rate controls; establishment of a free trade area by 2008; establishment of a customs union by 2010; establishment of a common market by 2012; and establishment of a monetary union by 2016.

There is enormous disparity between the economies of SADC countries, in terms of income levels and distribution; macroeconomic performance, fiscal deficits; public debt-to-GDP ratios; rates of inflation; financial sector development and stability; human resources; and infrastructure development. In addition, there is no strong political commitment to implement and monitor concrete programmes of action to improve the macroeconomic environment in the SADC zone.

Despite the challenges, there are success stories from the Southern African Customs Union (SACU) and Common Monetary Area (CMA), whose members are also in SADC, and where a customs union has been established and de facto monetary integration exists among four of the five members. [3] In recent years, SADC has embarked on programmes that would improve efficiency and effectiveness and macroeconomic policy coordination among its member States. These actions have contributed to sound policies in the SACU member States and Mauritius, with low rates of inflation and convergence of key macroeconomic variables. Post-conflict economies in SADC are also moving rapidly towards lower levels of inflation, with a notable exception being Zimbabwe, which has the highest level of inflation in the SADC zone as well as poor economic performance. Some of the poorer economies in the SADC zone, including the Democratic Republic of Congo and Tanzania, have attained the regional inflation targets. Angola,

Malawi, Mozambique, Zambia and Zimbabwe are yet to achieve single-digit inflation rates, but some of them could do so by 2008 if the current inflation reduction trends are maintained, except for Zimbabwe, which would have to halt and reverse the trend and make much more marked progress in this regard. SACU member States, Tanzania and Mauritius have already achieved the targets ahead of the 2008 schedule.

For other indicators of convergence, the performance is again mixed. The poorer member States have their current fiscal deficit-to-GDP ratio above the target level. These countries tend to be highly donor-dependent and tend to have high fiscal deficits (excluding grants), which would be unsustainable if donor support were not available. The fiscal imbalance is partly the result of expansionary fiscal policies or serious economic crises and delays in the poor economies receiving Highly Indebted Poor Country (HIPC) debt relief. As a result of the poor fiscal imbalance, most of the economies also show weak current account balances as well as high debt-to-GDP ratios. Against the background of the macroeconomic targets set up by SADC, an assessment of the macroeconomic performance of the Members States of the community shows mixed results.

Table 8.2 reports on the growth performance of member States from 2001 to 2005. The table shows that Angola, Botswana, Democratic Republic of Congo, Mozambique and Tanzania have registered strong growth performances in recent years, growing above 6 percent in the last few years. Factors responsible for this strong showing include sound macroeconomic policies; strong world demand for commodities such as diamond (Botswana), oil (Angola) and copper (Democratic Republic of Congo); and relative peace and security (Angola, Democratic Republic of Congo, and Mozambique). The poor-performing economies in the zone are those of Zimbabwe and Seychelles, where growth rates have declined.

Table 8.2: Growth Performance in SADC

Country	2001	2002	2003	2004	2005
Angola	3.14	14.49	3.31	11.18	20.61
Botswana	5.18	5.59	6.32	5.92	6.19
Congo, Dem. Rep.	-2.10	3.50	5.70	6.60	6.50
Lesotho	3.21	3.50	3.09	3.15	1.20
Malawi	-4.97	2.86	6.07	7.12	2.55
Mauritius	5.56	2.71	3.19	4.70	4.57
Mozambique	13.10	8.16	7.90	7.49	7.70
Namibia	2.40	6.67	3.48	5.95	3.50
Seychelles	-2.21	1.30	-6.30	-1.99	-2.30
South Africa	2.74	3.69	2.98	4.47	4.87
Swaziland	1.79	2.90	2.40	2.10	1.80
Tanzania	6.24	7.24	7.12	6.69	6.97
Zambia	4.89	3.30	5.12	5.41	5.20
Zimbabwe	-2.70	-4.40	-2.40	-3.80	-6.50
SADC	2.59	4.39	10.86	4.64	4.49

Source: UNECA and World Development Indicators.

Like most developing countries of the world, SADC region is also plagued by bouts of inflation which cause considerable hardships to the population at large. Price stability, therefore, is at the heart of economic policies.

Table 8.3 clearly shows that inflation in the SADC region remains very high, averaging around 36 percent between 2001 and 2005. Zimbabwe experienced extremely high inflation during the period under review, perhaps due to the consequences of the sanctions imposed by Western governments on the country. Angola is also experiencing very high inflation, due to excessive demand for goods and services generated by higher oil and commodity revenues. It must be noted that Lesotho, Mauritius, Namibia, Seychelles, South Africa and Tanzania registered single-digit inflation in recent years due to the pursuance of aggressive monetary policies by their respective monetary authorities. It is very important that member States of SADC should be encouraged to pursue aggressive price stability policies so as to create the enabling environment needed for sustainable economic activities.

Table 8.3: Inflation Rates in SADC

Country	2001	2002	2003	2004	2005
Angola	108.48	120.51	102.54	42.71	43.52
Botswana	6.31	-0.05	2.79	6.10	8.73
Congo, Dem. Rep.	383.92	31.93	13.15	6.15	21.51
Lesotho	6.66	8.47	6.00	6.33	3.17
Malawi	25.62	16.38	9.25	12.52	15.45
Mauritius	4.04	6.61	5.93	5.88	4.76
Mozambique	15.98	17.02	8.96	9.04	6.43
Namibia	14.13	11.42	-0.63	2.92	2.00
Seychelles	5.46	4.25	5.91	3.91	0.98
South Africa	7.67	10.51	4.44	5.59	4.75
Swaziland	10.56	12.54	12.14	10.44	4.88
Tanzania	7.17	6.45	5.62	8.07	3.74
Zambia	24.31	19.86	19.81	20.05	19.02
Zimbabwe	76.57	123.25	411.10	349.87	237.74
SADC	49.78	27.80	43.36	34.97	26.91

Source: UNECA and World Development Indicators.

FDI inflows have been playing an important role in the development process of emerging economies in recent years. SADC region has also attracted considerable amount of FDI to boost the domestic rate of investment.

In assessing the net FDI inflow in the SADC sub-region, the literature suggests that stable macroeconomic environments encourage such flows. SADC region attracts substantial levels of FDIs, with South Africa and Angola accounting for most in recent years. The economic growth performance of South Africa and Angola is related to the net inflow of FDI, although Angola has registered high inflation in recent years. Democratic Republic of Congo, Mozambique and

Tanzania appear to also attract high levels of FDI. Mozambique and Democratic Republic of Congo FDI flows go the development of their extractive industry.

Tanzania's attraction of FDIs is due to its stable macroeconomic environment, as attested by its relative low inflation and the sustainable and moderate growth of its economy.

8.3.2 Monetary Arrangements of Common Market for Eastern and Southern Africa (COMESA): COMESA has embarked on a monetary cooperation arrangement that aims to establish a common monetary zone with strong monetary stability to support its integration and sustained economic growth agenda. Ultimately, COMESA hopes to transform the zone into a monetary union.

The decision to create a monetary union within the Preferential Trade Area of Eastern and Southern African States (PTA) was taken as far back as 1989, even though the Heads of State and Government concretized it only in 1992 with the adoption of a Monetary and Fiscal Policies Harmonization Programme. Based on a gradualist approach, this programme constituted the framework of economic integration in the region and was articulated around four stages spanning a period of more than 30 years:

- **Stage 1 (1992-1996):** Consolidation of existing instruments of monetary cooperation and implementation of policy measures aimed at achieving macroeconomic convergence.
- **Stage 2 (1997-2000):** Introduction of limited currency convertibility and an informal exchange rate union.
- **Stage 3 (2000-2024):** Formal exchange rate union and coordination of economic policies by a common monetary institution.
- **Stage 4 (2025 onwards):** Full monetary union involving the use of one common currency issued by a common central bank.

The four-stage programme of economic integration

adopted by the PTA was endorsed by COMESA, when the PTA was officially transformed into COMESA in 1994. Its implementation was reviewed with the definition of specific criteria to achieve macroeconomic convergence (COMESA, 1995 and Harvey et al. 2001). Since COMESA was conceived as an instrument of a comprehensive programme of cooperation and integration, its activities covered a variety of fields beyond trade and macroeconomic policies, including research in science and technology, peace and security and physical infrastructures development.

The fundamental rationale of macroeconomic and monetary integration in COMESA is to create the conditions for sustained economic development of the sub-region. The objective is thus to achieve deep forms of integration and, most notably, to establish a monetary union and a full economic community through the following:

- Liberalization of the exchange systems of member States to promote intraregional trade and cross-border capital flows;
- Harmonization of national policies to correct misalignments, strengthen macroeconomic adjustment and performance;
- Achievement of currency convertibility;
- Mobilization of financial resources to expand trade and support development projects (COMESA, 2003); and
- Promotion of intraregional trade and cross-border capital flows in COMESA started with the restructuring of the Clearing House into a Regional Payment and Settlement System (REPSS). The REPSS, which was launched in 2007, is a multilateral system that converts all payments in local currencies to a "settlement currency" based on a fixed daily rate for transfer between countries. With a view to encouraging sustainable monetary stability in the zone, COMESA promotes monetary harmonization programmes on a consistent basis. Specific convergence targets based on agreed criteria are used to monitor progress by each

Member State. The criteria address macroeconomic policies, external debt situations and adapted Maastricht criteria. Each criterion has a number of quantitative indicators serving as targets. In a number of cases, efforts are made to coordinate national programmes so as to help meet the targets.

The revised macroeconomic convergence criteria that were adopted by the seventh meeting of Ministers of Finance held in Lusaka, Zambia on 17 November 2005 contain the following elements:

A. Primary Criteria: Budget Deficit: Fiscal imbalances are generally the result of spending growing faster than revenues. COMESA countries continue to be challenged by their resource needs to reduce poverty as set out in their Poverty Reduction Strategy and their commitment to achieve macroeconomic stability in the context of their limited national resources. Despite these difficulties, most members of COMESA are on the right track. In 2004, the average fiscal deficit-to-GDP ratio (excluding grants) for COMESA was 5.9 percent. Comoros, Kenya, Seychelles and Swaziland registered a ratio of less than 5 percent, which is in compliance with COMESA's revised macroeconomic convergence criteria.

These countries managed to achieve fiscal adjustment through revenue-enhancing and expenditure-cutting measures, even though the overall result varied from country to country. Where most countries fared poorly was in the availability of deep financial markets and domestic savings to finance large budget deficits. Data on deficits suggests that fiscal stabilization still has to be achieved in most countries (Democratic Republic of Congo, Eritrea and Zimbabwe).

B. Inflation: On the average, inflation in the COMESA sub-region remains very high, exceeding 20 percent for each year under review. However, it must be pointed out that inflation has been decreasing since 2001, from 35 percent in 2001 to 22.40 percent in 2005. Despite the negative impact of high oil prices on inflation, Burundi, Comoros, Djibouti,

Egypt, Ethiopia, Kenya, Mauritius, Namibia, Rwanda, Sudan and Uganda have managed to keep inflation generally in single digits, mainly due to prudent monetary policies. The inflation performance of Zimbabwe needs to improve drastically so as to spur sound economic growth.

On the contrary, countries such as Kenya (11.5 percent), Madagascar (13.8 percent), Malawi (11.6 percent), Rwanda (12 percent), Zambia (18 percent) and Zimbabwe (282 percent) went through double-digit inflation primarily due to higher food prices. Excluding the Democratic Republic of Congo and Zimbabwe, which were affected by hyperinflation, the number of countries with single-digit inflation rose significantly between the first and second half of the 1990s. According to the figures of the 1990s up to 2004, the overall regional dispersion of inflation seemed to be on a decreasing trend. Madagascar, Malawi and Zambia were able to curb inflation relative to the previous sub-period.

In particular, Zambia made a strong correction to its inflationary stance, which had degenerated into hyperinflation between 1992 and 1993. The Democratic Republic of Congo was a conflict-affected country that needed to finance high levels of fiscal spending through an inflation tax, which contributed to hyperinflation in that country. Zimbabwe bucked the regional trend and exhibited ramping inflation coupled with a variety of other problems, including a large budget deficit.

C. External Reserves: On the average, the level of reserves in COMESA could cover three months of imports of goods and services in 2004 as compared to just under three months in 2003. This result was possible because of higher levels of capital flows (official development assistance and debt relief measures). Countries such as Ethiopia, Rwanda, Mauritius and Uganda were able to meet COMESA's requirement by maintaining external reserves that could cover four months of imports of goods and services.

D. Secondary Criteria: Exchange Rate Policy: The

COMESA monetary harmonization programme calls for a progressive dismantling of exchange controls and the introduction of a market- determined exchange rate regime. Accordingly, most COMESA countries have made progress in moving towards market-determined exchange rates. Overvaluation of currencies that characterized the 1980s and early 1990s has been reduced. Different exchange regimes exist in COMESA. Swaziland has its currency pegged to the South African rand, which floats independently. Nine countries have freely floating exchange rate regimes, although it is difficult to confirm that there is no government interference.

Exchange rate arrangements in COMESA (except for the EAC countries) vary from country to country. This heterogeneity reflects the different views by countries about currency exchange regimes. The process of economic integration is ultimately aimed at the formation of currency unions. It implies that countries engaged in the process must move towards a system of fixed – and later irrevocable – parities. The process of implementation of a system of fixed exchange rates in a REC must be gradual. Flexible exchange rates have the advantage of easing the impact of fiscal adjustment and absorbing exogenous shocks. Pegging the exchange rate is a strategy to lock in the progress achieved on macroeconomic stabilization. Furthermore, the risk that the peg would be a target of speculative attacks is quite limited, since most African countries are not significantly integrated into global financial markets. However, to avoid distortions of the path of domestic development, countries are advised to move to a peg only once some basic conditions have been met:

- Domestic inflation must have been stabilized to a relatively low level, so as to avoid the negative real exchange rate consequences of the inflation gap vis-à-vis the reference country;
- Fiscal stabilization must have been achieved;
- A consistent stock of international reserves must exist; and

- The economic institutions and arrangements such as an independent central bank and strong budgetary procedures must have been established. It is also desirable that appropriate instruments for banking supervision and surveillance should have been put in place.

The domestic currency should be pegged to a major international currency (euro, US dollar or yen). The consistency of international trade flows suggests that most African countries ought to peg to the euro, especially if Great Britain joins the EMU.

However, to avoid fluctuations among the major currencies generating undesirable appreciations or depreciations of the domestic currency, the peg could be referred to a composite basket. All countries in each REC should move towards a stable peg against an international reference currency. This will occur at different speeds for different countries, depending on their initial situation and on the time required to achieve the conditions for the sustainability of the peg. The adoption of a bilateral peg against the international reference will de facto produce a system of fixed exchange rates within the REC, and one where parities between members of the REC are determined based on the bilateral exchange rates against the international reference. Before creating a currency union, it would be desirable to let the fixed exchange rate system work for several years (seven to ten years are advised). The long transition period will also allow RECs and member States to set up the institutional and technical arrangements required by a currency union.

Eventually, following the example of the European Monetary System, fluctuation bands (in the range of no more than ±15 percent around the central parity) could be established to provide a minimum margin for stabilization. Only countries that, for the last three years, have been able to maintain that parity without the need to impose restrictions on the free flow of foreign exchange would be admitted to the currency union.

A hard-peg arrangement against an international currency (or a basket of currencies) should also be adopted by the common central bank as an anchor for regional monetary policy. Countries in the union should be continuously monitored in their adherence to convergence criteria, with sanctions applied to non-complying countries. Mechanisms for flexibility of the type previously discussed should, however, remain in place. Countries that did not initially qualify for participation in the union could be admitted subsequently once they have satisfied the convergence criteria and have maintained a stable parity against the reference international currency for a period of at least three years.

The target for limited currency convertibility among COMESA member countries has not materialized yet throughout the sub-region. Swaziland, which belongs to the Common Monetary Area (CMA) or the rand zone, operates on the basis of a limited currency convertibility arrangement. The same applies to the members of the East African Community (EAC), Kenya, Tanzania and Uganda, which have adopted and implemented a policy making their national currencies fully convertible against one another. The acceptance of each other's currency not only facilitates the flow of trade and investment by reducing transaction costs, but also serves as an important instrument that promotes regional cooperation and economic integration and lays the groundwork for a smooth transition to a single currency.

The policy of convertibility in EAC is so far considered to be a success story, although EAC authorities acknowledge that there are potential risks that could be attributed to increased counterfeiting and losses arising from exchange rate fluctuations. Such risks are, however, deemed inherent in the nature of dealings involving convertible international currencies.

As for the removal of exchange restrictions, many COMESA member countries have accepted Article VIII of IMF and have removed restrictions on their current account.

Efforts are also being made to remove restrictions on intra-COMESA trade. Byand large, COMESA member States have made significant efforts to liberalize their financial markets.

8.3.3 Interest Rate Policy: All countries in COMESA have liberalized their interest rates. In some countries, real lending rates are still high and the margin between lending and deposit rates is quite wide, indicating inefficiencies in the financial system.

E. Growth: Between 2001 and 2005, the COMESA bloc grew at an average rate of about 4 percent (Table 8.4). This is below the required 7 percent level of growth to achieve the MDGs, and is also low when compared to other developing countries and emerging economies.

Except for 2002 and 2003, Ethiopia's economy has been growing at a rate of over 7 percent each year. The Democratic Republic of Congo has also been experiencing very high growth, perhaps due to increased external demand for its commodities. The strong global demand for oil is contributing to the robustness of Sudan's economy, which is growing above 5 percent each year. Modest economic growth has been posted by Mauritius, Rwanda and Egypt. Overall, improved macroeconomic stability, higher external demand for commodities, better agricultural production, significant increase in ODA, debt relief measures and improved peace and security account for part of the improved growth performance in the COMESA zone. Debt service has been on a decreasing trend at the regional level since the mid-1980s. The average external debt-to-GDP ratio of COMESA fell from 62.4 percent in 2003 to 55.4 percent in 2004, because some countries (Ethiopia, Madagascar and Uganda) have reached the HIPC completion point regarding their debt relief. Many countries have also seen their ODA shares increase substantially.

Several COMESA countries participate, or are expected to participate, in the HIPC initiative for debt relief. This is likely to have a significant impact on debt service statistics at both the national and the regional level. As projected by IMF for the period 2001-2003, debt service as a percentage of Gross Domestic Product (GDP) in countries with debt relief arrangements was expected to be 50 percent lower than the others.

A similar effect was predicted for debt service as a percentage of export earnings. Despite these encouraging signals, the Millennium Development Goals (MDGs) remain underfinanced and most COMESA countries have not made real progress on most of the goals as scheduled.

Table 8.4: Growth Performance in Common Market for Eastern and Southern Africa (COMESA)

Country	2001	2002	2003	2004	2005
Burundi	2.06	4.45	-1.22	4.83	0.91
Comoros	3.33	4.15	2.47	-0.24	4.23
Congo, Dem. Rep.	-2.10	3.50	5.70	6.60	6.50
Eritrea	9.23	0.66	6.09	1.86	0.50
Ethiopia	7.93	-0.01	-3.09	12.30	8.73
Kenya	3.80	0.55	2.98	4.85	5.81
Madagascar	6.02	-12.67	9.79	5.26	4.60
Malawi	-4.97	2.86	6.07	7.12	2.55
Mauritius	5.56	2.71	3.19	4.70	4.57
Rwanda	6.72	9.38	0.95	3.95	5.99
Seychelles	-2.21	1.30	-6.30	-1.99	-2.30
Sudan	6.10	6.40	5.60	5.20	8.00
Swaziland	1.79	2.90	2.40	2.10	1.80
Uganda	4.94	6.34	4.72	5.49	6.57
Zambia	4.89	3.30	5.12	5.41	5.20
Zimbabwe	-2.70	-4.40	-10.40	-3.80	-6.50
Djibouti	2.05	2.62	3.20	3.84	3.20
Egypt, Arab Rep.	3.52	3.19	3.11	4.18	4.94
COMESA	3.07	2.92	2.36	4.44	4.47

Source: UNECA and World Development Indicators.

F. Current Account Deficit: Most COMESA countries are running deficits on their current account, excluding grants. Exports of goods and services as a percentage of GDP increased from 34.9 percent to 39.5 percent, while imports of goods and services also increased from 41.2 percent of GDP to 43.8 percent.

G. Domestic Investment and Savings Rates: Average investment performance in COMESA has improved from 13.8 percent of GDP in 2003 to 16.3 percent in 2004. This achievement is below the COMESA target ratio of 20 percent of GDP and varies from country to country. However, most countries registered a performance of less than 20 percent of GDP, suggesting that COMESA countries need to implement a set of policies to achieve higher investment and growth.

The average COMESA savings rate as a percentage of GDP was 12.6 percent in 2004 as compared to 7.4 percent in 2003. Most countries have a performance in savings of less than 10 percent of GDP, which is not sufficient to finance the level of investment required for rapid and sustained growth. Furthermore, it is important to note that the relatively high interest rates observed above did not improve domestic savings and possibly hurt domestic investment.

Net FDI into the COMESA zone shows that Egypt and Sudan have been attracting most of the FDI to the zone in recent years. Sudan's FDIs are for the development of its oil industry. Democratic Republic of Congo attracts substantial FDI to its extractive industry. The FDI into Ethiopia is also very substantial. Not surprisingly, the FDIs into Democratic Republic of Congo, Sudan and Ethiopia account for their strong growth performance in recent years. It must be noted that despite the recent stability in Burundi, FDI flow into the country remains very low.

8.3.4 Monetary Arrangements of the Economic Community of West African States (ECOWAS): Monetary cooperation in the West African sub-region began in 1975 with the Economic Community of West African States (ECOWAS) establishing the West African Clearing House (WACH) to provide a multilateral clearing mechanism for trade within the sub-region. The key objectives of the WACH were to promote the use of the currencies of member countries in intra-ECOWAS trade and to encourage the member States to pursue trade liberalization schemes that support and strengthen monetary and economic cooperation in the sub-region. Under the operations of the WACH, the use of foreign exchange was substituted for an artificial currency unit, the West African Unit of Account (WAUA). The WAUA was linked to the special IMF drawing right. The WAUA served as the benchmark for determining the relative strength of the currencies in the WACH payment and clearing system. The operations of the WACH required that member States commit to unrestricted conversion of their national currencies into the WAUA for transactions so as to avoid currency inconvertibility in the sub-region.

In 1996, the WACH was transformed into the West African Monetary Agency (WAMA), paving the way for a single monetary zone in the sub-region and making the multilateral settlement, clearing and payment system more efficient. With the collaboration of the Committee of Central Bank Governors and the WAMA, the ECOWAS traveller's cheque was introduced in 1998 and went into circulation the following year to facilitate intra-community trade and other business transactions. However, it was phased out in the aftermath of less restrictive exchange controls accompanying increased economic liberalization under the structural adjustment programmes in member States.

Despite the good intentions of the leadership of ECOWAS, the WACH had a number of difficulties. Ojo (2003) suggests that these challenges included operational inadequacies; the ineffectiveness of the system as cumbersome documentation requirements by central banks delayed crediting exporters' accounts; the absence of a short-term financing facility; and the absence of trade promotion instruments such as bills of exchange and traveller's cheques. WACH also failed to promote the use of national currencies in intraregional trade.

In its effort to create a common currency in the zone, ECOWAS in 1987 adopted a comprehensive Monetary Cooperation Programme (MCP). The main objective of the MCP is to promote a harmonized monetary system that would support the sustainable growth of the economies in the ECOWAS zone. Through the MCP, the sub-region is expected to achieve a common convertible currency that would subsequently be managed by a common central bank.

To achieve the objectives of the MCP, ECOWAS has implemented a number of measures, including exchange rate realignment and harmonization; adoption of an ECOWAS exchange rate mechanism; liberalization of exchange controls and maintenance of fiscal discipline; and adoption of a market-oriented approach to monetary management. Consequently, member States are expected to follow a set of primary and secondary convergence criteria, as presented in Table 8.5.

Table 8.5: ECOWAS Macroeconomic Convergence Criteria

Convergence criteria	Priority	Parameter	Target date
Budget deficit	Primary	4 percent, maximum	2003
Central bank finance of fiscal deficit	Primary	10 percent, maximum	2003
Inflation rate, annual	Primary	5 percent, maximum	2003
External reserves	Primary	6-months imports, minimum	2003
Domestic debt	Secondary	Liquidate outstanding	Open
Tax revenue/GDP	Secondary	20 percent, maximum	Open
Wage bill/tax revenue	Secondary	35 percent, maximum	Open
Exchange rate	Secondary	Stabilize real rate	Open
Interest rate	Secondary	Maintain positive real rate	Open
Capital expand/Tax revenue	Secondary	20 percent, maximum	Open

Source: UNECA and the ECOWAS Secretariat

It should be noted that the maximum budget deficit does not include grants and the maximum central bank financing of the budget deficit is based on the previous year's tax revenue. The MCP has faced a number of challenges that have delayed its implementation. Member States, perhaps due to the lack of political commitment, have failed to adopt the desired policy frameworks that would lead to convergence. Furthermore, the required monetary harmonization has not been achieved. Consequently, the date for the single monetary zone was shifted three times from 1992 to 1994, to 2000 and again to 2004.

Assessing the performance of the economy of the ECOWAS zone shows that the growth performance was modest, averaging about 4 percent between 2001 and 2005, which is clearly below the 7 percent needed to achieve the MDG (Table 8.6). Post-conflict Sierra Leone is experiencing high growth due to sound macroeconomic management and strong external demand for its extractive commodities. Strong external demand for crude oil has boosted Nigeria's growth performance, averaging above 6 percent every year from 2003.

Sound fiscal and monetary management of the Ghanaian economy has yielded great benefits, as witnessed by its average GDP growth of about 5 percent between 2001 and 2005. The political uncertainty in Cote d'Ivoire appears to be hurting the economy as its real GDP shrunk during 2001-2003. The growth performance of the Gambia and Senegal has also been very strong since 2003, with solid agriculture yields, good macroeconomic policy and tourism accounting for part of the strength in the economies.

The inflation performance of the ECOWAS region is relatively good, averaging less than 9 percent each year from 2001 to 2005. Benin, Burkina Faso, Cote d'Ivoire, Mali, Niger, Senegal and Togo, all member States of the CFA zone, registered very low rates of inflation during the years in review. This is due primarily to the peg of the CFA to the euro, which itself accounts for the low and stable inflation of

Europe. The central banks of the Gambia, Ghana, Guinea and Nigeria have to work hard to improve the inflation rate in their respective countries, as they all posted double-digit inflation in the years under review.

Table 8.6: Growth Performance in ECOWAS

Country	2001	2002	2003	2004	2005
Benin	5.00	4.50	3.90	3.10	3.90
Burkina Faso	5.90	4.50	6.50	3.90	4.80
Cape Verde	3.80	4.60	6.20	4.50	5.80
Cote d'Ivoire	-0.03	-1.44	-1.56	1.76	1.80
Gambia, The	5.80	-3.25	6.95	5.10	5.00
Ghana	4.00	4.50	5.20	5.60	5.90
Guinea	4.00	4.20	1.20	2.67	3.33
Guinea-Bissau	0.20	-7.10	0.60	2.20	3.50
Liberia	2.90	3.70	-31.30	2.60	5.30
Mall	12.10	4.15	7.44	2.19	6.08
Niger	7.10	3.00	5.32	0.00	4.50
Nigeria	3.10	1.55	10.69	6.00	6.94
Senegal	4.69	1.12	6.55	6.17	5.13
Sierra Leone	18.20	27.40	9.20	7.40	7.50
Togo	-0.18	4.14	2.70	3.00	2.80
ECOWAS	5.11	3.70	2.64	3.75	4.82

Source: UNECA and World Development Indicators.

The ECOWAS sub-region attracts substantial levels of FDIs, with Nigeria taking full advantage to strengthen its oil-producing sector. Despite the political uncertainty, Cote d'Ivoire attracted high levels of FDIs during the period under review. Surprisingly, inflow of FDIs did not translate into strong growth performance in Cote d'Ivoire. Ghana, Liberia and Mali also received modest levels of FDIs that coincided with their strong economic performance.

To support investment and promote financial cooperation in the region, ECOWAS has established a number of regional banks. In 1975, it formed the ECOWAS Fund for Cooperation, Compensation and Development (EFCCD), to serve as a source of finance for the compensation of revenue losses accompanying regional trade liberalization. It is also responsible for the promotion of balanced regional economic development, providing support to less-developed member States of the community. EFCCD has been reconstituted as the ECOWAS Bank for Investment and Development (EBID). The two subsidiaries of EBID are the ECOWAS Regional Development Fund (ERDF) and the ECOWAS Regional Investment Bank (ERIB), which focus on public and private sector financing respectively.

The ECOWAS Bank Group (Ecobank) has also been established to strengthen regional financial cooperation. Ecobank, a parent holding company, has subsidiaries in twelve countries across West and Central Africa. It was established to provide commercial banking and other financial services to individuals and private and public sector organizations. The ERDF is the major shareholder of Ecobank. The Ecobank Foundation, a philanthropic arm of the bank, is also involved in supporting scientific, cultural and humanitarian causes across the region.

8.3.5 Monetary Arrangements of East African Community (EAC): In 1993, Kenya, Tanzania and Uganda, the three original members of the EAC, signed the agreement establishing the Permanent Tripartite Commission for East African Cooperation.4 In 1996, the East African Cooperation Secretariat was inaugurated in Arusha, Tanzania. The Treaty establishing the East African Community was signed in November 1999 and entered into force in July 2000. In Article 5(2), the Treaty states that, "... the Partner States undertake to establish among themselves and in accordance with the provisions of this Treaty, a customs union, a common market, subsequently a monetary union and ultimately a political federation in order to strengthen and regulate the industrial, commercial, infrastructure, cultural, social, political and other relations of the Partner States to the end that there shall be accelerated, harmonious and balanced development and sustained expansion of economic activities, the benefit of which shall be equitably shared".

More specifically, Article 82(1) says that, "….Partner States undertake to cooperate in monetary and fiscal matters in accordance with the approved macroeconomic policies harmonization programmes and convergence framework of the Community in order to establish monetary stability within the Community aimed at facilitating economic integration efforts and the attainment of sustainable economic development of the Community. To this end the Partner States shall:

- Cooperate in monetary and financial matters and maintain the convertibility of their currencies as a basis for the establishment of a monetary union
- Harmonize their macroeconomic policies especially in exchange rate policy, interest rate policy, monetary and fiscal policies
- Remove obstacles to the free movement of goods, services and capital within the Community".

Furthermore, Article 83(2) adds that "….Member States undertake to:

- Remove all exchange restrictions on imports and exports within the Community
- Maintain free market determined exchange rates and enhance the levels of their international reserves
- Adjust their fiscal policies and net domestic credit to the government to ensure monetary stability and the achievement of sustained economic growth
- Liberalize their financial sectors by freeing and deregulating interest rates with a view to achieving

positive real interest rates in order to promote savings for investment within the Community and to enhance competition and efficiency in their financial systems

- Harmonize their tax policies with a view to removing tax distortions in order to bring about a more efficient allocation of resources within the Community".

In pursuit of the objectives of the Treaty mentioned above, Partner States agreed on a number of macroeconomic convergence criteria aimed at integrating their economies for a sustainable monetary union as follows:

- Low and stable inflation rate at single digit of less than 5 percent;
- High and sustainable rate of growth of real GDP at 7 percent as the minimal annual target;
- Reduce current account deficit-to-GDP ratio to a sustainable level;
- Reduce budget deficit-to-GDP ratio (excluding grants) to less than 5 percent;
- Raise national savings-to-GDP ratio to at least 20 percent in the medium term;
- Build gross foreign exchange reserves to a level equivalent to six months of imports in the medium term;
- Maintain low market-determined interest rates;
- Maintain stable market-determined exchange rates;
- Pursue debt reduction initiatives to reduce both domestic and foreign debt; and
- Maintain prudential norms of banking regulation, strict supervision, improved corporate governance and transparency of all financial transactions.

The policy reform programmes adopted by Partner States to achieve the above macroeconomic criteria helped in getting the following results:

A. Currency convertibility of the shilling of the three Partner States: The Kenyan, Tanzanian and Ugandan shillings are freely convertible within the East African sub-region. This has facilitated the flow of trade and investment by reducing transaction costs and has also served as an important instrument for promoting regional cooperation and economic integration. It is paving the way for a smooth transition to a single currency in the sub-region in a foreseeable future.

B. Harmonization of macroeconomic policies: Priority is being given to the harmonization of macroeconomic policies, particularly in exchange rate, interest rate, monetary and fiscal policies. The central banks of the three Partner States meet regularly to harmonize their policies and share experiences and information regarding budget, revenue and other economic policies.

C. In the area of growth, the result achieved is mixed: The growth performance of the EAC zone has been modest, recording around 5 percent each year, from 2001 to 2005 (Table 8.7). The economies of Tanzania and Uganda have been growing very strongly since 2001. Kenya's growth in 2002 was very slow, posting a mere 0.55 percent. However, the Kenyan economy has been robust since 2003 as is evident from Table 8.7.

Table 8.7: Growth Performance in the EAC Region

Country	2001	2002	2003	2004	2005
Kenya	3.80	0.55	2.98	4.85	5.81
Tanzania	6.24	7.24	7.12	6.69	6.97
Uganda	4.94	6.34	4.72	5.49	6.57
EAC	5.00	4.71	4.94	5.68	6.45

Source: UNECA and World Development Indicators

D. Inflation: Compared to other parts of Africa, the EAC zone continued to post single-digit inflation throughout the years under review. Inflation rates posted by the member States are also very impressive, indicating that their respective central banks are pursuing very sound monetary polices. It is important for the central banks to continue with their policies so that EAC can achieve its target of keeping inflation below 5 percent.

E. Current account and fiscal deficits: Current account and fiscal deficits (excluding grant) were contained below 5 percent in 2002 in Kenya and Tanzania, whereas Uganda's twin deficits rose to more than 13 percent in the same year. Several reasons could be given for the mixed macroeconomic performance of Partner States, including:

- Lack of enforcement, as there is no penalty for defaulting countries;
- Relevance of some variables is questionable;
- Terms such as "sustainable" or "stable" need to be clearly defined, since they are of a general nature and are difficult to measure;
- The computation and definition of the variables need to be harmonized in all three Partner States; and
- There is no clear roadmap (milestone) leading to a single currency.

In a bid to improve the sub-region's macroeconomic performance, the EAC Ministers of Finance in 2006 approved the terms of reference for a comprehensive study on the EAC monetary union and single currency. Among other things, the study is expected to take into consideration the experiences of other sub-regions such as the rand zone, the CFA zone, the euro convergence criteria, the stability and growth pact of the euro zone and Gordon Brown's five economic tests for the United Kingdom to join the euro zone.

Has the stable macroeconomic environment in the EAC zone translated into FDI flows into the zone? The zone attracts modest levels of FDI, with Tanzania attracting the most, followed by Uganda. Despite its strong business environment, Kenya does not attract sufficient FDI.

8.3.6 Monetary Arrangements of the Economic and Monetary Union of Central Africa (CEMAC): CEMAC is one of the oldest sub-regional groupings in Africa. Member countries are Cameroon, Central African Republic, Chad, Republic of Congo, Equatorial Guinea and Gabon. It was established under French colonial rule as a way of forging monetary and economic integration between the member States.

Although the countries are contiguous, the infrastructure network in the region is very poor, making intra-CEMAC trade very difficult and isolating the countries from one another. Indeed, some of the countries have more economic links with Nigeria and Democratic Republic of Congo, both of which are not in the grouping, than with each other.

The steep history of CEMAC and UEMOA is rooted in French colonial Africa. It began with the formation of the Afrique Occidentale Francaise (AOF) in 1898, made up of Senegal, Guinea, Cote d'Ivoire, the Sudan (later Mali), Dahomey (later Benin), Upper Volta (later Burkina Faso), Mauritania and Niger. The Afrique Equatoriale Francaise (AEF) was also created in 1910 and was made up of Chad, Oubangi-Chari (later the Central African Republic), Congo and Gabon. The French part of Cameroon was governed separately by France under a United Nations mandate and remained outside the federation. France's African colonies began to assert their right to self-determination after World War II, and their formal arrangements with France ended with their independence. Despite the newly gained independence of the French colonies in Africa, the CFA franc created under colonial rule continued to be used.

In December 1945, the Colonies Francaise d'Afrique (CFA) franc was created to maintain the exchange rates for AEF and AOF with the dollar. The acronym CFA was later renamed as the Cooperation Financiere Africaine in Central Africa and Communaute Financiere Africaine in West Africa. It must be noted that while most colonies severed their monetary relationships with the former colonial power after independence, the CFA zone's monetary arrangements remained largely unchanged after independence. In the mid-1980s, severe domestic policy and exogenous shocks hit the CEMAC area hard. However, the CFA was devalued to mitigate the negative shock and provide stability. Consequently, the area went into a protracted depression that saw per capita income fall by over 17 percent. Member States reacted to the macroeconomic imbalances by pursuing an "internal adjustment strategy," as an alternative to devaluation. However, as explained in box 4, the strategy failed and forced the countries to devalue the CFA franc in 1994, which allowed the economies in the region to recover.

The coordination of monetary programmes in the region is carried out by the Central Bank of Central African States (BEAC), which was created in 1972 as a regional central bank. BEAC was charged with the responsibility of issuing currencies and pooling the external reserves of member States. It functions through an operations account with the French Treasury, which is used to manage the fixed parity between the CFA franc and the French franc and is governed by monetary accords between France and BEAC. Some of the accords require BEAC to abide by a set of rules of monetary and fiscal discipline designed to reduce the risk of accumulating large balance of payments deficits that would have to corrected by extensive financing from the operations account. BEAC is also responsible for overseeing macroeconomic and financial stability in the zone. In order to preserve the value of the CFA and ensure macroeconomic stability, CEMAC in 2002 adopted a macroeconomic framework, which requires member States to ensure that:

- Inflation does not exceed 3 percent;
- Total debt as a percentage of GDP is not greater than 70 percent;
- External debt payment arrears are not negative;
- Domestic debt payment arrears are not negative;
- Budget deficit as a percentage of GDP is not negative;
- Deficit financed by the central bank is less than 20 percent of the previous year's fiscal revenue;
- Wage bill as a percentage of tax revenue is less than 35 percent; and

- There are no domestic and external arrears on the current account.

The average growth performance of CEMAC was very modest between 2001 and 2005 (Table 8.8). With the exception of 2002 and 2004, growth for the entire zone remained below 5 percent. The high-performing countries in the zone are Chad and Equatorial Guinea, which posted double-digit GDP growth during the years in review, mainly due to the performance of the oil sector. The growth performance of Central African Republic and Gabon is very weak, with the former posting negative growth rates in 2002 and 2003.

Table 8.8: Growth Performance in the CEMAC Region

Country	2001	2002	2003	2004	2005
Cameroon	4.51	4.01	4.03	3.70	2.04
Central African Republic	1.50	-0.80	-7.60	1.30	2.20
Chad	10.42	8.38	14.91	29.50	5.57
Congo, Rep.	3.80	4.60	0.80	3.60	9.20
Equatorial Guinea	1.45	17.62	14.70	9.98	Na
Gabon	2.50	0.00	2.60	1.40	2.20
CEMAC	4.03	5.63	4.91	8.25	4.24

Source: UNECA and World Development Indicators.

Although the zone as a whole has not been able to keep inflation below 3 percent, it has managed to post single-digit inflation. In 2001, 2004 and 2005, Chad registered double-digit inflation, partly due to increased pressures for goods and services to support increased activities in the oil sector. The top inflation performers in the zone are Cameroon, Congo, Gabon and Central African Republic.

As regards net FDI flows into the CEMAC zone between 2001 and 2005, Chad and Equatorial Guinea attracted most of the FDIs mainly for the development of their oil sectors. Despite Cameroon and Gabon being the biggest economies in the zone, they do not attract substantial levels of FDIs.

8.3.7 Monetary Arrangements of West African Economic and Monetary Union (UEMOA): UEMOA was established in 1994, and comprises the following countries: Benin, Burkina Faso, Cote d'Ivoire, Guinea Bissau, Mali, Niger, Senegal and Togo. The history of UEMOA dates back to 1962 with the establishment of the West African Monetary Union (UMOA), composed of the French colonies in West Africa. UEMOA was born in 1994 out of a merger between the West African Monetary Union (UMOA) and the West African Economic Community (CEAO).

The main objectives of UEMOA are the following:

- To reinforce the competitiveness of the economic and financial activities of member States in the context of an open and rival market and a rationalized and harmonized judicial environment;
- To ensure the convergence of the macroeconomic performance and policies of member States with the institution of a multilateral control procedure;
- To create a common market among member States based on the free movement of people, goods, services and capital and on the right of people exercising an independent or remunerated activity;
- To establish a common external tariff as well as a common commercial policy;
- To institute coordination of national sector-based policies with the implementation of common market actions, especially in the following domains: community-based land reclamation, environment, transport, infrastructure, telecommunications, human resources, energy, industries, mines and crafts; and
- To harmonize the legislations, especially, the fiscal systems of the member countries. UEMOA is a single monetary zone backed by a convertible currency, the CFA

franc, which is issued by the Central Bank of West African States (BCEAO). BCEAO is the common central bank for the eight member States. Besides the issue of the common currency, BCEAO is also responsible for the pooling of foreign exchange reserves; the unrestricted circulation of the common currency and freedom of capital movements within the territory of the member States; the harmonization of monetary and banking legislation; the free and unlimited convertibility of CFA franc into euros at a fixed parity guaranteed by France; the concentration of the Union's foreign currency–denominated assets in the operations account of the French Treasury; and the application of a common regulation against third-party countries. The credibility and international convertibility of the CFA franc are guaranteed through the euro, to which it is anchored. To ensure convertibility between the CFA franc and the euro, the French Treasury maintains an operations account on behalf of BCEAO. Recently, the need to maintain a common monetary policy called for financial discipline on the part of each country belonging to the Union. Accordingly, UEMOA, with the endorsement of the Heads of State and Government of the member States, has adopted the Convergence, Stability, Growth and Solidarity Pact. The Pact establishes a multilateral surveillance system aimed at ensuring greater economic policy cohesiveness among members and outlines a set of primary and secondary criteria to be satisfied.

The macroeconomic convergence policy of UEMOA consists of the primary and secondary criteria referred to earlier. The primary criteria focus on the budget deficit; the reduction of inflation; the ceiling on total public external debt; and the internal and external arrears. The secondary criteria deal with variables such as the wage bill to- tax revenue ratio; public investment; fiscal revenues and current account deficits. The macroeconomic policies of member States are coordinated through the multilateral surveillance mechanism.

A monetary union calls for some coordination of budgetary policies of member countries. Divergent budgetary policies can lead to tensions within the monetary union, especially when they can give rise to competitive capital movements between countries. The convergence provisions in the UEMOA zone are encapsulated in the multilateral surveillance mechanism. In applying these provisions, the Union pursues general as well as specific objectives. Article 4 of its treaty stipulates that the Union is aimed at:

- "Reinforcing the competitiveness of economic and financial activities of member States within the framework of an open and competitive market and a rationalized and harmonized juridical environment"; and
- "Ensuring the convergence of performances and of economic policies by the institution of a multilateral surveillance procedure".

To ensure budgetary discipline as well as macroeconomic stability, UEMOA has imposed the following convergence criteria on its member States:

Primary criteria:

- A ratio of global budgetary deficit to GDP of no more than 4 percent
- An annual inflation rate of less than 5 percent
- A budgetary deficit financed by the central bank of no more than 10 percent of the previous year's fiscal revenues; and
- Some exchange reserves (gross external reserve) representing at least six months of import of goods and services.
- Secondary criteria:
- A fiscal revenue/GDP ratio of at least 20 percent;
- A wage bill/fiscal revenue ratio of no more than 35 percent;
- Real exchange rate stabilization; and
- Investment on own resources/fiscal revenue of at least 20

percent.

A review of the current inflation performance of the UEMOA zone indicates that the zone as a whole is meeting its inflation target of less than 3 percent. With the exception of 2001, most of the member States stayed below the target for most of the period under review. It is remarkable to observe that throughout the period, all member States posted single-digit inflation rates, due to the strong linkage between the CFA franc and the euro, with the countries registering similar low levels of inflation as those in the euro zone. This clearly demonstrates the advantage of a monetary union.

Table 8.9 reports on the budget deficits of member States as a percentage of their GDP. The minimum primary target is set at zero. The region as a whole has not been very successful in achieving this objective, although it has not deviated too far from the target. The best performers are Mali, Senegal and Togo, which maintained budget surpluses for most of the period under review. Guinea-Bissau is the only member State that had difficulties in meeting the target for each year under review.

Table 8.9: Budget Deficit/GDP (percent) in the UEMOA Region

Country	2001	2002	2003	2004	2005
Benin	1.0	0.8	-0.2	0.5	1.1
Burkina Faso	-2.7	-2.3	-0.7	-1.5	-1.7
Cote d'Ivoire	1.4	0.2	-2.0	-1.1	-0.6
Guinea-Bissau	-106.	-4.4	-5.1	-9.1	-9.5
Mali	-0.6	-0.1	1.0	0.1	0.3
Niger	-3.2	-2.6	-2.2	-2.2	-1.7
Senegal	-1.0	1.5	1.5	1.5	0.5
Togo	1.3	0.3	2.6	2.6	0.6
UEMOA	0.2	0.0	-0.5	-0.3	0.4

Source: UNECA, BCEAO and UEMOA Commission.

One of the primary targets of UEMOA is for each Member State to ensure that its total public debt as a percentage of GDP does not exceed 70 percent. The zone has been struggling to achieve this target, although it was successful in 2004 and 2005. Benin, Burkina Faso, Mali and Senegal have performed very well in achieving this target. However, Guinea-Bissau, and to a lesser extent Cote d'Ivoire and Togo, would have to work hard to keep their debt level at less than 70 percent of GDP.

Had it not been for the poor performance of Cote d'Ivoire, Guinea-Bissau and Togo, the entire zone would have achieved the target of non accumulation of internal and external arrears. These countries, particularly Cote d'Ivoire and Guinea-Bissau, would have to take corrective measures so as to achieve the target.

As pointed out earlier, UEMOA also maintains secondary convergence criteria. The variables monitored are: wage bills-to-tax revenue; public investment-to-tax revenue; tax revenue-to-GDP; and current account deficit-to-GDP.. Assessing the growth performance of the economies of the UEMOA zone shows that growth has been very modest, averaging around 3.4 percent between 2001 and 2005, which is clearly below the 7 percent needed to achieve the MDG (Table 8.10). Senegal and Mali are the best-performing economies in the zone, followed by Burkina Faso and Benin. The performance of Cote d'Ivoire was lacklustre, perhaps due to its political uncertainty. Overall, the sound macroeconomic convergence criteria do not appear to have translated into good economic performance.

The UEMOA zone attracts modest levels of FDI. It is pertinent that most of the FDI goes to Cote d'Ivoire and Mali. However, the inflow of FDIs into Cote d'Ivoire did not translate into strong growth performance. Mali's FDI appears to be correlated to its modest economic performance. Guinea-Bissau attracts the least FDI in the UEMOA area.

The analysis shows that the convergence performance in UEMOA falls short of expectations. None of the member

States has succeeded in meeting the eight targets set for the convergence pact, the stability and the growth and solidarity objectives. The general impression is that budgetary targets are difficult to achieve.

Senegal is the only economy that met five budgetary criteria in 2005, namely the budget deficit-to-GDP ratio, the non-accumulation of internal and external arrears, the public investment-to-tax revenue ratio, the wage bill-to-tax revenue ratio and the tax revenue-to-GDP ratio.

Table 8.10: Growth Performance in UEMOA

Country	2001	2002	2003	2004	2005
Benin	5.00	4.50	3.90	3.10	3.90
Burkina Faso	5.90	4.40	6.50	3.90	4.80
Cote d'Ivoire	-0.03	-1.44	-1.56	1.76	1.80
Guinea-Bissau	0.20	-7.10	0.60	2.20	3.50
Mali	12.10	4.15	7.44	2.19	6.08
Niger	7.10	3.00	5.32	0.00	4.50
Senegal	4.69	1.12	6.55	6.17	5.13
Togo	-0.18	4.14	2.70	3.00	2.80
UEMOA	4.35	1.60	3.93	2.79	4.06

Source: UNECA and World Development Indicators.

Mali met four; Benin, Niger and Togo met three each, while Burkina Faso met two. Guinea Bissau met one, while Cote d'Ivoire achieved none of the budgetary targets. This poor performance could be due to the weak economic growth in the zone; the fragile public finances reflected by the accumulation of debt arrears; the deterioration of budget balances; and socio-political instability in some member States.

8.3.8 Progress Report on the West African Monetary Zone: In 2000, as part of a process of "fast-tracking" its integration agenda, ECOWAS established a second monetary zone in the region. Under the declaration, five non- UEMOA members of the community (Gambia, Ghana, Guinea, Nigeria and Sierra Leone) would form a common currency union by 2003. However, the launch date of the common currency for the non-CFA zone, which was pushed back to 2005, would now be in 2009. Under the ECOWAS programme of monetary union, the two monetary zones (the CFA and non-CFA zones) would be merged into one monetary union under a common currency and a common central bank-designated as the West African Central Bank (WACB)-at a future date. The process towards the establishment of the West African Monetary Zone (WAMZ) gave rise to the West African Monetary Institute (WAMI), which is responsible for preparing the groundwork for the launch of a single West African monetary union. WAMI, which is based in Ghana, started its operations in March 2001 to prepare member States for monetary union. WAMI has been carrying out a number of technical studies for the establishment of a common central bank and the introduction of a common currency. These studies include the monitoring of the macroeconomic performance and movement towards convergence of member States and harmonization of laws governing financial institutions in the zone. WAMI is also charged with the design of an exchange rate mechanism; a foreign exchange reserve management system; a payment system; and the design and technical preparation of a common currency and common central bank for the zone.

Since the establishment of the WAMZ in 1999, many efforts have been made towards the establishment of a single currency for the zone. The initial phase of the WAMZ programme (2001-2003) was characterized by generally poor macroeconomic performance, evidenced by the persistence of fiscal instability, high inflation and low levels of foreign exchange reserves accumulation. The dismal performance was due mainly to domestic and sub-regional factors, rather than developments in the global economy. During the second phase

(2004-2005), macroeconomic performance improved markedly over the level in Phase 1, but that was not sufficient to launch the currency.

The Banjul Declaration of 2005, which postponed the introduction of the common currency to 2009, required member countries to meet, in addition to the primary and secondary quantitative convergence criteria, specific qualitative/structural benchmarks. These included the adoption of a common payment and settlement system anchored on the Real-Time Gross Settlement (RTGS) platform; integration of financial/capital markets; harmonization of statistical databases of the WAMZ; implementation of the ECOWAS Common External Tariff (CET) and the ECOWAS Trade Liberalization Scheme (ETLS); and use of WAMZ national currencies to finance intraregional trade on a bilateral basis (as a stop-gap measure), pending the introduction of the common currency in 2009.

Assessment of the status of convergence revealed that, for the first time since the project started in 2001, two countries-the Gambia and Nigeria-met all the four primary convergence criteria in 2006. Even in the countries that failed to meet all four criteria, significant progress was made towards convergence, a clear testimony to the markedly improved macroeconomic environment in the WAMZ, in sharp contrast to the situation in 2003 and 2005. Ghana and Sierra Leone met two criteria each, with Ghana narrowly missing the single-digit inflation criterion, while Guinea met one. Both Ghana and Sierra Leone did not achieve the fiscal benchmarks, partly reflecting their continued and increased reliance on external grants.

Indeed, the appropriate fiscal convergence ratio to be targeted continues to be a subject of debate in the WAMZ. In most of the countries (Ghana, Sierra Leone and the Gambia), donor (HIPC) grants are expected to continue to feature prominently in budgetary operations. Thus, the argument has been made that the exclusion of such grants in the definition of the criteria limits the ability of member countries to observe and sustain them. However, the history of lapses in fiscal management and the vulnerability of member countries to external and internal shocks have made the WAMZ authorities focus more on fiscal consolidation through improved revenue mobilization and efficient management.

A. Financial Sector Integration: An integrated financial system is a prerequisite for an efficient and effective monetary policy in ECOWAS. The key strategy for financial sector integration in ECOWAS is predicated on the harmonization of banking regulations in accordance with the Basle Core Principle (BCPs), and the integration of the capital markets. Currently, all the WAMZ countries have adopted the BCPs as the basis for banking supervision. Also, work is currently under way on the integration of the Ghana and Nigeria stock exchanges, driven by the financial grant from the United States Department of Trade (USTDA). Furthermore, the WAMZ Convergence Council, which met in May 2007, gave approval for WAMZ national currencies to be used to finance intraregional trade, pending the introduction of the common currency.

B. Payments System Integration: The WAMZ has made good progress in harmonizing the payment and settlement system of all its member countries. Two countries (Ghana and Nigeria) have an operational Real-Time Gross Settlement (RTGS) system. Acting on WAMI's request, the African Development Bank has agreed to finance the RTGS infrastructure for The Gambia, Guinea and Sierra Leone, in preparation for the adoption of a common payment system platform in the zone. WAMZ has also adopted a common cheque standard and a common payment system statute will soon be adopted.

C. Statistical Harmonization: Work is ongoing in the area of statistical harmonization in the WAMZ. The Gambia, Guinea and Sierra Leone are working toward improved coverage for the consumer price index to cover both the rural and urban areas. The process of statistical harmonization is being driven by AFRISTAT and the ECOWAS Commission.

D. Legal Instruments: Significant work has been done in this area. The West Africa Central Bank (WACB), the West African Monetary Zone (WAMZ) and the WAMZ Secretariat statutes have been signed by the Authority of Heads of State and Government of the WAMZ and are awaiting ratification and domestication by member States. Statutes for the payment and banking systems of the West African Financial Services Authority (WAFSA) and non-bank regulations have been drafted, but are yet to be signed by the Authority of Heads of State and Government.

Overall, the WAMZ project has regained the needed momentum and progress is rapidly being made towards satisfying the quantitative and structural criteria. The critical success factor remains stronger political support for the project.

8.3.9 Monetary arrangements of Arab Maghreb Union (UMA): The Arab Maghreb Union has not formally established a set of convergence criteria for its member States. However, it is currently making efforts to establish one. Among the issues being considered by AMU are:

- Harmonization of private rules and procedures, such as market conventions, self-regulations and contractual arrangements for producing, pricing, delivering and acquiring various payment instruments and services;
- Harmonization of laws and regulations governing the payment system, particularly inter-bank transfers within the community; and
- Harmonization of technical standards, network arrangements for transacting and clearing payment instruments, processing and communicating payment information, transferring funds between institutions, and payment instruments such as debit and credit cards as well as direct debit.

Despite the absence of formal targets, the economic

performance of member States in the Union is very good. Inflation in the zone is very low and the growth performance is also very strong. The Union also attracts a great deal of foreign direct investments (FDIs) to support its manufacturing and oil-based industries.

8.4 Comparative Analysis

This section attempts to summarize the discussion so far as well as to compare and contrast the performances of the regional economic communities (RECs) and the inter-governmental organizations (IGOs). The analysis presented in Section 3 shows that, out of the fourteen RECs and IGOs, only six have convergence criteria (COMESA, EAC, ECOWAS, SADC) or monetary unions (CEMAC and UEMOA), due perhaps to the historical past of the member States.

The legal arrangements supporting the participation by member countries in the arrangements during the colonial period ranged from treaties (SADC), decrees and conventions (CEMAC, ECOWAS and UEMOA) to specific ordinances (EAC). During the colonial era, the main features of the arrangements ranged from currency boards based on the French franc or the pound sterling to free access to member States' capital markets or convertibility of member States' currencies. As noted earlier, the monetary arrangements in the colonial era were purely to support the administration of the colonies and were not based on economics.

Despite their desire to dismantle most of the colonial arrangements, several of the member States of the RECs and IGOs continued the monetary and financial arrangements immediately after their independence. This decision was made in order to promote internal and external stability of the economies within the communities as well as to increase the flow of goods, services and capital, and to increase economic growth. Furthermore, the ultimate objective of these programmes and activities of monetary cooperation is to establish monetary unions.

The main features of the framework governing the monetary cooperation arrangement of the RECs and IGOs are convertibility of member countries' currencies and harmonization of macroeconomic policies as well as the establishment of institutional organs. In the case of member countries of CEMAC and UEMOA, the established macroeconomic cooperation framework allows for the free circulation of capital and the use of common currencies.

To ensure that member States adhere to the macroeconomic convergence programmes and activities, most of the RECs and IGOs have put in place a multilateral surveillance mechanism, to monitor coherence and convergence of the macroeconomic policies of member States.

The primary and secondary convergence criteria established by the RECs include agreed targets for macroeconomic variables such as budgetary balance, inflation and public debts. Although the principles are the same, there are some variations in the criteria from REC to REC.

The RECs and the IGOs have set up statutory organs with responsibility for carrying out and monitoring the macroeconomic convergence activities in the RECs. These organs include councils of ministers, RECs commissions/secretariats, convergence councils/secretariats, central banks, regional development banks and national committees.

The organs take their job very seriously, meeting at least once a year and in some cases once every month to review the programmes and activities of the member States.

Attendance by member States at the mandatory meetings is very high. Despite the challenges, the organs have been able to promote monetary cooperation and discipline within the RECs by setting up regional payment systems and clearing houses within the communities.

Although all the member States of the RECs have committed to macroeconomic stability, most the RECs do not have legal enforcement mechanisms that ensure compliance with the objectives of the macroeconomic convergence by member States. However, in UEMOA, during ordinary sessions, the Council of Ministers reviews the programmes and activities of the member States to see if the programmes conform to community objectives. The Chairperson of the Council then notifies non-performing member States, which are then required to revise their programmes. The decisions of the Council of Ministers are published in the official bulletin of UEMOA and the relevant countries are notified accordingly. The analysis carried out so far suggests that there is no mechanism designed by the RECs and IGOs for imposing sanctions on member countries that fail to meet the convergence criteria. However, in the CEMAC area, the Council of Ministers publishes a *communiqué* on the performance of member States and announces publicly the withdrawal of support for non-performing member States.

Like CEMAC, UEMOA also imposes sanctions by publishing a *communiqué* of the Council of Ministers on the performance of the member States. The *communiqué* also stipulates measures that non-performing member countries should follow, with the Community withdrawing support to the countries that fail to comply. Although UEMOA and CEMAC have these sanctions enshrined in their protocols, the sanctions are yet to be implemented. However, the RECs have indicated a desire to strengthen the surveillance mechanism as well as the capacity to impose strong sanctions on member States that fail to adhere to the criteria.

Despite the modest achievements, the RECs and the IGOs face significant challenges, although they are taking measures to address them. These measures include capacity-building, technical assistance to member countries, harmonization of statistics, and the organization of seminars and workshops to sensitize member States.

8.5 Conclusion

In this chapter, we have taken a critical look at monetary

cooperation and the performance of selected regional economic communities on macroeconomic convergence criteria. It was argued in the chapter that regional economic communities generally impose macroeconomic convergence criteria to guide the economic policies of member States. Member States are required to adopt sound macroeconomic policies and to commit to low inflation and prudent fiscal policies. The rationale for imposing macroeconomic convergence criteria on all member States of a REC is to avoid the distortionary negative economic effects that may arise from member States pursing variant and inconsistent policies.

This is why the criteria force member States to implement policies that lead to convergence of key macroeconomic variables such as inflation, the budget deficit and the stock of public debt. In order to guarantee monetary stability, member States would have to undertake tough anti-inflationary policies and bear the associated output loss. Limits on budget and debt requirements ensure that member States adjust their fiscal policies in order to maintain an overall balance between spending and revenues from taxation and ensure fiscal prudence. This analysis shows that African countries are experiencing enormous difficulties in meeting the desired macroeconomic convergence criteria set by the regional economic communities. Whereas some member States, particularly those that belong to monetary unions (CEMAC and UEMOA), have done well in maintaining relatively low single-digit inflation, most countries are posting double-digit inflation and consequently struggling to achieve their desired inflation targets. By the same token, most of the countries have not been able to achieve the desired fiscal targets, due in part to negative external shocks, large budget deficits, lack of reliable statistics and poor growth performance.

This raises the issue of the relevance of the convergence criteria. Macroeconomic convergence mechanisms are needed because the success of regional integration also hinges on member countries pursuing convergent macroeconomic policies. Misalignments of tariffs, inflation, exchange rates, debt-to-GDP ratios, rate of money growth and other vital macroeconomic variables between member countries would be disruptive to the regional integration process. In addition, these misalignments could lead to rent-seeking activities by governments and private individuals that could stifle legitimate investment opportunities.

This could contribute to the demise of the economy of a member country, thereby weakening the whole integration process. It is therefore imperative that the process of strengthening regional integration should include guidelines for the convergence of macroeconomic and trade polices of the entire regional space so as to strengthen the overall regional integration agenda. However, for the coordination of macroeconomic policies in the RECs to succeed, African countries should have a clear sense of their own development objectives and strategies and be fully committed to these goals. Member States should muster the political will to mainstream regional monetary and macroeconomic objectives into their national development strategies.

Notes

1. A study by Mr. Blumenthal (a German banker) in 1962 recommended the continuation of the East African currency area with a supranational central bank replacing the EACB and with each country establishing its own central bank. Another study by the IMF made a similar recommendation.
2. The nine founding members of SADC are Angola, Botswana, Lesotho, Malawi, Mozambique, Swaziland, Tanzania, Zambia and Zimbabwe. The current members of SADC are the nine founding members and Democratic Republic of Congo, Madagascar, Mauritius, Namibia and South Africa.
3. The four countries are Lesotho, Namibia, South Africa and Swaziland. The fifth member of SACU, which is not part of the CMA, is Botswana. Under the CMA, Lesotho, Namibia and Swaziland have their currencies tied to the South African Rand.

References

Chamley, Christophe and Patrick Honohan. (1993.) Financial Repression and Bank Intermediation. Savings and Development 17(3): 301-308.

Collier, Paul. (1991.) Africa's External Relations: 1960-90. African Affairs 90: 339-56.

Honohan, Patrick and Philip Lane. (January 2000.) Will the Euro Trigger More Monetary Unions in Africa? *World Bank* Mimeo.

Honohan, Patrick and Stephen O'Connell. (1997.) Contrasting Monetary Regimes in Africa. *IMF Working Paper*, WP/97/64.

Mothae Maruping (2005.) Challenges for Regional Integration in Sub-Saharan Africa: Macroeconomic Convergence and Monetary Coordination. Chapter 11 of: *Africa in the World Economy - The National, Regional and International Challenges,* Fondad, The Hague, www.fondad.org.

Michael Ojo (2004.) Regional currency areas and use of foreign currencies: the experience of West Africa. *Bank of International Settlements Papers* # 17.

9

Mercosur: Mercado Commum de Sur (The Southern Cone Common Market): Economic Integration in Latin America

9.1 Introduction

In 1991, Brazil, Argentina, Paraguay and Uruguay created a trading zone among their nation-states. The agreement was formulated by the Treaty of Asunción (1991) which allowed these nations to establish common markets, promote scientific and technical development, establish common external tariffs, and coordinate economic policies After several failed attempts of regional and economic integration among Latin American nations-exemplified by ineffective measures such as the Latin American Free Trade Association (1960), the Latin American Common Market (1965) and the current Latin American Integration Association (1979)-Mercosur was established as Latin America's Southern Cone Common Market by the Asuncion Treaty of 1991. This regional-state is known as the *Mercado Commum de Sur* (MERCOSUR in Portuguese, MERCOSUL in Spanish), which means the Southern Cone Common Market. As a sub-regional common market, Mercosur sought to not merely reduce tariffs but also promote free trade and movement of capital and resources among its constituents: Brazil, Argentina, Uruguay and Paraguay.

Later, in the Treaty of Ouro Preto (1995), other countries were added as associate members (Bolivia, Chile, Colombia, Ecuador, Peru, and Venezuela). Mexico was also included into the treaty as an associate member. However, as the European Union has so notably demonstrated, the long road leading to economic integration is filled with complexities and obstacles. In fact monetary unification among EU members has taken more than 25 years. Yet although Mercosur should have expected challenges and growing pains similar to the EU, the lack of institutional and macroeconomic coordination among its members has hindered its primary goal to advance economic and monetary integration in the region, and therefore Mercosur's over-arching success.

This chapter aims to explore the institutional and macroeconomic coordination among Mercosur's members and its effects on Mercosur's primary goal to successfully achieve economic integration in the region. Using the framework presented by Dorruci, Firpo, Fratzscher and Mongelli (2002), who argue that this lack of coordination has been Mercosur's most detrimental downfall, it will be shown that how this lack of institutional integration among Mercosur nations has inhibited further economic integration in this sector of Latin America. Dorruci, Firpo, Fratzscher and Mongelli (2002) sustain that in order for a regional trade bloc to achieve full economic integration it must first achieve institutional integration; that is, in order for a sustainable common market to be successfully implemented on an economic basis, there must be a set of joint policies that outline, support and enforce the economic objectives of the countries in question. Accordingly, institutional integration is defined "as the outcome of joint policy decisions designed to affect the depth and breadth of regional integration over time" (Dorruci, Firpo, Fratzscher and Mongelli, 2002) and exemplified through the five stages of regional integration among regional trade blocs developed by Balassa (1961): Free Trade Area (FTA), Customs Union (CU), Common Market (CM), Economic Union (EUN) and Total Economic Integration (TEI). Mercosur is currently classified as an imperfect customs union or an FTA setting up common tariffs and quotas (if any) for trade with non-members (Balassa, 1961).

Furthermore, Dorruci, Firpo, Fratzscher and Mongelli (2002) measure the depth of economic integration in a regional trade bloc, based on the Optimal Currency Area Theory, according to the synchronization of the business cycle, convergence of inflation rates, exchange rate variability, trade openness and integration, convergence of interest rates, and income convergence between members of a regional trade bloc. The study must address two significant caveats relative to these measures of economic integration. First, it should be discussed that the integration process of real variables (business cycle, trade and income) is generally much slower than the integration process of nominal variables (exchange rates, inflation, interest rates, and financial markets). That is, these variables must be analyzed with the knowledge that usually the nominal measures of economic integration will be stronger than the real variables according to the specific time period analyzed. Thus, the degree of economic integration in regional trade blocs is relatively quickly evident in nominal variables when compared to real variables.

However, with respect to Mercosur, while the convergence of nominal variables since 1991 show significant increases in economic integration in the region, there is nevertheless much to be desired in regards to exchange rate, inflation and interest rate convergence, which will be actively discussed throughout the chapter. Indeed the correlation of nominal interest rates has been around 60 percent within the euro area during the pre-EMU period when the EU was an imperfect customs union similar to Mercosur currently], but only around 30 percent for the Latin American countries. Secondly, there are various authors such as Busse, Hefeker and Koopman (2004), Larrain and Tavares (2003), and Belke and Gros (2002) who argue that the countries of Mercosur do not constitute an optimum currency area-thereby questioning the validity of applying the measures of economic integration to Mercosur-because "trade interdependence and intra-regional financial and labour market integration are low," (Busse, Hefeker and Koopman, 2004) and member nations exhibit a high degree of both asymmetric shocks and exchange rate variability.

However, Dorruci, Firpo, Fratzscher and Mongelli (2002) explain that the endogeneity hypothesis-which states that monetary integration reduces trading costs much beyond the elimination of the costs arising from exchange rate variability-implies "that a group of countries adopting a single currency might develop into an OCA ex-post even if this group does not constitute an OCA ex-ante". In other words, although Mercosur as an imperfect customs union is not in a stage where it can successfully adopt a single currency for member nations and be deemed an OCA, because an OCA can develop after the implementation and coordination of macroeconomic policies, we can apply the concepts and ideals behind the OCA theory in our analysis of Mercosur. In essence, while Mercosur does not currently consistently exhibit the characteristics of an OCA, it can develop these characteristics over time through the enactment of the proper institutional and monetary policies.

Hence, with these definitions of both institutional and economic integration in mind, Dorruci, Firpo, Fratzscher and Mongelli's (2002) main argument can be summarized as follows: institutional integration leads to deeper economic integration and economic integration further reinforces institutional integration in a circular fashion. Using the European Union as their comparative standard they propose:

'The more institutional integration goes beyond the creation of a customs union and moves towards a common market and an economic and monetary union, the deeper economic integration turns out. Increasing economic integration, in turn, corroborates and sustains the process of institutional integration.

While scholars such as Barry Eichengreen (2004) claim that the Mercosur and EU comparison is not viable due to the unique political, historical and economic circumstances behind the development of both regional blocs, because the EU is the most successful common market which Mercosur implicitly seeks to emulate-Mercosur seeks to become a common market in Latin America similar to the EU-for the development of this paper the comparison is valid and concrete. Thus, in order for

Mercosur to succeed in economically integrating this sub-regional common market, like the EU, it must seek to achieve institutional integration through the coordination of macroeconomic policies among its members (i.e. coordinating monetary and exchange rate policies), and strong political commitments to the goals in question from the nations involved (i.e. creating laws and independent supranational governing institutions to enforce Mercosur objectives).

Accordingly, this chapter explored the specific obstacles that hinder Mercosur's institutional and economic integration such as the differences in trade, exchange rate, price and inflationary policies, and the remaining tariffs and protectionist measures among member nations as result of lobbying interest groups.. These differences are detrimental to Mercosur's success since Baer, Cavalcanti and Silva (2001) find these specific policies affect international trade and the allocation of investments among members of a trade area bloc. Furthermore, this chapter will also discuss Mercosur's lack of authority-since the Mercosur Treaty does not preside over national governments being intergovernmental and not supranational in nature-and its critical effects on the institutional and economic integration between Mercosur member nations. Therefore, this chapter analyzed the reasons behind the lack of institutional and economic integration in Mercosur, along with the unique economies and characteristics of Brazil, Argentina, Uruguay and Paraguay and the formation of Mercosur.

9.2 Mercosur: Overview of Progress

The international environment, specifically the combination of a series of forces including the computer revolution, advanced manufacturing technologies, and genetic engineering, paved the way for regional integration plans for Latin American countries that sought to achieve a "meaningful role in the international economic system" (Zerio, 1992). Indeed Mercosur was based on the notion of "open regionalism" and neo liberal economic reform, which were designed not to only facilitate trade but also to "enhance the potential for countries to attract foreign direct investment (FDI), as a result of the lure of larger markets to Multinational corporations (MNCs) eager to take advantage of economies of scale" (Phillips, 2003). However, Mercosur was not solely created as a strategic response to the globalization processes imminent in the international environment, but also to promote the national capitalist project in the domestic political economy of member nations; it involved the relocation of decision-making authority and a consequent contraction in space for discretionary government policy.

More specifically, in a hemispheric environment controlled by the United States, the Mercosur alliance was a response against the US hegemony in the Western Hemisphere; Mercosur was also formed to resist and offset US dominance. In general, "regional integration was sought as a political tool to consolidate broader goals aimed at reversing the dark ages of authoritarianism, intraregional antagonism, economic crisis, and international marginalization" (Hirst, 1999).

However, many of these simplistic neo-liberal assumptions concerning globalization and the formation of Mercosur are intricately complicated by the reasons behind each individual nation's entrance into the Treaty of Asuncion. Kaltenthaler and Mora (2002) discuss how the primary motivation for regional integration in South America was Argentina and Brazil's desire to end their century long trade and military rivalry and conflict, thereby dissolving the security dilemma and threat each nation presumed in one another. Indeed once an agreement was reached between the two nations-fostering a positive and non-threatening relationship-both nations, and the regional bloc in general, aspired to strengthen democracy, democratic rule and the domestic economies of the region (Kaltenthaler and Mora, 2002). As a matter of fact, Mercosur, like the European Community itself placed consolidating democracy and preserving peace in the Southern Cone among its paramount objectives.

Besides promoting democracy, as the years progressed, for Argentina, Uruguay and Paraguay the motivation behind joining Mercosur and ensuring its success became economic gain—evident in Argentina's desire to widen and expand Mercosur. On the other hand, Brazil consistently emphasized political interests and the need to strengthen civilian democratic interests over economic gain.

Furthermore, while the economic motive was prevalent in Argentina, Uruguay and Paraguay, there were still important dissimilarities in the reasons why each of these members sought to create a regional trade bloc and common market. On the one hand, while Argentina actively pursued its economic interests through Mercosur after the Brazilian conflict was resolved, for Paraguay in particular the democratic imperative reigned supreme. Paraguay's primary and consistent motivation was the institutionalization of democracy; it sought external support against persistent antidemocratic forces threatening the fragile regime after more than three decades of General Alfredo Stroessner's authoritarian regime (1954-89).

Both Paraguay and Uruguay also pose a special case for analysis since as the smaller Mercosur partners, they did not join the integration process until after Argentina and Brazil agreed in July 1990 (Buenos Aires Act) to establish a common market by the end of 1994. Uruguay in particular was not interested in regional integration efforts with Brazil and Argentina because it feared being absorbed economically by the two sub-regional giants. In consequence, the impetus behind Uruguay's decision to join Mercosur was political in nature: President Luis Alberto Lacalle desired to "strengthen and enhance the power of the leadership on issues related to economic policy and integration". President Luis Alberto Lacalle and former Uruguayan foreign minister, Hector Gros Espiell, wanted to avoid the potential economic costs associated with Uruguay's lack of involvement in the Argentine-Brazilian integration, especially since Argentina and

Brazil were and remain Uruguay's largest trade partners. Basically, Uruguay's motivations were largely of a domestic political and economic nature, initiated by political elites determined to achieve integration as a means of consolidating popular support for economic reform and democracy.

While Brazil, Argentina and Uruguay played an active role in the integration process, Paraguay was more of a passive observer in the establishment of Mercosur. Precisely because it was a weak and newly established democracy itself, it lacked the power and ability to become an active participant in the integration process. Thus, the improvisation and immobilism of Paraguay's foreign ministry and relative weakness and disorientation of political elites and societal groups (legacy of authoritarianism) contributed to Paraguay being 'dragged' by its neighbours (principally Uruguay) into the regional economic system.

Accordingly, Paraguay had a minimal role, if any, in the long road leading to the Treaty of Asuncion. Consequently, due to the lack of knowledgeable experts on economic integration and negotiation in Paraguay's foreign ministry, Uruguay defined and outlined Paraguay's interests in the process, although their interests and objectives did not always match .Conclusively, Paraguay's primary reason for attaining membership in Mercosur was to advance democracy in its domestic politics. Paraguay's President Andres Rodriguez's main foreign policy objective was to "re-insert Paraguay into the community of democratic nations" In essence, Mercosur offered Paraguay the opportunity to:

- end Paraguay's international isolation from which it suffered during the latter years of the Stroessner regime ,
- reactivate a ravaged economy by joining regional economic
- integration systems and attracting foreign investments; and
- perhaps the most important objective, seek international support for his government (Kaltenthaler and Mora, 2002).

Mercosur provided an open door for the Paraguayan

government to both legitimize its regime and re-introduce Paraguay into the democratic Latin American community for its advancement, growth and recovery from the Stroessner dictatorship. As these diverse motivations behind Mercosur's creation illustrate, Mercosur itself did not originate from economic or business sectors but from the governments or state elites who had their specific agendas and political inducements to create and join Mercosur.

9.2.1 Mercosur's Main Provisions and Subsequent Successes and Failures: With the process of integration beginning as early as 1985-1986 through the advent of the Program for Integration and Economic Cooperation (PICE) between Brazil and Argentina, Mercosur was created through the Treaty of Asuncion in1991-when Uruguay and Paraguay joined the agreement. Mercosur seeks to create a common market with a common industrial policy, thereby coordinating the economic policies of member nations while simultaneously harmonizing competition policy, national investment regimes, and achieving a set of coordinated social policies dealing with security, drugs, the environment and democracy for example (Phillips, 2003).

Thus, the Treaty, based upon concepts of deregulation and integration efforts, hopes to achieve "the free circulation of goods, services, and production factors, reinforced by the attainment of a uniform external tariff (Arrighi, 1992). From its inception, with a population of over 220 million and a GDP in excess of USD 900 billion. Mercosur became the third largest trading bloc in the world after the European Union and the North American Free Trade Agreement, NAFTA (Carranza, 2003). In fact, Mercosur became second to the European Union in terms of the depth of the integration process.

Successfully completing its transition phase from 1991-19940-wherein import tariffs between member nations were gradually eliminated-it was decided in the Buenos Aires presidential summit of 1994 that Mercosur would become an imperfect customs union, diverting the bloc from its over-arching goal of creating a common market according to Carranza (2003). However, it is significant to understand that this was actually a step toward its final objective as indicated by the five stages of regional integration discussed in Section 1. Indeed, signifying advancement and growth, the Mercosur Trade Commission was established by the Protocol of Ouro Preto of December 1994, thereby creating an institution which administers trade relations between the members and serves as a forum of first instance for the settlement of trade disputes. Thus, the 1991 Free Trade Agreement-that entailed semi-annual, progressive, linear and automatic tariff reductions, lists of products temporarily excluded from such reductions, to be reduced by the end of each of year, and the progressive elimination of non-tariff restrictions or equivalent measures.

It became an imperfect customs union through the implementation of a Common External Tariff on imports from third countries ranging from 0 to 20 percent in January 1995. However, there were a great number of exception lists in this CET for Mercosur members, which explains why Mercosur is deemed an imperfect customs union. These exceptions include up to 300 tariff items for Argentina, Brazil and Uruguay until 2001 and 399 items for Paraguay until 2006, reflecting that a convergence process is needed for the CET as of now, the time periods have been extended. As a sign of success however, intra-regional trade in aggregate Mercosur exports rose throughout the decade from 9 percent in 1990 to 25 percent in 1998. Demonstrating the magnitude of this increase, Brazil accounted for one third of Argentina's exports by the end of the 1990s, 40 percent of Paraguay's exports and 35 percent of Uruguay's exports (Inter-American Development Bank, 2000). It is also imperative to note that in 1996 Chile and Bolivia became associate members of Mercosur, which was an important step in expanding Mercosur markets while moving in the direction of broadening regional integration.

However, despite this success, due to the differing

economic structures and political profiles of Mercosur members-the more industrial and diversified economic profile of Brazil (which also has a higher index of extra regional trade relative to the other Mercosur members) coexists with the agricultural specializations of Argentina, Paraguay and Uruguay. Mercosur has faced various challenges and trade crises that have undermined its efforts in deepening both institutional and economic integration in the region. In fact, Mercosur's largest economies, Brazil and Argentina, have differing and to a large extent conflicting political goals: Brazil favours the idea of 'deepening' Mercosur while Argentina favours the extension of the Mercosur and the construction of wider regionalist arrangements, reflecting its much greater relative dependence on regional markets. In essence, while Brazil desires to deepen the regional integration among Mercosur members, Argentina seeks to widen and increase Mercosur's membership because it depends more heavily on trade in the South American region than Brazil.

Due to the differing economic profiles and political goals for Mercosur among its constituents-evident also in the diverse motivations behind each nation's entrance into the Mercosur Treaty discussed in Section 2 political tensions and fragility, exacerbated by the lack of supranational institutions in Mercosur, jeopardize its goal to harmonize economic policies and achieve a common market in the region. Basically, each member is pursuing the domestic and political agenda that is optimal for its domestic goals, while disregarding the effects these agendas inflict on Mercosur as a whole. This tendency to place the national goals and sovereignty over Mercosur objectives is explicitly exemplified in one of Mercosur's major underlying problems: its lack of macroeconomic and exchange rate policy coordination (institutional integration), which is also directly measured through the exchange rate variability in the region-one of the nominal variables representing the depth of economic integration between members of a regional bloc.

9.3 Macroeconomic and Exchange Rate Policy Coordination in Mercosur

In order for Mercosur to be successful as both a regional trade bloc and potential common market, it must synchronize the macroeconomic policies of member nations, particularly those of Brazil and Argentina. As the largest and most powerful Mercosur economies, macroeconomic coordination between Brazil and Argentina is essential for Mercosur's success as Latin America's southern cone market. This is especially significant since Uruguay and Paraguay will implement monetary policies in line with these sub-regional giants to sustain positive trade relations with both nations and advance economic integration in the region-also evident in both Uruguay's and Paraguay's reasons for joining Mercosur mentioned in Section 2. Indeed coordinating macroeconomic policies is a prerequisite to sustain the unhindered operation of market forces in Mercosur. In fact, regional trade arrangements cannot flourish in the face of high levels of exchange rate and financial volatility. Sharp misalignments leading to import surges and distress for concentrated interests can provoke sharp reactions against liberalization, encouraging protectionist interventions that stymie regional integration.

The effects of these misalignments in macroeconomic and exchange rate policies on both trade relations and economic integration in Mercosur, are highly evident in two important crises: Brazil's currency devaluation in 1999 and Argentina's subsequent recession and devaluation in 2001-2002. These events (which will be discussed in the following section) have significantly hampered both institutional and economic integration in the region-thereby threatening Mercosur's viability and existence-and exemplify the importance of synchronizing exchange rate policies between members of a regional trade bloc. Indeed, in comparison to the EU-6-which is the stage wherein the EU most resembled Mercosur's current status and progress—real exchange rate variability in Mercosur was almost 7 times higher, while nominal exchange rate variability was nearly 10 times higher.

However, before we can accurately analyze and understand the workings and effects of the aforementioned crises, we must further explore the nature of the divergent monetary policies pursued by Argentina and Brazil. Specifically, throughout Mercosur's progression both countries have operated under divergent exchange rate regimes and macroeconomic policies; Brazil has pursued a free-floating exchange rate regime while Argentina has followed a fixed exchange rate regime, pegging its peso to the US dollar.

Argentina's exchange rate regime in the 1990s was sustained and implemented by the Convertibility Law and Plan of 1991, which explicitly pegged the peso one-to-one to the US dollar—the Argentinean central bank could only issue new currency if backed by US dollars. Simultaneously, Argentina also implemented 'far reaching' economic goals in accordance to the Washington Consensus. The Washington Consensus is a very important agreement to understand since it also influenced Brazil's macroeconomic policy, which simultaneously adhered to and challenged the main provisions of the Washington Consensus. Specifically: the Washington Consensus favours full reliance on market forces to allocate resources. It features three main areas of economic policymaking: macroeconomic stability ("fiscal discipline"), a reduced government role in the economy (deregulation and privatization of state enterprises), and greater openness to the outside: elimination of barriers to trade while attracting foreign direct investment (Williamson, 1990).

Thus, Brazil's decision to adopt a floating exchange rate while maintaining state support for domestic industry and a long-term industrial policy. Both the countries supports and undermines the Washington Consensus. It is no wonder that the striking differences between Brazil's free floating exchange rate regime and Argentina's fixed exchange rate regime would hinder Mercosur's goals of institutional and economic integration as a common market. Accordingly,

Carranza (2003) explains: individually, Brazil upheld an active industrial policy; but Argentina abandoned all state- sponsored industrial initiatives, partly for ideological reasons and for the fiscal restraints inherent in maintaining a fixed exchange rate. The simultaneous implementation of trade liberalization and opening of domestic financial markets made the four member states vulnerable to external crises, such as the Mexican "tequila" effect in 1995, without pursuing the minimum of "developmental protectionism" that would have allowed them to overcome technological obsolescence and become competitive in world markets. As Mercosur's exchange rate problem became increasingly unmanageable, what emerged as Mercosur's 'common industrial policy' was a set of ad hoc initiatives aimed at smoothing out the very erratic swings in the current account balance between Argentina and Brazil, especially given the two countries' lack of progress in achieving macroeconomic coordination.

Therefore, it is evident that the divergence between Argentina and Brazil's macroeconomic policies has been detrimental to Mercosur, making the regional trade bloc vulnerable to external crises due to its lack of solid and sustainable common policies and unified objectives-which prevent Mercosur from institutionally advancing from an imperfect customs union to a common market. Indeed if Mercosur is practically struggling to survive under the pressures and crises created due to the conflicting policies of Argentina and Brazil, it cannot actively advance neither institutional nor economic integration in the region. Here, we can see the circular relationship between institutional and economic integration once more: because there is a high variability in exchange rates (lack of economic integration) between Mercosur's two most powerful economies, the regional trade bloc is unable to further integrate institutionally- and implement joint and harmonized fiscal and supra-governmental policies-into a common market.

Similarly, Baer, Cavalcanti and Silva (2002) discuss how

uncoordinated macroeconomic policies lead to excessive price and exchange rate fluctuations that affect international trade and the allocation of investments among members of a regional trade bloc. They specifically classify two main channels through which international trade is affected: First, there is an increased level of risk in international transactions (risk channel), which induce producers to refrain from exporting or importing and, therefore, causing an allocation of resources different than what would be suggested from comparative advantage. Second, it also stimulates lobbying for protection from imports when there exists a substantial increase in the import penetration ratio (lobbying channel).

Thus, not only does the lack of macroeconomic coordination hinder institutional integration, but it also further inhibits economic integration as well, precisely because it distorts trade relations among Mercosur members by producing a framework that violates the theory of comparative advantage. Furthermore, these fluctuations in the real exchange rate may increase or decrease the returns on investments and thus induce shifts in the location of new production plants and the reallocation of existing ones. This is particularly important for Mercosur nations since this reallocation of investments may cause strains between Brazil, Argentina, Uruguay and Paraguay—because they heavily rely on foreign direct investment (FDI). Moreover, Argentina and Brazil's divergent exchange rate policies have hampered commercial integration, which results in and reinforces the formation of lobby groups demanding the introduction of trade barriers (when the level of import penetration increases) to protect domestic industry from external competition. Indeed the effects of lobbying further shift trade volumes as changes in import penetration ratios increase the demand for protectionist measures in order to decrease the adjustment costs of the loss of competitiveness.

In essence, the uncoordinated macroeconomic policies between Mercosur's Argentina and Brazil serve as obstacles to institutional and economic integration by hindering trade relationships (causing trade imbalances), increasing the prevalence and uprising of lobbying interest groups and protectionist measures in member nations, affecting the flows of FDI to member nations thereby increasing strains among them, intensifying the effects of external and internal currency crises, and hindering the pursuit of unified goals, objectives and policies that promote and advance Mercosur's overarching goal to become Latin America's southern cone common market. Here it is interesting to contrast that usually regional integration, in general, reduces the impact of exchange rate volatility on trade (Bevilaqua, 1997) by implementing policies to promote macro coordination. One of the stated purposes of the EU, for instance, was to reduce exchange rate uncertainty and to avoid exchange rate misalignment among European countries to promote intra-trade and investments.

Thus, simply the mere fact that Argentina and Brazil have pursued such divergent exchange rate policies illustrates the persistent lack of institutional and economic integration in Mercosur, and the long and difficult road Mercosur countries must travel in order to successfully become a common market.

9.4 Brazil's Real Devaluation and the Argentinean Crisis

As previously mentioned the detrimental effects of the uncoordinated macroeconomic policies of Argentina and Brazil on Mercosur are particularly exemplified through the effects of both the 1999 devaluation of the Real and the subsequent Argentinean crisis in the early 2000s. Beginning with the Brazilian devaluation, in 1999 Brazil was considered the latest victim of the global financial crisis that had broken out in Southeast Asia in July 1997 and had spread to Russia in the summer of 1998 (Carranza, 2003). As a matter of fact, the crisis occurred in spite of a US$ 41.5 billion economic support package announced by the International Monetary Fund (IMF) and the Clinton administration in November 1998 to prevent the 'Asian flu' from spreading to Latin America. Many economists explain that in January 1999 the Brazilian government had to terminate its policy of periodic small devaluations of the Real vis-à-vis the US. Dollar due to the accelerated loss of foreign reserves, resulting from a combination of capital outflows and trade deficits (Inter-American Development Bank, 2000). As result the Real was allowed to undergo a drastic devaluation of 40 percent vis-à-vis the US. Dollar, and hence the Argentinean Peso.

This devaluation had several important effects on Brazil, Argentina and Mercosur. Firstly, it spurred an economic recession in both Brazil and Argentina, which reduced the amount of trade between both countries thereby jeopardizing economic integration in the region (Carranza, 2003)-in the first eight months of 1999, Argentine exports to Brazil were down 28.4 percent from the comparable period in 1998; Brazilian exports to Argentina were down 26.9 percent (LAWR 1999c). Thus, the devaluation devastated the Argentinean economy as Argentinean exports (particularly automobiles, steel, rice, and fruit) became less competitive on the Brazilian market-for example by August 1999, the giant auto plants in Argentina (such as Fiat) were operating at less than a quarter of their capacity. The devaluation produced a much-feared 'flood' of cheap Brazilian imports to Argentina, from chickens to footwear. This led to implementation of protectionist measures from the Menem administration, which imposed a variety of restrictions on trade with Brazil such as a surcharge of US$ 410 per ton on imports of Brazilian iron, quotas for imports of five categories of Brazilian textile products, and prior licensing for imports of paper (LAWR 1999b).

The Brazilian government in turn responded with similar countermeasures, such as a requirement of prior licenses for foodstuffs, boarder sanitary controls of Argentine products, and an import licensing system for industrial imports, which greatly hurt Argentina since 50 percent of Argentine exports to Brazil are manufactured goods. Therefore, while Brazil threatened to go to arbitration over Argentina's 23 percent tariff on sugar and antidumping actions against Brazilian steel, Argentina, Uruguay and Paraguay were complaining over the newly implemented trade restrictions. This was especially serious because Argentina sells 30 percent of all of its exports to Brazil and 35 percent and over 40 percent of Uruguayan and Paraguayan exports, respectively, go to Brazil. The crisis escalated to such a degree that Brazil threatened to dissolve Mercosur unless Argentina removed some of its tariffs. Fortunately, however, both countries were able to solve the disputes through the help of the industrial associations of both countries who set limits on mutually protectionist measures.

However, while these issues were temporarily resolved, due to Argentina's fixed exchange rate regime and its lack of an independent monetary policy, it continued to suffer as a result of its overvalued peso. As Carranza (2003) describes, Argentina's fixed exchange rate regime "was a big obstacle to achieving macroeconomic harmonization in Mercosur". In fact, the overvaluation of Argentina's real exchange rate and the devaluation of the Real in 1999, negatively impacted Argentina's automotive sector as they caused both a switch in components purchases to Brazil and also a migration of FDI to the latter due to lower costs of production—thereby increasing tensions between the two countries. Specifically, as a result of the Brazilian devaluation and Argentina's over valued peso, Chrysler closed its plant in Cordoba and GM closed one of its Argentinean plants thereby concentrating its remaining production in Rosario (another Argentinean city).

Thus, Argentinean executives feared that the parent offices of multinationals would continue to transfer operations to Brazil, where production costs were 25 to 30 percent lower than in Argentina-especially since no new investment plans were made in the Argentinean automotive sector in the subsequent years following the Real's 1999 devaluation.

In general, by March 2001, Argentina's economy was on the verge of collapse, while the Brazilian economy entered its own recession. Furthermore, with the scarce ability to meet its debt payments, the Argentinean recession grew worse when Brazil once again devalued its currency by 32 percent in the first quarter of 2001. This economic crisis motivated another set of trade disputes as Argentina raised a tariff of 35 percent on imports of consumer goods from outside Mercosur, and eliminated tariffs on imports of capital goods from outside the bloc to encourage domestic investment. These measures-supported by Mercosur's Common Market Council through December 31, 2002-clearly violated Mercosur's common external tariff, causing a temporary suspension of the customs union, once again threatening Mercosur's existence. Consequently, a reduction in bilateral trade between both nations followed once more as a result of these protectionist measures-Argentinean exports to Brazil in September 2001 fell 26.7 percent (US$ 447 million) from September 2000, while imports of Brazilian products fell 39.2 percent (US$ 330 million) in the same period (Business and Information Community 2001).

Further complicating the tensions between Argentina and Brazil, Domingo Cavallo-author of the Convertibility Plan, came to power on March 20, 2001, appointed by President De La Rua, as Argentina's economy minter. Cavallo undeniably preferred a trade agreement with the US instead of completing the customs union precisely because Brazil did not want to dollarize its currency. Therefore, due to Brazil's periodic devaluations and the negative impact on the Argentinean economy, political and economic tensions were high between Mercosur's most powerful economies. Yet after a meeting of the Common Market Council on October 8, 2001-following an informal Cardoso-de la Rua (the presidents of Brazil and Argentina during that period) summit-the disputes were resolved. Argentina and Brazil agreed to "create a 'temporary bilateral mechanism of safeguards inspired by the rules of the World Trade Organization' allowing Argentina to compensate Argentine industries by imposing temporary tariffs on any products that it could show to have been affected by a surge in imports caused by the Brazilian currency's fall" (Carranza, 2003). Though this served as a temporary solution to the trade disputes, the economic pressures of the overvalued peso were so high that in December 2001 Argentina's currency board collapsed and the peso was devalued in January 2002. In Argentina, convertibility was regarded as a sacred contract between the government and the public and the linchpin of national economic policy, but when it came to be seen as incompatible with the pursuit of full employment and growth, it lost public support and then investor confidence.

Indeed, the Argentinean devaluation shows the difficulty in defending exchange rate bands or pegs in the face of highly liquid international financial markets (Eichengreen, 2004). As these crises illustrate, it was precisely the lack of macroeconomic policy coordination that led to the profound conflicts among all four Mercosur nations and threatened Mercosur's existence. Exhibiting the detailed characteristics and effects of uncoordinated macroeconomic policies detailed in Section 3, we can clearly observe how these crises exacerbated and emphasized the lack of both institutional and economic integration in the region. By constantly questioning and making exceptions to the customs union, the regional bloc's institutional integration was persistently undermined along with its economic integration, as illustrated by the reduction in bilateral trade between Argentina and Brazil during these crises. As Carranza (2003) concludes: Argentina and Brazil have managed to iron out their trade disputes while upholding Mercosur as a 'strategic project'. Yet what is left of a customs union when member states can establish so many temporary exceptions to the common external tariff?

Furthermore, as Carranza (2003) explicitly discusses, these temporary resolutions were-as is customary for Mercosur-accomplished through presidential diplomacy. The presidential summits paved the way for reconciliation between the foreign and finance ministers of Brazil and Argentina, thereby ensuring Mercosur's survival. The following section will briefly discuss the power of presidential diplomacy in Mercosur's creation and survival.

9.5 Mercosur's Progress towards Common Market

Presidential power and diplomacy have played a significant role in Mercosur's creation and survival in the face of various threatening critical crises exemplified in Section 4. Simultaneously hindering and promoting Mercosur's progress to become a common market, presidential diplomacy and involvement are consistently highlighted throughout Mercosur's most historically detrimental and significant moments. Specifically, through Malamud's (2005) detailed discussion of how the meetings between Argentinean and Brazilian presidents Menem and Cardoso respectively, were the impetus behind the temporary resolution adopted between Brazil and Argentina-after the Brazilian devaluation in 1999 threatened Mercosur's existence—we can see the important role presidents serve in Mercosur. In this respect, presidents employ the tasks that usually correspond to foreign ministers, chief executives, and supranational institutions-if they existed in the regional trade bloc. In fact, Malamud (2005) explicitly discusses how the final-dispute-settlement mechanism in Mercosur conflicts is inter-presidential bargaining.

However, Malamud (2005) also consistently emphasizes that "presidential interventions were successful because they were backed by institutional capabilities such as veto and decree powers and because the presidents were not accountable to the legislative branch". In other words, because the presidents of Brazil, Argentinean, Uruguay and Paraguay were capable of exercising their political will and power freely-for the benefit of Mercosur-due to the institutions in their national governments, Mercosur survived and surpassed its most detrimental moments. Indeed in order to solve the Argentinean-Brazilian crisis after the devaluation of the Real: Menem affirmed his supremacy vis-à-vis the cabinet and the diplomatic corps. Under his personal supervision, his right-hand man had gone above the heads of politicians and bureaucrats to arrange a meeting with the Brazilian president, one that incidentally also contravened the public position of the Brazilian foreign minister. Thereafter, the presidents settled the dispute alone (Malamud, 2005).

Furthermore, as explored in Section 2, it was the presidents of Brazil, Argentina, Uruguay and Paraguay that spurred the creation of Mercosur and their respective nations' involvement in the regional trade bloc and the Treaty of Asuncion. As Malamud (2005) describes, "Mercosur arose from the political will of national governments, and only thereafter generated public demand for further integration." As a result, Mercosur presidents have acquired the popular legitimacy and determination to intervene in Mercosur issues in order to promote regional integration in the southern cone. Specifically: while increasing interdependence has created the need to manage a growing number of crises and coordination problems in Mercosur, transactors seem to demand particular decisions rather than general rules. For such a task, by and large, national presidents have been perceived as more able-more accessible, more responsive, more effective, faster-than any other actors to reach decisions (Malamud, 2005).

By delegating such power and influence on Mercosur to the national presidents, it is obvious that Mercosur presidents are sovereign as policy-crafters and decision-makers-presiding over both Mercosur as an institution itself and any other regional institutions that might be created to support Mercosur and further integration in the region. According to Malamud (2005) Mercosur presidents have been successful as chief executives and decision makers of the bloc because: the constitutional capabilities of the presidents vis-à-vis other actors have made it credible that their polices would not be blocked, [and secondly] the pre-eminence of the presidents has provided social actors with a single, non bureaucratic target through which to channel their interests, allowing for a faster decision-making process. Consequently, presidential intervention in Mercosur conflicts and activities has become a structural element of the integration process.

Indeed as critical actors in the integration process, oftentimes presidents were even able to compromise national sovereignty without facing serious vetoes from other relevant actors for two reasons. Firstly, a high degree of concentration of power in the hands of the chief executives enabled them to overcome or circumvent potential veto players. Secondly, foreign policy typically offers chief executives more room to manoeuvre than domestic politics do.

Precisely because presidents have played such a crucial role in Mercosur negotiations from its inception, it is no wonder that they are also reluctant to build up regional institutions or to relinquish their competencies to the regional institutions that do exist.

This unwillingness to create regional institutions for Mercosur further illustrates and explains not only the lack of macroeconomic and fiscal policy coordination in the region, but also the lack of supranational governing institutions that would help advance economic and institutional integration. Certainly, while presidents have advanced integration in Mercosur by refusing to give up their sovereignty, they have also hindered the process-exemplified in the lack of effective supranational institutions in Mercosur and the lack of appeals to the institutions, such as the Protocol of Brasilia, already in place. Indeed as Kaltenthaler and Mora (2002) proclaim: rather, loose regulations and shallow institutionalism have been maintained at a relatively low political cost. The trepidation of political elites is due to their unwillingness to cede any domestic policy autonomy that a harmonization of macroeconomic policy and supranational institutions would produce.

In this case, we see the real objective political elites and national presidents sought through regional integration; they sought to strengthen the power and authority of elites and their fragile states that faced significant domestic political and economic challenges. Thus, societal and state elites will continue to hamper the integration process-by impeding the coordination of macro and fiscal policies and obstructing the creation of supranational institutions-for fear of losing their autonomy and power to Mercosur.

Basically, Mercosur nations and presidents seek to obtain the benefits of both worlds: the member states of Mercosur want the maximum economic and political benefits from integration while foregoing as little sovereignty as possible. Conclusively, Mercosur's strong reliance and dependence on presidential diplomacy as a final dispute settlement mechanism reflects the fear member nations experience from the possibility of losing national autonomy and sovereignty to Mercosur.

However, this fear inhibits the integration process among Mercosur's members as Zerio (1992) accurately portrays: The stark reality is that as long as the integration effort rests solely on the initiative of presidents and a few ministries, Mercosur's success will be linked too directly to the fortunes and misfortunes of the individual administration that is attempting to implement the process. This further explains why over a decade later, Mercosur has yet to achieve total economic and institutional integration among its constituents. As previously mentioned, this precise desire to have the best of both worlds is a primary reason why Mercosur lacks supranational institutions that would further advance both institutional and economic integration in the region, which will be explored in greater depth in the following section.

9.6 Mercosur's Deficiency: Lack of Supranational Institutions

Mercosur's lack of supranational institutions is another one of the main reasons-besides the lack of synchronized macroeconomic and fiscal policies among member nations-that Mercosur has failed to fully achieve its common market status. Historically, whereas the Europeans created supranational institutions to avoid the threat of declaring war against one another, Mercosur nations, specifically Brazil and Argentina, overcame their security dilemma-discussed in Section 2-without the need or desire to surrender their sovereignty to supranational institutions. Accordingly, as detailed in Section 5, Mercosur has relied on presidential diplomacy to stay afloat during its most difficult times instead of relying on supranational institutions to effectively solve disputes between member nations and advance regional integration. Part of the reasons for this phenomenon, also discussed in Section 5, is the desire of political and states elites to retain and consolidate their autonomy and power.

These conflicting interests-Mercosur members seek to advance institutional and economic integration while retaining individual power—serve as significant obstacles to the creation of a 'mini-Maastricht', in European terms, and supranational institutions. However, these supranational institutions are necessary to advance both economic and institutional integration in the region. Indeed the differences between member nations and their divergent and uncoordinated macroeconomic policies are exacerbated by the lack of supranational decision-making authority, "which necessitates the transfer of legislation entirely to the national level" (Phillips, 2003). As Mercosur lacks these institutions to enforce a code of set standards and regulations to further integration between Mercosur members, it is no wonder that laws pertaining to Mercosur must be enforced and created at the individual national levels. Undoubtingly, this inspires conflicting and divergent perspectives, laws, and polices between member nations that lack the capability to coordinate and enforce their laws without supranational institutions.

Precisely because the Treaty of Asuncion is intergovernmental in nature, not supranational, Mercosur's decisions have no force as such and need to be implemented by corresponding national measures, with no obligation for member states to comply with common market rules. There is indeed no supranational court through which either a member country or the Mercosur Secretariat can enforce treaty provisions on another member or a private party. The lack of an institution, similar to the European Commission, that would serve to hold Mercosur members accountable to Mercosur laws and policies prevents the convergence of interests, fiscal and economic policies between Brazil, Argentina, Uruguay and Paraguay. Thus, any possible solutions to the uncoordinated macroeconomic polices of Mercosur nations will be greatly undermined due to the lack of a supranational body to preside over Mercosur.

Furthermore, the actual institutions created by the Treaty of Asuncion are also intergovernmental organs where decisions are made by consensus. Specifically, the Common Market Council (CMC) is composed of ministers of foreign affairs and economy; it is the highest ranking body, responsible for political direction. Furthermore, in December 1994, the Joint Parliamentary Commission made up of legislators from the member countries and the Advisory Forum on Economic and Social Matters were created. Neither body has the power or capacity to make decisions; they only have responsibility for monitoring and making recommendations.

Evidently, these institutions themselves lack decision-making and coordinating power thereby sustaining the decision-making powers of the presidents and foreign economic ministers in Mercosur. Indeed the lack of supranational institutions exacerbates Mercosur's complicated arbitration process—implemented when the Common Market Group cannot solve the dispute in question. In fact, since private companies cannot get involved in Mercosur trade disputes, when they have a complaint against a member state, they can only resort to the national agency of the concerned regional organ, such as the National Section of the Common Market Group and the Mercosur Trade Commission (MTC). Should they wish to move further to the arbitral phase, they need the support of their own state. Therefore, in order to successfully achieve economic and institutional integration in the region, Mercosur must create supranational institutions to support the regional trade bloc and imperfect customs union.

9.7 Possible Solutions to Diverging Macroeconomic Policies

Various scholars have proposed diverse solutions to solve Mercosur's problems rising from the lack of macroeconomic policy coordination among its four members. Some, specifically Busse, Hefeker and Koopmann (2004) have incorporated their understanding of the prevalence of fixed exchange rate regimes in Latin American nations into their solutions. Evident in various examples ranging from El Salvador's full dollarization regime to Argentina's Convertibility Plan, it is significant to discuss these nations' preference for fixed exchange rate regimes over free floating regimes. One, if not, the most significant reason for this tendency and preference is that fixed exchange rate regimes lead to more stable exchange rates. On the other hand, free floating regimes imply, encourage and produce a higher degree of exchange rate variability, thereby leading to risk and adverse economic effects on foreign investment and trade between significant external trade partners for the region-such as the United States and the European Union. Accordingly, stable exchange rates are also important for the sustainability of deep integration as the vulnerability of trade and investment flows to exchange rate movements grows in line with rising interdependence among partner countries. Consequently, one can conclude that stable exchange rates are known to foster healthier and more prosperous relationships among and between trade partners. It would follow then that achieving a stable exchange rate through diverse degrees of dollarization, as evident in Argentina's case, would favour trade relations with the US.

Latin American nations such as Argentina have also leaned towards a stable or fixed exchange rate regime in order to "import monetary stability". That is, by pegging their currencies to a more established and credible currency such as the U.S. Dollar, these countries hope to increase the credibility of their own currency and monetary policy in order to avoid higher expected inflation and interest rates-caused by a lack of credibility in a country's monetary policy. However, though there is some validity to this theory today it is often stressed that fixed rates provide a natural target for speculators whereas flexible rates, at least under (nearly) full capital mobility, appear less inviting to speculators. Thus, though fixed rate regimes may seem appealing, especially since capital inflows to emerging markets are typically denominated in foreign currencies, most long-term debt in these nations has been issued in US dollar or euro terms-the threat of speculation may undermine the very purposes and goals of monetary and exchange rate stability these nations are seeking. These ideals explain the motivations behind Argentina's Convertibility Plan and the subsequent devaluation of the Argentinean peso after the currency board collapse in December 2001.

In fact, according to Busse, Hefeker and Koopmann (2004) because Mercosur nations are greatly dependent and linked to both the US dollar and the euro-demonstrating the ill approach of the Convertibility Plan which only considered the US as Argentina's principal trading partner-Mercosur should implement a dual currency board that could at the same time provide a stabilizing anchor to domestic policy, be credible, and solve the problem that trading patterns do not accommodate a single currency peg to either the dollar or the euro. They also propose that such a dual currency board could further contribute to the stabilization of exchange rates within Mercosur. In this sense, a dual currency will both favour trade relations and agreements between Mercosur and its two largest trading partners, and contribute to further economic integration between Mercosur members.

Indeed the benefits of a dual currency board are highlighted through the significant figures that demonstrate Mercosur's deep trade relations with Europe and the US:

nearly 50 percent of the region's total trade is with the EU, with regard to Mercosur's own total trade (including internal trade) nearly one-fourth of its trade is with the EU and one-fifth of its overall trade is with the US, the US being its second largest trading partner. Thus, a dual currency board would lend higher credibility and promote further regional integration in Mercosur since the currency board should be less vulnerable to exchange rate movements between the currencies of main trading partners, i.e. the dollar-euro rate, than a standard currency board [and] it should restrict exchange rate movements between the members of Mercosur to a significant degree. Furthermore, because both major international currencies will be considered, there will be no problems with financial flows, thereby making a strong case for the dual currency board.

Whereas Busse, Hefeker and Koopmann (2004) advocate a dual currency board, Malamud and Label (2002) argue for the implementation of the Merco as a common currency for Mercosur. Malamud and Label (2002) support the idea of "a floating currency that leaves room for independent monetary policy and wage and price flexibility", while maintaining monetary discipline. Malamud and Label (2002) discuss how "a flexible rate regime averts the currency crisis that besets target zone and crawling peg arrangements", i.e. the Argentinean crisis. Presenting, a path for total monetary union in the region, Malamud and Label (2002) propose, "when managed by an independent central bank committed to holding down inflation, this alternative affords the stability advantages of dollarazation." In addition, they argue that as a floating currency, the Merco's flexibility vis-à-vis other currencies provides a cushion against external shocks, a cushion that dollarization lacks. Malamud and Label (2002) also discuss additional advantages of the Merco, which will also serve to secure seignorage revenues—purchasing power that a government secures by creating money at essentially no cost that it can use to buy real things—for the members of the

Merco zone. However, realizing that the Merco cannot be instituted overnight, Malamud and Label (2002) also describe a process similar to Busse, Hefeker and Koopmann (2004) whereby:

Argentina would tie its peso to a shrinking basket of dollars and euros while Brazil retains an inflation targeting-floating exchange rate regime with an inflation target somewhat above the US-euro zone average. With the peso tied by formula to the dollar and the euro and the real linked more loosely to these currencies, narrow spreads between Argentine and Brazilian inflation rates and interest rates should maintain over time. Brazil would adjust its inflation target to achieve convergence with Argentina before a common currency is inaugurated. The suggested path offers Argentina an exit strategy from its current hard fix to the dollar. Other Merco zone candidates could follow similar paths as Argentina (Malamud and Label, 2002).

Thus, both models, the dual currency board and the Merco, reflect the importance of achieving some form of reconciliation between the Euro and the US dollar necessary to stabilize the high exchange rate variability in Mercosur. Indeed as Zerio (1992) foreshadows: "unless the economies of Argentina and Brazil succeed in controlling inflation, and put in place monetary policies that maintain a certain level of currency parity, integration is unlikely to be successful".

On the other hand, rejecting monetary union in the region while simultaneously favouring the synchronization of macroeconomic policies between Mercosur members, Barry Eichengreen (2004) advocates a common policy of inflation targeting for Mercosur members. Arguing that it is not likely for Mercosur countries to forego their individual sovereignty through the adoption of a single currency, such as the Merco proposed by Malamud and Label (2002), he argues that the best alternative for Mercosur nations is harmonized inflation targeting. Barry Eichengreen (2004) contends that inflation targeting would "reduce exchange rate volatility to levels more compatible with the operation of their free trade areas, but would not require ambitious commitments to coordinate policies that, at the end of the day, cannot be successfully met". Thus, Mercosur nations would be able to solve the problems resulting from unsynchronized macroeconomic policies while both retaining their national sovereignties, and employing reachable goals and objectives regarding both institutional and economic integration in the region. In essence, through harmonized inflation targeting, Mercosur nations will resolve the problems dealing with exchange rate instability while reconciling monetary autonomy with economic integration. Furthermore, discrediting the basket-peg or dual currency board approach endorsed by Busse, Hefeker and Koopmann (2004), Eichengreen (2004) sustains that, as the Argentinean case exemplifies.

If there is one clear lesson in international financial history, it is that so-called adjustable pegs grow rigid in an environment of high capital mobility. That rigidity, in turn, limits the scope for foreign support. And with absent foreign support, the defensibility of such pegs is dubious. Thus, Eichengreen argues that instead of promoting institutional and economic integration in Mercosur, such an approach would undermine regional integration in its entirety. The main provisions of inflation targeting are: an institutionalized commitment to price stability as the primary goal of monetary policy; mechanisms rendering the central bank accountable for attaining its monetary policy goals; the public announcement of targets for inflation; and a policy of communicating to the public and the markets the rationale for the decisions taken by the central bank .

In summary, as a policy framework, inflation targeting is designed to provide a clear and credible anchor for monetary policy that stabilizes both expectations and foreign exchange markets themselves.

However, while these three viable solutions for Mercosur's unsynchronized macroeconomic policies have great validity, it is nevertheless important to note that the fiscal policies of these nations must also be coordinated-and institutional integration enhanced in the regional trade bloc-in order for such frameworks to produce their desired effects. Specifically in terms of the three solutions, all authors respectively mention and discuss the importance of institutional and fiscal integration: Firstly, Busse, Hefeker and Koopmann (2004) discuss that it is clear, however, that a dual currency board cannot solve [all] of a country's macroeconomic problems. A currency board alone does not force politicians, as the Argentine example demonstrated, to run prudent fiscal policy. It does not avoid that countries run up debts that are ultimately not consistent with a fixed exchange rate, and it does not solve the free-rider problems of fiscal federalism. Hence, currency boards will only survive if these problems can be solved. Similarly, Malamud and Label (2002) also proclaim:

Following the euro zone's example, cross currency exchange rates should be stabilized and inflation rates, interest rates, and government debt to GDP ratios should converge before a common currency is instituted. Uniform financial regulations must also be designed and a credible commitment to low inflation must be demonstrated.

Accordingly, Eichengreen agrees that Mercosur countries: [m]ust follow prudent fiscal and financial policies, not just adopting appropriately balanced budgets but also minimizing their dependence on short-term, foreign currency-denominated and indexed debt. With such policies in place, exchange rate volatility can be reduced to levels compatible with regional integration.

As demonstrated in the preceding statements and as supported by Dorruci, Firpo, Fratzscher and Mongelli (2002), in order to achieve economic integration through macroeconomic policy harmonization, Mercosur members must advance institutional integration through the synchronization of fiscal policies in order to further promote regional integration among Mercosur's constituents—again showing the circular relationship between institutional and economic integration.

9.8 Conclusion

This chapter has shown the intricate and inter-related reasons and obstacles that prevent Mercosur from successfully implementing a common market in Latin America's southern cone. Discussing the historical and diverse motivations for Mercosur's creation from the perspective of Brazil, Argentina, Uruguay and Paraguay, along with the inherent differences in their economic profiles, we can clearly observe some of the fundamental reasons why Mercosur has been unable to achieve total economic integration among its constituents similar to the European Union. By using the framework provided by Dorruci, Firpo, Fratzscher and Mongelli (2002), this chapter has demonstrated that Mercosur cannot achieve its goal of total economic integration in the region unless it makes the efforts to achieve institutional integration through the coordination of currently divergent macroeconomic and monetary polices, and the implementation of a successful common market through the creation of supranational institutions.

In fact, unless Mercosur nations take the necessary measures to reduce the role of presidential diplomacy during Mercosur crises, implement supranational institutions, and coordinate fiscal policies among its members (institutional integration), the solutions discussed in Section 7 will be ineffective and incapable of resolving Mercosur's uncoordinated macroeconomic policies-thereby hindering the region's economic integration. Yet as Dorruci, Firpo, Fratzscher and Mongelli (2002) discuss, in order for institutional integration to further advance in the region it must be supported by economic integration, which has been deterred as a result of the lack of institutional integration in the first place-evident in the Brazilian and Argentinean economic crises wherein the lack of macro coordination hindered economic integration.

However, Mercosur has made substantial process in these issues as well. During a Mercosur summit on December 15, 2000 a Macroeconomic Monitoring Group (GMM) was established to monitor the compliance of member nations to a set of macroeconomic convergence targets endorsed by Mercosur (Eichengreen, 2004). Indeed, currently all Mercosur nations have adopted a free floating exchange rate regime. Furthermore, the implementation and creation of the Protocol of Olivos for Dispute Settlement, signed by the presidents of the bloc's member countries on February 18, 2002, also shows signs of advancement for institutional integration in the region. Through this agreement, a permanent tribunal, made up of 5 arbitrators, was created to review the awards issued by ad hoc arbitration tribunals. This tribunal's awards are considered 'final judgment' and 'will be binding on the state parties involved in the dispute' (INTAL 2002, 7; Carranza 2003). In essence, while Mercosur has the power to become irreversible if it continues on the right path towards achieving full economic and institutional integration, if it fails to overcome and resolve the obstacles that impede these processes, "the Mercosur customs union risks becoming an empty shell, even if it remains politically important as an instrument to negotiate free trade agreements with European Union and the United States" (Carranza, 2003).

References

Alberola, E., Buisan, A., Fernandez, S., 2002. The quest for nominal and real convergence through integration in Europe and Latin America. Working paper no. 2013. Madrid: Banco de Espana.

Alimonda, H., 1994. Mercosur, democracy, and labour. Latin American Perspectives 21, 21-33.

Arrighi, J.M., 1992. Integration and consumer protection: the case of Latin America. Journal of Consumer Policy 15, 179-190.

Baer, W., Silva, P.A., Cavalcanti, T., 2002. Economic integration without policy coordination: the case of Mercosur. Emerging Markets Review 3, 269-304.

Balassa, B., 1961. The Theory of Economic Integration. Irwin,

Homewood, Illinois.

Belke, A., Gros, D., 2002. Monetary integration in the southern cone. North-American Journal of Economics and Finance 13, 323-349.

Bevilaqua, A.S., 1997. Macroeconomic coordination and commercial integration in Mercosur. PUC/Rios, Texto Para Discussao No. 378. Departamento de Economia, Outubro.

Bizzozero, L., Lujan, C., 1992. La politica exterior del gobierno de transicion en Uruguay (1985-1990). Documento de trabajo. Facultad de Ciencias Sociales, Montevideo.

Bleaney, M., 2004. Argentina's currency board collapse: weak policy or bad luck? The World Economy 27, 699-714.

Business and Information Community, 2001. Se acuenta caida en intercambio entre Argentina y Brazil. October 10. <www.mercosur.com/info/articuloimp.jsp?noticia>

Busse, M., Hefeker, C., Koopmann, G., 2004. Between two poles: matching trade and exchange rate regimes in Mercosur. HWWA Discussion Paper No. 301.

Carranza, M.E., 2003. Can Mercosur survive? Domestic and international constraints on Mercosur. Latin American Politics and Society 42, 67-104.

Cheibub, J.A., Limingi, F., 2002. Democratic institutions and regime survival: parliamentary and presidential democracies reconsidered. Annual Review of Political Science 5, 151-79.

Child, J., 1985. Geopolitics and Conflict in South America: Quarrels Among Neighbours. Praeger, New York.

Chudnovsky, D., Porta, F., 1989. On Argentine-Brazil economic integration. CEPAL Review 39, 115-33.

Dorrucci, E., Firpo, S., Fratzscher, M., Mongelli, F.P, 2002. European integration: what lessons for other regions? The Case of Latin America. ECB Working Paper No. 185.

Edwards, S., 1989. Real Exchange Rates, Devaluation, and Adjustment: Exchange Rate Policy in Developing Countries. MIT press, Cambridge, MA.

Eichengreen, B., 2004. What macroeconomic measures are needed for free trade to flourish in the western hemisphere? Latin American Politics & Society 46, 1-27.

Ferguson, Y., 1986. Cooperation in Latin America: the politics of regional integration. In: Lincoln, J.K., Ferris, E.G. (Eds.), The Dynamics of Latin American Foreign Policies: Challenges for the 1980s. Boulder, Westview Press, pp. 37-38.

Figueiredo, A.C., Limongi, F., 2000. Presidential power, legislative organization, and party behaviour in Brazil. Comparative Politics 32, 151-70.

Fleming, J.M., 1971 On exchange rate unification. The Economic Journal 81, 467-88.

Fraga, A., Goldfain, I., Minella, A., 2003. Inflation targeting in emerging market economies. NBER Working Paper no. 10019.

Frankel, J., Shang-Jin Wei, 1993. Trade blocs and currency blocs. NMER Working Paper 4335.

Frankel, J., Rose, A.K., 1998. The endogeneity of the optimum currency area criteria. Economic Journal 108, 10009-1025.

Garcia, A. Glocker G., 2000. Options for Latin America in a globalized world: a regional monetary union versus dollarization. Unpublished mss. Frankfurt: European Central Bank.

Gonzaga, G., Terra, M., 1997. Equilibrium real exchange rate, volatility, and stabilization. Journal of Economic Development 54, 77-100.

Haines-Ferrari, M., 1998. Mercosur: individual access and the dispute settlement mechanism. In: Cameron, J., Campbell, K. (Eds.), Dispute Resolution in the World Trade Organization. Cameron May, London, pp. 270-85.

Hirst, M., 1999. Mercosur's complex political agenda. In Roett, R. (Ed.), Mercosur: Regional Integration, World Markets. Boulder, Westview Press, pp.35-49.

Institute for the Integration of Latin America and the Caribbean (INTAL), 2002. Monthly Newsletter no.67 (February). Buenos Aires: Inter-American Development Bank/INTAL.

Inter-American Development Bank, 1999. Integration and trade in the Americas. Periodic Note, October.

Inter-American Development Bank, 2000. Informe Mercosur.

International Monetary Fund, 1994, 1997, 2000. Directions of Trade.

Kaltenthaler, K., Mora, F.O., 2002. Explaining Latin American economic integration: the case of Mercosur. Review of International Political Economy 9, 72-97.

Kenen, P., Rodrik, D., 1986. Measuring and analyzing the effects of short-term variability in real exchange rates. Review of Economics and Statistics 68, 311-319.

Lael, B., Thierry, V., 1994. Lobbying and the adjustment in declining industries.

European Economic Review 38, pp. 586-595.

Larrain, F., Tavares, J., 2003. Regional currencies versus dollarization: Options for Asia and the Americas. Journal of Policy Reform, 6, 35-49.

Latin American Weekly Report (LAWRb), 1999. Brazilian threat is changing stances of Argentine businessmen on key policies. August 24, 385.

Latin American Weekly Report (LAWRc), 1999. Brazil escalates tit-for-tat measures: latest restriction affects 400 Argentinean products. September 21, 434.

Malamud, A., 2001. Presidentialism in the southern cone. A framework for analysis. EUI SPS Working Paper.

Malamud, A., 2005. Presidential diplomacy and the institutional underpinnings of Mercosur: an empirical examination. Latin American Research Review 40, 136-164.

Malamud, B., Label, W.A., 2002. The merco: A common currency for Mercosur and Latin America. American Business Review 20, 132-139.

Manzetti, L., 1993-4. The political economy of Mercosur. Journal of Interamerican Studies and World Affairs 35, 101-42.

Mora, F., 2000. Paraguay y el sistema interamericano: de dictadura y paralisis a democracia y la resolucion 1080. In: Tickner, A., Perina, R. (Eds.), El Sistema Interamericano y Democracia en America Latina. Bogota/Washington, Universidad de los Andes/OEA.

Oppers, S., 2000. Dual currency boards-a proposal for currency stability, IMF Working Paper 00/199.

Pereira, L.V., 1999. Toward the common market of the South: mercosur's origins, evolution and challenges. In: Roett, R. (Ed.), Mercosur: Regional Integration, World Markets. Boulder, Westview Press, pp.7-25.

Phillips, Nicola, 2003. Hemispheric integration and subregionalism in the Americas. International Affairs 79, 327-349.

Prasad, E., Rogoff, K., Wei Shang-Jin, Kose M.A., 2003. Effects of financial globalization on developing countries: some empirical evidence. Unpublished mss. Washington, DC: International Monetary Fund.

Rogowski, R., 1999. Institutions as constraints on strategic choice. In: Lake, D., Powell. R. (Eds.), Strategic Choice and International Relations. Princeton, New Jersey, Princeton

University Press, 115-36.

Sauer, C., Bohara, A.K., 2001. Exchange rate volatility and exports: regional differences between developing and industrialized countries. Review of International Studies 9, pp.133-152.

Schlesinger, A.M., Jr., 1974. The Imperial Presidency. Andre Deutsch Limited, London.

Silva, P., 1989. Democratization and foreign policy: the cases of Argentina and Brazil. In: Galjart, B., Silva, P. (Eds.), Democratization and the State in the Southern Cone. Essays on South American Politics. Amsterdam, CEDLA.

Simon, J.L., 1995. Los deficit de la actual politica exterior paraguaya frente los avances diplomaticos de las democracies vecinas. In: Simon, J.L. (Ed.), Politica Exterior y Democracia en el Paraguay y sus vecinos. Asuncion: Fundacion Hans Seidel/Universidad Nacional de Asuncion, 201-16.

Smith, P.H., 1993. The politics of integration: concepts and themes. In: Smith, P.H. (Ed.), The Challenge of Integration: Europe and the Americas. New Brunswick, 1-15.

Tavlas, G.S., 1993, The theory of monetary integration. Open Economics Review 5, 211-230.

Urbiztondo, S., 1998. Direct foreign investment in Argentina: evolution, new challenges and perspectives. The Quarterly Review of Economics and Finance 38, 459-482.

UNCTAD, 1999. Foreign Direct Investment and the Challenge of Development. World Investment Report.

UNCTAD, 2000. FDI Determinants and TNC strategies: The Case of Brazil.

Williamson, J., 1990. The progress of policy reform in Latin America. Policy Analyses in International Economics no. 28 Washington, D.C.: Institute for International Economics.

Zerio, J.M., 1992. Southern cone common market and north atlantic blocs (EC and NAFTA): problems and perspectives. The International Executive 34, 57-74.

Index

Index